J. M. SYNGE : PLAYS

Sketch of J. M. Synge, 1905, by Jack B. Yeats

J. M. SYNGE : PLAYS

EDITED BY ANN SADDLEMYER

OXFORD UNIVERSITY PRESS

LONDON   OXFORD   NEW YORK

Oxford University Press

LONDON   OXFORD   NEW YORK
GLASGOW   TORONTO   MELBOURNE   WELLINGTON
CAPE TOWN   IBADAN   NAIROBI   DAR ES SALAAM   LUSAKA   ADDIS ABABA
DELHI   BOMBAY   CALCUTTA   MADRAS   KARACHI   LAHORE   DACCA
KUALA LUMPUR   SINGAPORE   HONG KONG   TOKYO

ISBN 0 19 281042 1

*First published as an Oxford University Press paperback by
Oxford University Press, London, 1969 and reprinted 1974*

The text of this edition of Synge's *Plays* is taken from
volumes III and IV of J. M. Synge, *Collected Works* (General
Editor, Robin Skelton), first published by Oxford University
Press, London, 1968. These two volumes, edited by Ann
Saddlemyer and subtitled *Plays* Book I and Book II, contain
in addition to the texts of the plays here reproduced, introduc-
tions notes on the texts, and appendices, including a section of
unpublished scenarios, dialogues, and fragments, and Synge's
worksheets on each of the plays, with a commentary

*Printed in Great Britain
at the University Press, Oxford
by Vivian Ridler
Printer to the University*

TO

LILO STEPHENS

AND THE MEMORY OF

NED STEPHENS

CONTENTS

INTRODUCTION

I was born in 1871 near Dublin—my father was a barrister and land-lord. I went to various local schools and had private tutors till 1887 when I entered Trinity College Dublin, taking my degree (B.A.) in 1892. Meanwhile I had given a great deal of my time to music—I took the scholarship of Harmony and Counterpoint in the royal Irish Academy of Music about the same time—and in 1893 I went to Germany (partly for a holiday), but I stayed there studying music for nearly a year. I saw that the Germans were so much more innately gifted with the musical faculties than I was that I decided to give up music and take to literature instead. I went back to Germany for a few months to work at the language only, and then on the first day of 1895 I went to Paris for six months. The next year I went to Italy and learned Italian, and then I spent six or seven winters in Paris going back to Ireland for half the year. In 1898 I went to the Aran Islands to learn Gaelic and lived with the peasants. Ever since then I have spent part of my year among the Irish speaking peasantry in various localities as I am now doing once more. I have the MS of a book giving an account of my life on the Aran Islands which Mr. Elkin Mathews has promised to publish shortly. During the last 10 years I have written a certain number of short articles and reviews for various papers, but my first real success was with the two little plays—which I suppose you have seen or heard of—'Riders to the Sea' and 'The Shadow of the Glen' which were played in Dublin by our Society and also in London March, 1904, where they were very well received. Since then I have given up Paris and give all my time to writing for the little Theatre we have in Dublin. I hope to have another play ready before very long. . . .

When John Millington Synge[1] wrote these words from a little country inn in County Kerry on a wet September day in 1905, he was thirty-four years old. Some months earlier at Dublin's new Abbey Theatre the Irish National Theatre Society had produced his third play, *The Well of the Saints*, which was now being translated into German by his correspondent, Dr. Max Meyerfeld.[2]

---

[1] Synge's surname is pronounced as in the verb 'to sing'.

[2] The original letters from Synge to Meyerfeld are in the possession of the National Library of Ireland. Synge's comments and instructions concerning the translation are in the Academic Center Library, University of Texas.

He was shortly to be made Director, along with William Butler Yeats and Lady Gregory, of that 'little Theatre' in Dublin.

The new play he mentions, *The Playboy of the Western World*, was not ready until January 1907, when the reaction to its first production in Dublin proved one of the stormiest in theatre history since Ibsen's *Ghosts*. Yet another play, *The Tinker's Wedding*, begun at the same time as his two one-act plays, was finally published late in 1907 but considered too dangerous to be acted at the Abbey. The same year saw the publication of his travel book, *The Aran Islands*, long after he had turned from Aran to explore other parts of western Ireland. And in 1909, his play *Deirdre of the Sorrows* still unfinished and a slim volume of poems and translations almost ready for publication, Synge died. He left behind him one other play, *When the Moon Has Set*, begun in 1900 but never published or produced, and two trunks full of thousands of pages of drafts, scenarios, dialogues, essays, and notes. From this material, much of it unpublished, it is possible to observe the writer at his craft and to determine exactly what Synge wished in the presentation of his work. The present edition is based upon a close study of those papers and of other manuscripts elsewhere.[1]

As he implies in the above autobiographical sketch, Synge's early training was far less theatrical than it was linguistic and musical. The same year he won the scholarship for Harmony and Counterpoint at the Academy of Music, he took prizes in Hebrew and Irish at Trinity College. During his years in Paris he enrolled in courses in language and literature at the Sorbonne and his diaries record extensive reading in four languages. But he records only two visits to the theatre, in September 1892 to see Beerbohm Tree's *Hamlet* in Dublin, and in March 1898 to see a production of Ibsen's *Ghosts* by Antoine's company in Paris. Nor did his family encourage an interest in drama. Apart from the pianist cousin who took him to Germany, Synge's relatives, evangelical Protestants boasting an impressive clerical lineage, frowned upon any professional connection with the arts. Consequently, although he showed an interest in dramatic expression well before the fateful encounter with Yeats in Paris in 1896 which Yeats

---

[1] For a detailed description of this unpublished material and examples of his revisions, see J. M. Synge, *Collected Works*, vols. III and IV, *Plays*, ed. Saddlemyer (Oxford University Press, 1968).

describes in his *Autobiographies*, Synge's early scenarios and even his first completed plays were composed far more for the reader than for the performer. Not until he had become involved in the management of the Abbey Theatre and set out to establish his own dramatic method do his manuscripts begin to indicate a conscious sense of stagecraft. In a very short time, however, the musician and dilettante student of languages and literature became a practical man of the theatre. From now on the material prepared for publication is treated with the careful eye of the producer, who points his directions with an intimate knowledge of the stage, and even punctuates rhetorically with an ear for the speech rhythms of the actor.[1] Finally, in 1906, Synge became engaged to Maire O'Neill, one of the Abbey's leading actresses and Sara Allgood's younger sister; his next two plays were written with major roles for Molly.

It is equally clear from his notebooks and worksheets, however, that the incessant revising and meticulous polishing of his plays took place in the study, not on the stage. He rewrote each scene over and over again, polishing the phrasing, balancing the dialogue, clarifying the action, until he had achieved the strong stage play he required. Although he did most of his work at the typewriter, lettering the various drafts as he went along, Synge frequently jotted down phrases and related ideas, sometimes entire scenes, in one of the small notebooks he always carried with him; these fragments would then be reworked into the fabric of the play. When he finally read the finished work to his colleagues, no revision beyond minor verbal alterations in rehearsal was possible; even the suggested alteration of a single passage would have upset the delicate balance of the whole. In an important sense then, although Synge undoubtedly learned much from his experience as a Director of the Theatre and adviser to would-be Abbey dramatists, play-writing remained

---

[1] One of the actresses in the first productions of his early plays remembered: 'At first I found Synge's lines almost impossible to learn and deliver. Like the wandering balladsinger I had to "humour" them into a strange tune, changing the metre several times each minute. It was neither verse nor prose. The speeches had a musical lilt, absolutely different to anything I had heard before. Every passage brought some new difficulty and we would all stumble through the speeches until the tempo in which they were written was finally discovered. I found I had to break the sentences—which were uncommonly long—into sections, chanting them, slowly at first, then quickly as I became more familiar with the words.' Maire Nic Shiubhlaigh and Edward Kenny, *The Splendid Years* (Dublin, Duffy, 1955), pp. 42–3.

for him very much the private composition of the lyric poet or musician, writing as much or more for the ear than the eye, imposing a balance of mood, tone, and colour on the material he distilled from the life about him rather than allowing characterization alone to control plot. In a letter to Frank Fay, one of the brothers responsible for the training of the company, he commented, 'The whole interest in our movement is that our little plays try to be literature first—i.e. to be personal, sincere, and beautiful —and drama afterwards.'[1]

The bulk of Synge's dramatic work was conceived over a surprisingly short period of time. In fact most of his plays were begun or contemplated during the first years of his association with the Abbey company. At the same time, ideas and plots for plays he had not time to write flocked to his mind and were sketched with some detail in his notebooks and diaries. The one exception both to his working methods and sense of stagecraft is his first completed play, *When the Moon Has Set*. He began it in 1900 a few years after his proposal of marriage to Cherrie Matheson was rejected on religious grounds, one of the incidents on which the play appears to be based. Synge completely revised this play three times during his lifetime; the text as presented here is a conflation of two incomplete one-act versions marked 'J' and 'K', both apparently separate revisions of the original three-act version. He left the play to be considered once more after his death, although both Yeats and Lady Gregory had already rejected it in earlier forms. Undoubtedly his colleagues were right to reject it, and Yeats's objection to the inclusion of Synge's *Manchester Guardian* articles on Ireland's Congested Districts in the 1910 collected edition of his work adequately explains his rejection of the play:

My feeling at the time however was chiefly of anxiety lest I should allow anything undistinguished to mar the effect upon posterity of a writer whose good fortune it should be to leave behind him a mass of perfectly distinguished work. The rest of us have had to make our experiments before the world. He alone, if he escape the commercial hand, will leave behind him work as perfect as a beautiful statue.[2]

---

[1] The letter, written from London in April 1904, is in the Fay papers, National Library of Ireland.

[2] Letter in the Synge papers to Joseph Hone, one of the directors of Maunsel and Company, the Dublin firm which published Synge's *Collected Works* in 1910.

When one considers the ruthlessness with which Synge perfected his later plays and criticized his fellow Directors' work, it is difficult to appreciate his reluctance to give up a work judged inferior by himself and his colleagues, especially after he had raided it so freely for both ideas and phrasing. For in addition to frequent verbal echoes, his later work far more effectively practises the belief he here preaches: Colm's plea for the individual's right to follow his own nature appears in all the plays, expressed perhaps most strongly in Mary Byrne's drunken soliloquies, the Tramp's poetic invitation to the life of the road, and the Playboy's blossoming spirit; while the Douls' insistence on their illusions in the face of reality becomes an ironic comment on Sister Eileen's belief in the beneficence of faith. However, despite Synge's later efforts to simplify and revise, the play clearly expresses the raw emotion of an immature young man hurt by a rigidity of life and narrowness of faith he believed immoral and unjust. It too has its place in the canon.

Synge's next two plays, *Riders to the Sea* and *The Shadow of the Glen*, were written during the summer of 1902, and at the same time he began work on *The Tinker's Wedding*. He still had not seen the Fays' company perform. But he had spent many weeks on the Aran Islands over the preceding five years, and he knew every inch of the Wicklow glens. Both plays were immediately accepted by the small Theatre Society, but alterations in staging were required for *Riders to the Sea*, so the little Wicklow play was presented first. And with that production the long battle between Synge and the Irish nationalists began.

The story of Synge's—or rather Yeats's, for Synge did not actively participate[1]—struggle with the press over *The Shadow of the Glen* has been fully described by David H. Greene and Edward M. Stephens in their detailed biography of Synge.[2] It seems likely, as Yeats and Lady Gregory always suspected, that the criticism was part of a premeditated attack on the entire theatre movement, which began over Yeats's *The Countess Cathleen* in 1899, and was to flare up again over *The Playboy of the Western World* in 1907. But it is clear also that the Dublin audience, trained on traditional melodrama at the old Queen's Theatre and led to

[1] Except for a brief note to the *United Irishman* enclosing the original story as he heard it from old Pat Dirane on Aran, and had printed it in *The Aran Islands*.

[2] *J. M. Synge 1871–1909* (New York, Macmillan, 1959).

expect another 'Celtic' play in the Yeatsian tradition, were
hardly prepared for the shock of reality to which Synge subjected
them. Furthermore, the production emphasized the reality of the
life he depicted. Dan Burke's cottage was scrupulously copied
from life, and Synge, who knew well the actual building and
site, could describe to the producer Willie Fay the exact setting:

His power of visualisation was perfect. . . . If I asked him, 'Was Dan
standing where he is on the right, behind the table, when he said
these lines?' he would say, 'No, he was on the right-hand side of the
table with his hand on it.' He was a great joy to work with, for he had
a keen sense of humour and plenty of patience, and above all he knew
what he wanted, and when he got it said so.[1]

Similarly, *Riders to the Sea* was produced with as much authen-
ticity as possible, Synge going so far as to order thick flannel and
pampooties, the traditional Aran footgear, from the west. This
fidelity to detail and simplicity of design, developed for the most
part in Synge's two one-act plays, combined to create the style
of acting and production which became known as 'the Abbey
method'. Although Lady Gregory was to make far more use of
'the Folk Play' than Synge, clearly his early work was the
inspiration as much as it was the product of the new movement
in Irish drama. It is hardly surprising, therefore, that the audience,
taken off guard by the realism of the productions in front of them,
should take the next step and accept literally the words and
situation presented there. Eventually this method hampered
Synge as well, for by the time he came to produce *The Playboy*,
his own theories in turn had become more sophisticated, and
neither the company nor the audience were trained to follow him.

Even before he had seen *Riders to the Sea* on stage, and perhaps
as early as the first rehearsals of *The Shadow of the Glen*, Synge had
begun work on *The Well of the Saints*, like most of his plays
based on his intimate knowledge of County Wicklow. 'I am very
well but in agony and horror over my play with the blind
people', he wrote to Frank Fay. 'It is exceedingly difficult to make
it work out.' The following month he wrote to Lady Gregory,
'I am hard at work overhauling my play and generally sharpening
dialogue, but the more I do the more there seems to be done.'[2]

[1] W. G. Fay and Catherine Carswell, *The Fays of the Abbey Theatre* (London, Rich and
Cowan, 1935), pp. 138–9.
[2] The original letters to Lady Gregory are in the Berg Collection, New York Public
Library.

He finally finished the play in July 1904, but it was not produced until the following February, and in the meantime he had become embroiled in the problems of converting the theatre company from an amateur group playing in halls into a semi-professional limited society with its own theatre, a gift to Yeats and his ideals from the English heiress Miss Horniman. Caught between the narrow nationalist fervour of some of the actors and his own determination to present the play as he saw it, Synge spent more time with the company and took further responsibilities for casting and rehearsing. He had already been attacked by the players, when several of the company, led by Maud Gonne, had ostentatiously walked out of the first performance of *The Shadow of the Glen*. Now more were objecting. Willie Fay complained of the consistent bad humour of the characters in *The Well of the Saints*, but Synge explained that he wanted to write 'like a mono-chrome painting, all in shades of one colour'.[1] To Frank Fay he wrote about a further complaint,

Tell Miss G.—or whoever it may be—that what I write of Irish country life I know to be true and I most emphatically will not change a syllable of it because A. B. or C. may think they know better than I do. . . . You understand my position: I am *quite ready* to avoid hurting people's feelings needlessly, but I will *not* falsify what I believe to be true for anybody. If one began that where would one end? I would rather drop play-writing altogether.

He provided brief notes for the company[2] and, still dissatisfied, later experimented with the dialogue in his own copy of the play. When the play was revived in the spring of 1908, he revised the third act.

The riots provoked by *The Playboy of the Western World* on its first production in January 1907 once again emphasized the playwright's refusal to allow emotions to blur the precision of his painfully acquired technique. Although the plot is based on a story current in Aran and strengthened by the notorious case of James Lynchehaun, who, like the Aran refugee, had been har-boured by peasants even though convicted of a brutal murder,[3]

---

[1] *The Fays of the Abbey Theatre*, pp. 167–8.

[2] Synge's letter and rehearsal notes are in the Fay papers, National Library of Ireland.

[3] Admitted by Synge in an interview with *The Freeman's Journal*, 30 January 1907. Synge quotes the Aran version in *The Aran Islands* and Yeats also describes hearing it when he and Arthur Symons visited Aran in 1896, in his *Autobiographies* and his essay 'J. M. Synge and the Ireland of his Time'.

far more of the flavour of the action and brilliance of the language come from Synge's delight in County Kerry, which he visited annually from 1904. His earliest drafts of the play date from this time, but he was still frantically revising when the play was put into rehearsal. In October 1906 he wrote to Yeats, 'My play, though in its last agony, is not finished and I cannot promise it for any definite day. It is more than likely that when I read it to you and Fay . . . there will be little things to alter that have escaped me. And with my stuff it takes time to get even half a page of new dialogue fully into key with what goes before it. The play, I think, will be one of the longest we have done, and in places extremely difficult.'[1]

When they did receive the finished play, both Directors and cast expressed anxiety over the strong language. However, no one could have been prepared for the uproar, now almost legendary, that the first production created.[2] The first-night audience, already made uneasy by the disturbing rumours circulating about the play, erupted at the word 'shifts', the line being made even more explosive by Willie Fay's substitution of 'Mayo girls' for Christy's 'drift of chosen females standing in their shifts'. At the second performance an angry audience forced Lady Gregory to call in the police and the actors were reduced to performing in dumb show. The following day, when Yeats returned from lecturing in Scotland, the three Directors decided as a matter of policy to continue the performances for the rest of the week, under police protection, until Synge's play was given its fair hearing. By the end of the week the players had earned their first uninterrupted performance and on the following Monday Yeats invited those interested to a public debate on 'the freedom of the theatre'.

It is clear from the early drafts and many scenarios that Synge had some doubts as to the players' capacity to provide the deliberately mannered production his concept of the play demanded. In a letter to Molly Allgood after the first performance he discussed the acting, and added,

I feel like old Maurya today, 'It's four fine plays I have, though it was a hard birth I had with every one of them and they coming to the world.'

---

[1] Original letters to Yeats in the Berg Collection, New York Public Library.
[2] See Greene and Stephens, *J. M. Synge*, chapter 13; Walter Starkie, 'The Playboy Riots', *Irish Times*, 7 October 1963.

It is better any day to have the row we had last night, than to have your play fizzling out in half-hearted applause. Now we'll be talked about. We're an event in the history of the Irish stage.[1]

However, the violence of the attacks against him and *The Playboy* upset Synge more than he was perhaps willing to admit. He denied the realism of the play, although the production by Willie Fay and further cutting by his colleagues tended to emphasize the realistic style of performance, and he even went so far as to say in an interview that his play was 'a comedy, an extravaganza made to amuse'.[2] That it was more than that his private comments indicate. To a Scottish friend he wrote, 'As to the point you raise as to a possible want of contrast in the moral attitude of my people, I am doubtful myself. I feel the want, and yet my instinct when I am working is always towards keeping my characters bound together as far as possible in one mood.'[3] To a criticism forwarded by his American patron John Quinn he replied,

He is quite right that early work, like 'Riders to the Sea', has a certain quality that more mature work is without. People who prefer the early quality are quite free to do so. When he blames the 'coarseness', however, I don't think he sees that the romantic note and a Rabelaisian note are working to a climax through a great part of the play, and that the Rabelaisian note, the 'gross' note, if you will, *must* have its climax no matter who may be shocked.[4]

And to a young aspiring playwright he wrote, '. . . you see—what it seems so impossible to get our Dublin people to see, obvious as it is—that the wildness and, if you will, vices of the Irish peasantry are due, like their extraordinary good points of all kinds, to the *richness* of their nature—a thing that is priceless beyond words.'[5] Later, while in Kerry in August 1907, he added a private postscript in his notebook: 'It is not impossible in Ireland to get a company of people who have no vulgarity and a few

---

[1] Original letter in the possession of Mrs. L. M. Stephens.

[2] Synge later retracted this in part by publishing a letter in the *Irish Times*, 31 January 1907, claiming that there were 'several sides to "The Playboy"'.

[3] Original letter to James Paterson, dated 12 March 1907, in the Synge papers.

[4] Original letter, dated 5 September 1907, in the Quinn papers, Manuscript Division, New York Public Library.

[5] Letter dated 19 February 1907 to M. J. Nolan, who had sent him an essay on the play. This letter, now in Trinity College Dublin, was published as 'A Letter to a Young Man' in the 1932 edition of the plays.

plays that are uncorrupted also but it is not proved that such work can bring together a few people to listen and look on.'

It could well be that this uproar influenced his decision to publish *The Tinker's Wedding* later that year, after six complete drafts in as many years, but the Directors still hesitated to produce it at the Abbey. However, by this time he was already at work on *Deirdre of the Sorrows*, although slowed down by the Hodgkins disease which was to kill him less than two years later. To John Quinn he enlarged on the difficulties of a new medium:

I don't know whether I told you that I am trying a three-act prose 'Deirdre', to change my hand. I am not sure yet whether I shall be able to make a satisfactory play out of it. These saga people, when one comes to deal with them, seem very remote; one does not know what they thought or what they are or where they went to sleep, so one is apt to fall into rhetoric. In any case, I find it an interesting experiment, full of new difficulties, and I shall be the better, I think, for the change.[1]

Daily letters to Molly Allgood record his struggles with the new play. In December 1906 he had written, 'My next play must be quite different from the P. Boy. I want to do something quiet and stately and restrained and I want you to act in it.' Almost a year later he was still making major revisions to the scenario and just completing the first rough draft of the play. Further illness intervened, however, and when Synge entered hospital for the last time he was still altering the action, strengthening various motifs and reworking the characterization. He died on 24 March 1909, and on the back of a fragment of Deirdre's keen over the grave of Naisi are scribbled the words, 'Unfinish[ed] play of "Deirdre", can be sent if desired to Mr W. B. Yeats'.

It would be a mistake to assume, then, that the play as it now stands is any more than half finished, either in mood or characterization. Synge was fairly satisfied with the third act, and thought the first act 'worth keeping', although certain specific alterations were required. His notebooks during the final months of revisions show many changes, as he sought to strengthen Owen's role in an effort to balance the 'poetic' with the equally necessary 'Rabelaisian' element. According to Yeats, Synge several times during his final illness asked that his fellow Directors should 'finish' the play, bringing Owen into the action of the

---

[1] Original letter, dated 4 January 1908, in the Manuscript Division, New York Public Library.

first act and giving him more business in the second. During the summer of 1909 Yeats, Lady Gregory, and Molly Allgood worked on the manuscript, trying to determine some order and form from the thousand typescript pages. But finally they decided to produce the play without any additional material or alterations, and the same assemblage of manuscripts was used for its first publication. The present edition for the first time takes into account additional notebook material belonging to Synge's last revisions of this play.

In an effort to present a definitive text for this edition, every available draft has been consulted for each of the plays, as well as Synge's marginalia and notes. Spelling and presentation of dialogue have been made consistent, but Synge's own punctuation is scrupulously followed in order to indicate his suggested rhythms to the actor and reader. The plays are arranged in the order of writing, with the exception of the unpublished *When the Moon Has Set*, given in the Appendix; the dates on the half-title pages indicate the period during which Synge worked on each play until he achieved his final version.

ANN SADDLEMYER

University of Victoria
Victoria, British Columbia
Canada
January 1969

ACKNOWLEDGEMENTS

I AM indebted to so many individuals and institutions on two continents over such a long period of time that it is impossible to thank by name each person who has made this edition possible. Mrs. Lilo Stephens gave me a home in Dublin and, together with the Synge family and officials and staff of the National City Bank of Dublin, made available to me all the papers held by the J. M. Synge Estate. The late Mrs. W. B. Yeats was a constant help and encouragement, as was her daughter Miss Anne Yeats; Mr. Austin Clarke helped in constructing the glossary and guide to pronunciation; the late Mr. Gerard Fay directed me to the Fay papers.

Further material was provided by the Academic Center Library, University of Texas; the Lilly Library, Indiana University; the Trustees of the New York Public Library; the Fellows of Trinity College Dublin; and the Trustees of the National Library of Ireland.

Permission has been graciously granted by Mrs. W. B. Yeats for quotations from her husband's unpublished letters; by Miss Anne Yeats and Macmillan & Co. Ltd. for W. B. Yeats's Preface to *Deirdre of the Sorrows*; and by Messrs. Rich and Cowan and Messrs. James Duffy and Co. Ltd. for quotations from copyright material.

Miss Anne Yeats kindly granted permission for the sketch of Synge by Jack B. Yeats reproduced as the frontispiece.

A. S.

RIDERS TO THE SEA

A PLAY IN ONE ACT

(1900–1905)

PERSONS

MAURYA, an old woman
BARTLEY, her son
CATHLEEN, her daughter
NORA, a younger daughter
MEN AND WOMEN

SCENE

An Island off the West of Ireland

Cottage kitchen, with nets, oil-skins, spinning wheel, some new boards standing by the wall, etc. CATHLEEN, *a girl of about twenty, finishes kneading cake, and puts it down in the pot-oven by the fire; then wipes her hands, and begins to spin at the wheel.* NORA, *a young girl, puts her head in at the door.*

NORA [*in a low voice*]. Where is she?

CATHLEEN. She's lying down, God help her, and maybe sleeping, if she's able.

[NORA *comes in softly, and takes a bundle from under her shawl.*]

CATHLEEN [*spinning the wheel rapidly*]. What is it you have?

NORA. The young priest is after bringing them. It's a shirt and a plain stocking were got off a drowned man in Donegal.

[CATHLEEN *stops her wheel with a sudden movement, and leans out to listen.*]

NORA. We're to find out if it's Michael's they are, some time herself will be down looking by the sea.

CATHLEEN. How would they be Michael's, Nora. How would he go the length of that way to the far north?

NORA. The young priest says he's known the like of it. 'If it's Michael's they are,' says he, 'you can tell herself he's got a clean burial by the grace of God, and if they're not his, let no one say a word about them, for she'll be getting her death,' says he, 'with crying and lamenting.'

[*The door which* NORA *half closed behind her is blown open by a gust of wind.*]

CATHLEEN [*looking out anxiously*]. Did you ask him would he stop Bartley going this day with the horses to the Galway fair?

NORA. 'I won't stop him,' says he, 'but let you not be afraid. Herself does be saying prayers half through the night, and the Almighty God won't leave her destitute,' says he, 'with no son living.'

CATHLEEN. Is the sea bad by the white rocks, Nora?

NORA. Middling bad, God help us. There's a great roaring in the west, and it's worse it'll be getting when the tide's turned to the wind. [*She goes over to the table with the bundle.*] Shall I open it now?

CATHLEEN. Maybe she'd wake up on us, and come in before we'd done [*coming to the table*]. It's a long time we'll be, and the two of us crying.

NORA [*goes to the inner door and listens*]. She's moving about on the bed. She'll be coming in a minute.

CATHLEEN. Give me the ladder, and I'll put them up in the turf-loft, the way she won't know of them at all, and maybe when the tide turns she'll be going down to see would he be floating from the east.

> [*They put the ladder against the gable of the chimney;* CATHLEEN *goes up a few steps and hides the bundle in the turf-loft.* MAURYA *comes from the inner room.*]

MAURYA [*looking up at* CATHLEEN *and speaking querulously*]. Isn't it turf enough you have for this day and evening?

CATHLEEN. There's a cake baking at the fire for a short space [*throwing down the turf*], and Bartley will want it when the tide turns if he goes to Connemara.

> [NORA *picks up the turf and puts it round the pot-oven.*]

MAURYA [*sitting down on a stool at the fire*]. He won't go this day with the wind rising from the south and west. He won't go this day, for the young priest will stop him surely.

NORA. He'll not stop him, mother, and I heard Eamon Simon and Stephen Pheety and Colum Shawn saying he would go.

MAURYA. Where is he itself?

NORA. He went down to see would there be another boat sailing in the week, and I'm thinking it won't be long till he's here now, for the tide's turning at the green head, and the hooker's tacking from the east.

CATHLEEN. I hear some one passing the big stones.

NORA [*looking out*]. He's coming now, and he in a hurry.

BARTLEY [*comes in and looks round the room; speaking sadly and quietly*]. Where is the bit of new rope, Cathleen, was bought in Connemara?

CATHLEEN [*coming down*]. Give it to him, Nora; it's on a nail by the white boards. I hung it up this morning, for the pig with the black feet was eating it.

NORA [*giving him a rope*]. Is that it, Bartley?

MAURYA [*as before*]. You'd do right to leave that rope, Bartley, hanging by the boards. [BARTLEY *takes the rope*.] It will be wanting in this place, I'm telling you, if Michael is washed up tomorrow morning, or the next morning, or any morning in the week, for it's a deep grave we'll make him by the grace of God.

BARTLEY [*beginning to work with the rope*]. I've no halter the way I can ride down on the mare, and I must go now quickly. This is the one boat going for two weeks or beyond it, and the fair will be a good fair for horses I heard them saying below.

MAURYA. It's a hard thing they'll be saying below if the body is washed up and there's no man in it to make the coffin, and I after giving a big price for the finest white boards you'd find in Connemara. [*She looks round at the boards.*]

BARTLEY. How would it be washed up, and we after looking each day for nine days, and a strong wind blowing a while back from the west and south?

MAURYA. If it isn't found itself, that wind is raising the sea, and there was a star up against the moon, and it rising in the night. If it was a hundred horses, or a thousand horses you had itself, what is the price of a thousand horses against a son where there is one son only?

BARTLEY [*working at the halter, to* CATHLEEN]. Let you go down each day, and see the sheep aren't jumping in on the rye, and if the jobber comes you can sell the pig with the black feet if there is a good price going.

MAURYA. How would the like of her get a good price for a pig?

BARTLEY [*to* CATHLEEN]. If the west wind holds with the last bit of the moon let you and Nora get up weed enough for another cock for the kelp. It's hard set we'll be from this day with no one in it but one man to work.

MAURYA. It's hard set we'll be surely the day you're drown'd with the rest. What way will I live and the girls with me, and I an old woman looking for the grave?

[BARTLEY *lays down the halter, takes off his old coat, and puts on a newer one of the same flannel.*]

BARTLEY [*to* NORA]. Is she coming to the pier?

NORA [*looking out*]. She's passing the green head and letting fall her sails.

BARTLEY [*getting his purse and tobacco*]. I'll have half an hour to go down, and you'll see me coming again in two days, or in three days, or maybe in four days if the wind is bad.

MAURYA [*turning round to the fire, and putting her shawl over her head*]. Isn't it a hard and cruel man won't hear a word from an old woman, and she holding him from the sea?

CATHLEEN. It's the life of a young man to be going on the sea, and who would listen to an old woman with one thing and she saying it over?

BARTLEY [*taking the halter*]. I must go now quickly. I'll ride down on the red mare, and the grey pony'll run behind me. . . . The blessing of God on you. [*He goes out.*]

MAURYA [*crying out as he is in the door way*]. He's gone now, God spare us, and we'll not see him again. He's gone now, and when the black night is falling I'll have no son left me in the world.

CATHLEEN. Why wouldn't you give him your blessing and he looking round in the door? Isn't it sorrow enough is on every one in this house without your sending him out with an unlucky word behind him, and a hard word in his ear?

[MAURYA *takes up the tongs and begins raking the fire aimlessly without looking round.*]

NORA [*turning towards her*]. You're taking away the turf from the cake.

CATHLEEN [*crying out*]. The Son of God forgive us, Nora, we're after forgetting his bit of bread. [*She comes over to the fire.*]

NORA. And it's destroyed he'll be going till dark night, and he after eating nothing since the sun went up.

CATHLEEN [*turning the cake out of the oven*]. It's destroyed he'll be, surely. There's no sense left on any person in a house where an old woman will be talking forever.

[MAURYA *sways herself on her stool.*]

CATHLEEN [*cutting off some of the bread and rolling it in a cloth, to* MAURYA]. Let you go down now to the spring well and give him this and he passing. You'll see him then and the dark word will be broken, and you can say 'God speed you', the way he'll be easy in his mind.

MAURYA [*taking the bread*]. Will I be in it as soon as himself?

CATHLEEN. If you go now quickly.

MAURYA [*standing up unsteadily*]. It's hard set I am to walk.

CATHLEEN [*looking at her anxiously*]. Give her the stick, Nora, or maybe she'll slip on the big stones.

NORA. What stick?

CATHLEEN. The stick Michael brought from Connemara.

MAURYA [*taking a stick* NORA *gives her*]. In the big world the old people do be leaving things after them for their sons and children, but in this place it is the young men do be leaving things behind for them that do be old. [*She goes out slowly.*]

[NORA *goes over to the ladder.*]

CATHLEEN. Wait, Nora, maybe she'd turn back quickly. She's that sorry, God help her, you wouldn't know the thing she'd do.

NORA. Is she gone round by the bush?

CATHLEEN [*looking out*]. She's gone now. Throw it down quickly, for the Lord knows when she'll be out of it again.

NORA [*getting the bundle from the loft*]. The young priest said he'd be passing tomorrow, and we might go down and speak to him below if it's Michael's they are surely.

CATHLEEN [*taking the bundle from* NORA]. Did he say what way they were found?

NORA [*coming down*]. 'There were two men,' says he, 'and they rowing round with poteen before the cocks crowed, and the oar of one of them caught the body, and they passing the black cliffs of the north.'

CATHLEEN [*trying to open the bundle*]. Give me a knife, Nora, the string's perished with the salt water, and there's a black knot on it you wouldn't loosen in a week.

NORA [*giving her a knife*]. I've heard tell it was a long way to Donegal.

CATHLEEN [*cutting the string*]. It is surely. There was a man in here a while ago—the man sold us that knife—and he said if you set off walking from the rocks beyond, it would be in seven days you'd be in Donegal.

NORA. And what time would a man take, and he floating?

[CATHLEEN *opens the bundle and takes out a bit of a shirt and a stocking. They look at them eagerly.*]

CATHLEEN [*in a low voice*]. The Lord spare us, Nora! Isn't it a queer hard thing to say if it's his they are surely?

NORA. I'll get his shirt off the hook the way we can put the one flannel on the other. [*She looks through some clothes hanging in the corner.*] It's not with them, Cathleen, and where will it be?

CATHLEEN. I'm thinking Bartley put it on him in the morning, for his own shirt was heavy with the salt in it. [*Pointing to the corner.*] There's a bit of a sleeve was of the same stuff. Give me that and it will do.

[NORA *brings it to her and they compare the flannel.*]

CATHLEEN. It's the same stuff, Nora; but if it is itself aren't there great rolls of it in the shops of Galway, and isn't it many another man may have a shirt of it as well as Michael himself?

NORA [*who has taken up the stocking and counted the stitches, crying out*]. It's Michael, Cathleen, it's Michael; God spare his soul, and what will herself say when she hears this story, and Bartley on the sea?

CATHLEEN [*taking the stocking*]. It's a plain stocking.

NORA. It's the second one of the third pair I knitted, and I put up three score stitches, and I dropped four of them.

CATHLEEN [*counts the stitches*]. It's that number is in it. [*Crying out.*] Ah, Nora, isn't it a bitter thing to think of him floating that way to the far north, and no one to keen him but the black hags that do be flying on the sea?

NORA [*swinging herself round and throwing out her arms on the clothes*]. And isn't it a pitiful thing when there is nothing left of a man who was a great rower and fisher, but a bit of an old shirt and a plain stocking?

CATHLEEN [*after an instant*]. Tell me is herself coming, Nora? I hear a little sound on the path.

NORA [*looking out*]. She is, Cathleen. She's coming up to the door.

CATHLEEN. Put these things away before she'll come in. Maybe it's easier she'll be after giving her blessing to Bartley, and we won't let on we've heard anything the time he's on the sea.

NORA [*helping CATHLEEN to close the bundle*]. We'll put them here in the corner. [*They put them into a hole in the chimney corner. CATHLEEN goes back to the spinning-wheel.*]

NORA. Will she see it was crying I was?

CATHLEEN. Keep your back to the door the way the light'll not be on you.

[NORA *sits down at the chimney corner, with her back to the door.* MAURYA *comes in very slowly, without looking at the girls, and goes over to her stool at the other side of the fire. The cloth with the bread is still in her hand. The girls look at each other, and* NORA *points to the bundle of bread.*]

CATHLEEN [*after spinning for a moment*]. You didn't give him his bit of bread?

[MAURYA *begins to keen softly, without turning round.*]

CATHLEEN. Did you see him riding down?

[MAURYA *goes on keening.*]

CATHLEEN [*a little impatiently*]. God forgive you; isn't it a better thing to raise your voice and tell what you seen, than to be making lamentation for a thing that's done? Did you see Bartley, I'm saying to you.

MAURYA [*with a weak voice*]. My heart's broken from this day.

CATHLEEN [*as before*]. Did you see Bartley?

MAURYA. I seen the fearfullest thing.

CATHLEEN [*leaves her wheel and looks out*]. God forgive you; he's riding the mare now over the green head, and the grey pony behind him.

MAURYA [*starts, so that her shawl falls back from her head and shows her white tossed hair. With a frightened voice*]. The grey pony behind him . . .

CATHLEEN [*coming to the fire*]. What is it ails you, at all?

MAURYA [*speaking very slowly*]. I've seen the fearfullest thing any person has seen, since the day Bride Dara seen the dead man with the child in his arms.

CATHLEEN and NORA. Uah. [*They crouch down in front of the old woman at the fire.*]

NORA. Tell us what it is you seen.

MAURYA. I went down to the spring well, and I stood there saying a prayer to myself. Then Bartley came along, and he riding on the red mare with the grey pony behind him [*she puts up her hands, as if to hide something from her eyes*]. The Son of God spare us, Nora!

CATHLEEN. What is it you seen?

MAURYA. I seen Michael himself.

CATHLEEN [*speaking softly*]. You did not, mother; it wasn't Michael you seen, for his body is after being found in the far north, and he's got a clean burial by the grace of God.

MAURYA [*a little defiantly*]. I'm after seeing him this day, and he riding and galloping. Bartley came first on the red mare; and I tried to say 'God speed you,' but something choked the words in my throat. He went by quickly; and 'the blessing of God on you,' says he, and I could say nothing. I looked up then, and I crying, at the grey pony, and there was Michael upon it—with fine clothes on him, and new shoes on his feet.

CATHLEEN [*begins to keen*]. It's destroyed we are from this day. It's destroyed, surely.

NORA. Didn't the young priest say the Almighty God won't leave her destitute with no son living?

MAURYA [*in a low voice, but clearly*]. It's little the like of him knows of the sea. . . . Bartley will be lost now, and let you call in Eamon and make me a good coffin out of the white boards, for I won't live after them. I've had a husband, and a husband's father, and six sons in this house—six fine men, though it was a hard birth I had with every one of them and they coming to the world—and some of them were found and some of them were not found, but they're gone now the lot of them. . . . There were Stephen, and Shawn, were lost in the great wind, and found after in the Bay of Gregory of the Golden Mouth, and carried up the two of them on one plank, and in by that door.

[*She pauses for a moment; the girls start as if they heard something through the door that is half open behind them.*]

NORA [*in a whisper*]. Did you hear that, Cathleen? Did you hear a noise in the north-east?

CATHLEEN [*in a whisper*]. There's some one after crying out by the seashore.

MAURYA [*continues without hearing anything*]. There was Sheamus and his father, and his own father again, were lost in a dark night, and not a stick or sign was seen of them when the sun went up. There was Patch after was drowned out of a curagh that turned over. I was sitting here with Bartley, and he a baby, lying on my two knees, and I seen two women, and three women, and four women coming in, and they crossing themselves, and not saying a word. I looked out then, and there were men coming after them, and they holding a thing in the half of a red sail, and water dripping out of it—it was a dry day, Nora—and leaving a track to the door.

[*She pauses again with her hand stretched out towards the door. It opens softly and old women begin to come in, crossing themselves on the threshold, and kneeling down in front of the stage with red petticoats over their heads.*]

MAURYA [*half in a dream, to* CATHLEEN]. Is it Patch, or Michael, or what is it at all?

B

CATHLEEN. Michael is after being found in the far north, and when he is found there how could he be here in this place?

MAURYA. There does be a power of young men floating round in the sea, and what way would they know if it was Michael they had, or another man like him, for when a man is nine days in the sea, and the wind blowing, it's hard set his own mother would be to say what man was in it.

CATHLEEN. It's Michael, God spare him, for they're after sending us a bit of his clothes from the far north.

[*She reaches out and hands* MAURYA *the clothes that belonged to Michael.* MAURYA *stands up slowly, and takes them in her hands.* NORA *looks out.*]

NORA. They're carrying a thing among them and there's water dripping out of it and leaving a track by the big stones.

CATHLEEN [*in a whisper to the women who have come in*]. Is it Bartley it is?

ONE OF THE WOMEN. It is surely, God rest his soul.

[*Two younger women come in and pull out the table. Then men carry in the body of* BARTLEY, *laid on a plank, with a bit of a sail over it, and lay it on the table.*]

CATHLEEN [*to the women, as they are doing so*]. What way was he drowned?

ONE OF THE WOMEN. The grey pony knocked him over into the sea, and he was washed out where there is a great surf on the white rocks.

[MAURYA *has gone over and knelt down at the head of the table. The women are keening softly and swaying themselves with a slow movement.* CATHLEEN *and* NORA *kneel at the other end of the table. The men kneel near the door.*]

MAURYA [*raising her head and speaking as if she did not see the people around her*]. They're all gone now, and there isn't anything more the sea can do to me. . . . I'll have no call now to be up crying and praying when the wind breaks from the south, and you can hear the surf is in the east, and the surf is in the west, making a great stir with the two noises, and they hitting one on the other. I'll have no call now to be going down and getting Holy Water in the dark nights after Samhain, and I won't care what way the sea is when the other women will be keening. [*To* NORA.] Give me the Holy Water, Nora, there's a small sup still on the dresser. [NORA *gives it to her.* MAURYA *drops Michael's clothes across* BARTLEY'S *feet, and sprinkles the Holy Water over him.*]. . . . It isn't that I haven't prayed for you, Bartley, to the Almighty God. It isn't that I haven't said prayers in the dark night till you wouldn't know what I'd be saying; but it's a great rest I'll have now, and it's time surely. It's a great rest I'll have now, and great sleeping in the long nights after Samhain, if it's only a bit of wet flour we do have to eat, and maybe a fish that would be stinking. [*She kneels down again, crossing herself, and saying prayers under her breath.*]

CATHLEEN [*to an old man kneeling near her*]. Maybe yourself and Eamon would make a coffin when the sun rises. We have fine white boards herself bought, God help her, thinking Michael would be found, and I have a new cake you can eat while you'll be working.

THE OLD MAN [*looking at the boards*]. Are there nails with them?

CATHLEEN. There are not, Colum; we didn't think of the nails.

ANOTHER MAN. It's a great wonder she wouldn't think of the nails, and all the coffins she's seen made already.

CATHLEEN. It's getting old she is, and broken.

[MAURYA *stands up again very slowly and spreads out the pieces of Michael's clothes beside the body, sprinkling them with the last of the Holy Water.*]

NORA [*in a whisper to* CATHLEEN]. She's quiet now and easy; but the day Michael was drowned you could hear her crying out from this to the spring well. It's fonder she was of Michael, and would any one have thought that?

CATHLEEN [*slowly and clearly*]. An old woman will soon be tired with anything she will do, and isn't it nine days herself is after crying, and keening, and making great sorrow in the house?

MAURYA [*puts the empty cup mouth downwards on the table, and lays her hands together on* BARTLEY'S *feet*]. They're all together this time, and the end is come. May the Almighty God have mercy on Bartley's soul, and on Michael's soul, and on the souls of Sheamus and Patch, and Stephen and Shawn [*bending her head*]. . . . and may He have mercy on my soul, Nora, and on the soul of every-one is left living in the world. [*She pauses, and the keen rises a little more loudly from the women, then sinks away. Continuing.*] Michael has a clean burial in the far north, by the grace of the Almighty God. Bartley will have a fine coffin out of the white boards, and a deep grave surely. . . .   What more can we want than that? . . . No man at all can be living for ever,   and we must be satisfied.

[*She kneels down again and the curtain falls slowly.*]

THE END

THE SHADOW OF THE GLEN

A PLAY IN ONE ACT

(1902–1905)

PERSONS

DAN BURKE, farmer and herd
NORA BURKE, his wife
MICHAEL DARA, a young herd
A TRAMP

SCENE

*The last cottage at the head of a
long glen in County Wicklow*

Cottage kitchen; turf fire on the right; a bed near it against the wall with a body lying on it covered with a sheet. A door is at the other end of the room, with a low table near it, and stools, or wooden chairs. There are a couple of glasses on the table, and a bottle of whiskey, as if for a wake, with two cups, a tea-pot, and a home-made cake. There is another small door near the bed. NORA BURKE *is moving about the room, settling a few things and lighting candles on the table, looking now and then at the bed with an uneasy look. Someone knocks softly at the door on the left. She takes up a stocking with money from the table and puts it in her pocket. Then she opens the door.*

TRAMP [*outside*]. Good evening to you, lady of the house.

NORA. Good evening kindly, stranger, it's a wild night, God help you, to be out in the rain falling.

TRAMP. It is surely, and I walking to Brittas from the Aughrim fair.

NORA. Is it walking on your feet, stranger?

TRAMP. On my two feet, lady of the house, and when I saw the light below I thought maybe if you'd a sup of new milk and a quiet decent corner where a man could sleep . . . . [*He looks in past her and sees the body on the bed.*] The Lord have mercy on us all!

NORA. It doesn't matter any way, stranger, come in out of the rain.

TRAMP [*coming in slowly and going towards the bed*]. Is it departed he is?

NORA. It is, stranger. He's after dying on me, God forgive him, and there I am now with a hundred sheep beyond on the hills, and no turf drawn for the winter.

TRAMP [*looking closely at the body*]. It's a queer look is on him for a man that's dead.

NORA [*half-humorously*]. He was always queer, stranger, and I suppose them that's queer and they living men will be queer bodies after.

TRAMP. Isn't it a great wonder you're letting him lie there, and he not tidied, or laid out itself?

NORA [*coming to the bed*]. I was afeard, stranger, for he put a black curse on me this morning if I'd touch his body the time he'd die sudden, or let anyone touch it except his sister only, and it's ten miles away she lives, in the big glen over the hill.

TRAMP [*looking at her and nodding slowly*]. It's a queer story he wouldn't let his own wife touch him, and he dying quiet in his bed.

NORA. He was an old man, and an odd man, stranger, and it's always up on the hills he was, thinking thoughts in the dark mist. [*She pulls back a bit more of the sheet.*] Lay your hand on him now, and tell me if it's cold he is surely.

TRAMP. Is it getting the curse on me you'd be, woman of the house? I wouldn't lay my hand on him for the Lough Nahanagan and it filled with gold.

NORA [*looking uneasily at the body*]. Maybe cold would be no sign of death with the like of him, for he was always cold, every day since I knew him,—and every night, stranger—[*she covers up his face and comes away from the bed*]; but I'm thinking it's dead he is surely, for he's complaining a while back of a pain in his heart, and this morning, the time he was going off to Brittas for three days or four, he was taken with a sharp turn. Then he went into his bed and he was saying it was destroyed he was, the time the shadow was going up through the glen, and when the sun set on the bog beyond he made a great lep, and let a great cry out of him, and stiffened himself out the like of a dead sheep.

TRAMP [*crosses himself*]. God rest his soul.

NORA [*pouring him out a glass of whiskey*]. Maybe that would do you better than the milk of the sweetest cow in County Wicklow.

TRAMP. The Almighty God reward you, and may it be to your good health. [*He drinks.*]

NORA [*giving him a pipe and tobacco from the table*]. I've no pipes saving his own, stranger, but they're sweet pipes to smoke.

TRAMP. Thank you kindly, lady of the house.

NORA. Sit down now, stranger, and be taking your rest.

TRAMP [*filling a pipe and looking about the room*]. I've walked a great way through the world, lady of the house, and seen great wonders, but I never seen a wake till this day with fine spirits, and good tobacco, and the best of pipes, and no one to taste them but a woman only.

NORA. Didn't you hear me say it was only after dying on me he was when the sun went down, and how would I go out into the glen and tell the neighbours and I a lone woman with no house near me?

TRAMP [*drinking*]. There's no offence, lady of the house?

NORA. No offence in life, stranger. How would the like of you passing in the dark night know the lonesome way I was with no house near me at all?

TRAMP [*sitting down*]. I knew rightly. [*He lights his pipe so that there is a sharp light beneath his haggard face.*] And I was thinking, and I coming in through the door, that it's many a lone woman would be afeard of the like of me in the dark night, in a place wouldn't be as lonesome as this place, where there aren't two living souls would see the little light you have shining from the glass.

NORA [*slowly*]. I'm thinking many would be afeard, but I never knew what way I'd be afeard of beggar or bishop or any man of you at all. [*She looks towards the window and lowers her voice.*] It's other things than the like of you, stranger, would make a person afeard.

TRAMP [*looking round with a half-shudder*]. It is surely, God help us all!

NORA [*looking at him for a moment with curiosity*]. You're saying that, stranger, as if you were easy afeard.

TRAMP [*speaking mournfully*]. Is it myself, lady of the house, that does be walking round in the long nights, and crossing the hills when the fog is on them, the time a little stick would seem as big as your arm, and a rabbit as big as a bay horse, and a stack of turf as big as a towering church in the city of Dublin? If myself was easily afeard, I'm telling you, it's long ago I'd have been locked into the Richmond Asylum, or maybe have run up into the back hills with nothing on me but an old shirt, and been eaten with crows the like of Patch Darcy—the Lord have mercy on him—in the year that's gone.

NORA [*with interest*]. You knew Darcy?

TRAMP. Wasn't I the last one heard his living voice in the whole world?

NORA. There were great stories of what was heard at that time, but would anyone believe the things they do be saying in the glen?

TRAMP. It was no lie, lady of the house . . . I was passing below on a dark night the like of this night, and the sheep were lying under the ditch and every one of them coughing, and choking, like an old man, with the great rain and the fog . . . Then I heard a thing talking —queer talk, you wouldn't believe at all, and you out of your dreams,—and 'Merciful God,' says I, 'if I begin hearing the like of that voice out of the thick mist, I'm destroyed surely.' Then I run, and I run, and I run, till I was below in Rathvanna. I got drunk that night, I got drunk in the morning, and drunk the day after,—I was coming from the races beyond—and the third day they found Darcy . . . Then I knew it was himself I was after hearing, and I wasn't afeard any more.

NORA [*speaking sorrowfully and slowly*]. God spare Darcy, he'd always look in here and he passing up or passing down, and it's very lonesome I was after him a long while [*she looks over at the bed and lowers her voice, speaking very clearly*], and then I got happy again—if it's ever happy we are, stranger—for I got used to being lonesome. [*A short pause; then she stands up.*] Was there anyone on the last bit of the road, stranger, and you coming from Aughrim?

TRAMP. There was a young man with a drift of mountain ewes, and he running after them this way and that.

NORA [*with a half-smile*]. Far down, stranger?

TRAMP. A piece only.

[*She fills the kettle and puts it on the fire.*]

NORA. Maybe, if you're not easy afeard, you'd stay here a short while alone with himself?

TRAMP. I would surely. A man that's dead can do no hurt.

NORA [*speaking with a sort of constraint*]. I'm going a little back to the west, stranger, for himself would go there one night and another, and whistle at that place, and then the young man you're after seeing

—a kind of a farmer has come up from the sea to live in a cottage beyond—would walk round to see if there was a thing we'd have to be done, and I'm wanting him this night, the way he can go down into the glen when the sun goes up and tell the people that himself is dead.

TRAMP [*looking at the body in the sheet*]. It's myself will go for him, lady of the house, and let you not be destroying yourself with the great rain.

NORA. You wouldn't find your way, stranger, for there's a small path only, and it running up between two sluigs where an ass and cart would be drowned. [*She puts a shawl over her head.*] Let you be making yourself easy, and saying a prayer for his soul, and it's not long I'll be coming again.

TRAMP [*moving uneasily*]. Maybe if you'd a piece of a grey thread and a sharp needle—there's great safety in a needle, lady of the house—I'd be putting a little stitch here and there in my old coat, the time I'll be praying for his soul, and it going up naked to the saints of God.

NORA [*takes a needle and thread from the front of her dress and gives it to him*]. There's the needle, stranger, and I'm thinking you won't be lonesome, and you used to the back hills, for isn't a dead man itself more company than to be sitting alone, and hearing the winds crying, and you not knowing on what thing your mind would stay?

TRAMP [*slowly*]. It's true, surely, and the Lord have mercy on us all!

[NORA *goes out.* THE TRAMP *begins stitching one of the tags in his coat, saying the 'De Profundis' under his breath. In an instant the sheet is drawn slowly down, and* DAN BURKE *looks out.* THE TRAMP *moves uneasily, then looks up, and springs to his feet with a movement of terror.*]

DAN [*with a hoarse voice*]. Don't be afeard, stranger; a man that's dead can do no hurt.

TRAMP [*trembling*]. I meant no harm, your honour; and won't you leave me easy to be saying a little prayer for your soul?

[*A long whistle is heard outside.*]

DAN [*listening, sitting up in his bed and speaking fiercely*]. Ah, the devil mend her . . . Do you hear that, stranger? Did ever you hear another woman could whistle the like of that with two fingers in her mouth? [*He looks at the table hurriedly.*] I'm destroyed with the drouth, and let you bring me a drop quickly before herself will come back.

TRAMP [*doubtfully*]. Is it not dead you are?

DAN. How would I be dead, and I as dry as a baked bone, stranger?

TRAMP [*pouring out the whiskey*]. What will herself say if she smells the stuff on you, for I'm thinking it's not for nothing you're letting on to be dead?

DAN. It is not, stranger, but she won't be coming near me at all, and it's not long now I'll be letting on, for I've a cramp in my back, and my hip's asleep on me, and there's been the devil's own fly itching my nose. . . . It's near dead I was wanting to sneeze, and you blathering about the rain, and Darcy [*bitterly*]—the devil choke him—and the towering church. [*Crying out impatiently.*] Give me that whiskey. Would you have herself come back before I taste a drop at all? [TRAMP *gives him the glass and he drinks.*] . . . Go over now to that cupboard, and bring me a black stick you'll see in the west corner by the wall.

TRAMP [*taking a stick from the cupboard*]. Is it that?

DAN. It is, stranger; it's a long time I'm keeping that stick, for I've a bad wife in the house.

TRAMP [*with a queer look*]. Is it herself, master of the house, and she a grand woman to talk?

DAN. It's herself, surely, it's a bad wife she is—a bad wife for an old man, and I'm getting old, God help me, though I've an arm to me still. [*He takes the stick in his hand.*] Let you wait now a short while, and it's a great sight you'll see in this room in two hours or three. [*He stops to listen.*] Is that somebody above?

TRAMP [*listening*]. There's a voice speaking on the path.

DAN. Put that stick here in the bed, and smooth the sheet the way it was lying. [*He covers himself up hastily.*] Be falling to sleep now and don't let on you know anything, or I'll be having your life. I wouldn't have told you at all but it's destroyed with the drouth I was.

TRAMP [*covering his head*]. Have no fear, master of the house. What is it I know of the like of you that I'd be saying a word or putting out my hand to stay you at all? [*He goes back to the fire, sits down on a stool with his back to the bed and goes on stitching his coat.*]

DAN [*under the sheet, querulously*]. Stranger.

TRAMP [*quickly*]. Whisht, whisht. Be quiet I'm telling you, they're coming now at the door.

[NORA *comes in with* MICHAEL DARA, *a tall, innocent young man, behind her.*]

NORA. I wasn't long at all, stranger, for I met himself on the path.

TRAMP. You were middling long, lady of the house.

NORA. There was no sign from himself?

TRAMP. No sign at all, lady of the house.

NORA [*to* MICHAEL]. Go over now and pull down the sheet, and look on himself, Michael Dara, and you'll see it's the truth I'm telling you.

MICHAEL. I will not, Nora, I do be afeard of the dead.

[*He sits down on a stool next the table facing* THE TRAMP. NORA *puts the kettle on a lower hook of the pot-hooks, and piles turf under it.*]

NORA [*turning to* TRAMP]. Will you drink a sup of tea with myself and the young man, stranger, or [*speaking more persuasively*] will you go into the little room and stretch yourself a short while on the bed. I'm thinking it's destroyed you are walking the length of that way in the great rain.

TRAMP. Is it go away and leave you, and you having a wake, lady of the house? I will not surely. [*He takes a drink from his glass which he has beside him.*] And it's none of your tea I'm asking either. [*He goes on stitching.*]

[NORA *makes the tea.*]

MICHAEL [*after looking at the tramp rather scornfully for a moment*]. That's a poor coat you have, God help you, and I'm thinking it's a poor tailor you are with it.

TRAMP [*looks up at him for a moment*]. If it's a poor tailor I am, I'm thinking it's a poor herd does be running back and forward after a little handful of ewes the way I seen yourself running this day, young fellow, and you coming from the fair.

NORA [*comes back to the table. To* MICHAEL *in a low voice*]. Let you not mind him at all, Michael Dara. He has a drop taken, and it's soon he'll be falling asleep.

MICHAEL. It's no lie he's telling, I was destroyed surely ... They were that wilful they were running off into one man's bit of oats, and another man's bit of hay, and tumbling into the red bogs till it's more like a pack of old goats than sheep they were ... Mountain ewes is a queer breed, Nora Burke, and I'm not used to them at all.

NORA [*settling the tea things*]. There's no one can drive a mountain ewe but the men do be reared in the Glen Malure, I've heard them say, and above by Rathvanna, and the Glen Imaal, men the like of Patch Darcy, God spare his soul, who would walk through five hundred sheep and miss one of them, and he not reckoning them at all.

MICHAEL [*uneasily*]. Is it the man went queer in his head the year that's gone?

NORA It is surely.

TRAMP [*plaintively*]. That was a great man, young fellow, a great man I'm telling you. There was never a lamb from his own ewes he wouldn't know before it was marked, and he'd run from this to the city of Dublin, and never catch for his breath.

NORA [*turning round quickly*]. He was a great man surely, stranger, and isn't it a grand thing when you hear a living man saying a good word of a dead man, and he mad dying?

TRAMP. It's the truth I'm saying, God spare his soul.

[*He puts the needle under the collar of his coat, and settles himself to sleep in the chimney-corner.* NORA *sits down at the table: their backs are turned to the bed.*]

MICHAEL [*looking at her with a queer look*]. I heard tell this day, Nora Burke, that it was on the path below Patch Darcy would be passing up and passing down, and I heard them say he'd never pass it night or morning without speaking with yourself.

NORA [*in a low voice*]. It was no lie you heard, Michael Dara.

MICHAEL [*as before*]. I'm thinking it's a power of men you're after knowing if it's in a lonesome place you live itself.

NORA [*slowly, giving him his tea*]. It's in a lonesome place you do have to be talking with someone, and looking for someone, in the evening of the day, and if it's a power of men I'm after knowing they were fine men, for I was a hard child to please, and a hard girl to please [*she looks at him a little sternly*], and it's a hard woman I am to please this day, Michael Dara, and it's no lie, I'm telling you.

MICHAEL [*looking over to see that* THE TRAMP *is asleep and then, pointing to the dead man*]. Was it a hard woman to please you were when you took himself for your man?

NORA. What way would I live and I an old woman if I didn't marry a man with a bit of a farm, and cows on it, and sheep on the back hills?

MICHAEL [*considering*]. That's true, Nora, and maybe it's no fool you were, for there's good grazing on it, if it is a lonesome place, and I'm thinking it's a good sum he's left behind.

NORA [*taking the stocking with money from her pocket, and putting it on the table*]. I do be thinking in the long nights it was a big fool I was that time, Michael Dara, for what good is a bit of a farm with cows on it, and sheep on the back hills, when you do be sitting, looking out from a door the like of that door, and seeing nothing but the mists rolling down the bog, and the mists again, and they rolling up the bog, and hearing nothing but the wind crying out in the bits of broken trees were left from the great storm, and the streams roaring with the rain?

MICHAEL [*looking at her uneasily*]. What is it ails you this night, Nora Burke? I've heard tell it's the like of that talk you do hear from men, and they after being a great while on the back hills.

NORA [*putting out the money on the table*]. It's a bad night, and a wild night, Michael Dara, and isn't it a great while I am at the foot of the back hills, sitting up here boiling food for himself, and food for the brood sow, and baking a cake when the night falls? [*She puts up the money, listlessly, in little piles on the table.*] Isn't it a long while I am sitting here in the winter, and the summer, and the fine spring, with the young growing behind me and the old passing, saying to myself one time, to look on Mary Brien who wasn't that height [*holding out her hand*], and I a fine girl growing up, and there she is now with two children, and another coming on her in three months or four [*she pauses*].

MICHAEL [*moving over three of the piles*]. That's three pounds we have now, Nora Burke.

NORA [*continuing in the same voice*]. And saying to myself another time, to look on Peggy Cavanagh, who had the lightest hand at milking a cow that wouldn't be easy, or turning a cake, and there she is now walking round on the roads, or sitting in a dirty old house, with no teeth in her mouth, and no sense, and no more hair than you'd see on a bit of a hill and they after burning the furze from it. [*She pauses again.*]

MICHAEL. That's five pounds and ten notes, a good sum, surely! . . . It's not that way you'll be talking when you marry a young man, Nora Burke, and they were saying in the fair my lambs were the best lambs, and I got a grand price, for I'm no fool now at making a bargain when my lambs are good.

NORA. What was it you got?

MICHAEL. Twenty pound for the lot, Nora Burke . . . We'd do right to wait now till himself will be quiet a while in the Seven Churches, and then you'll marry me in the chapel of Rathvanna, and I'll bring the sheep up on the bit of a hill you have on the back mountain, and we won't have anything we'd be afeard to let our minds on when the mist is down.

NORA [*pouring him out some whiskey*]. Why would I marry you, Mike Dara? You'll be getting old, and I'll be getting old, and in a little while, I'm telling you, you'll be sitting up in your bed—the way himself was sitting—with a shake in your face, and your teeth falling, and the white hair sticking out round you like an old bush where sheep do be leaping a gap.

[DAN BURKE *sits up noiselessly from under the sheet, with his hand to his face. His white hair is sticking out round his head.*]

NORA [*goes on slowly without hearing him*]. It's a pitiful thing to be getting old, but it's a queer thing surely . . . It's a queer thing to see an old man sitting up there in his bed, with no teeth in him, and a rough word in his mouth, and his chin the way it would take the bark from the edge of an oak board you'd have building a door . . . God forgive me, Michael Dara, we'll all be getting old, but it's a queer thing surely.

MICHAEL. It's too lonesome you are from living a long time with an old man, Nora, and you're talking again like a herd that would be coming down from the thick mist [*he puts his arm round her*], but it's a fine life you'll have now with a young man, a fine life surely . . .

[DAN *sneezes violently.* MICHAEL *tries to get to the door, but before he can do so,* DAN *jumps out of the bed in queer white clothes, with the stick in his hand, and goes over and puts his back against it.*]

MICHAEL. The Son of God deliver us . . . [*Crosses himself, and goes backward across the room.*]

DAN [*holding up his hand at him*]. Now you'll not marry her the time I'm rotting below in the Seven Churches, and you'll see the thing I'll give you will follow you on the back mountains when the wind is high.

MICHAEL [*to* NORA]. Get me out of it, Nora, for the love of God. He always did what you bid him, and I'm thinking he would do it now.

NORA [*looking at* THE TRAMP]. Is it dead he is or living?

DAN [*turning towards her*]. It's little you care if it's dead or living I am, but there'll be an end now of your fine times, and all the talk you have of young men and old men, and of the mist coming up or going down. [*He opens the door.*] You'll walk out now from that door, Nora Burke, and it's not to-morrow, or the next day, or any day of your life, that you'll put in your foot through it again.

TRAMP [*standing up*]. It's a hard thing you're saying, for an old man, master of the house, and what would the like of her do if you put her out on the roads?

DAN. Let her walk round the like of Peggy Cavanagh below, and be begging money at the cross roads, or selling songs to the men. [*To* NORA.] Walk out now, Nora Burke, and it's soon you'll be getting old with that life, I'm telling you; it's soon your teeth'll be falling and your head'll be the like of a bush where sheep do be leaping a gap.

[*He pauses; she looks round at* MICHAEL.]

MICHAEL [*timidly*]. There's a fine Union below in Rathdrum.

DAN. The like of her would never go there . . . It's lonesome roads she'll be going, and hiding herself away till the end will come, and they find her stretched like a dead sheep with the frost on her, or the big spiders, maybe, and they putting their webs on her, in the butt of a ditch.

NORA [*angrily*]. What way will yourself be that day, Daniel Burke? What way will you be that day and you lying down a long while in your grave? For it's bad you are living, and it's bad you'll be when you're dead. [*She looks at him a moment fiercely, then half turns away and speaks plaintively again.*] Yet, if it is itself, Daniel Burke, who can help it at all, and let you be getting up into your bed, and not be taking your death with the wind blowing on you, and the rain with it, and you half in your skin.

DAN. It's proud and happy you'd be if I was getting my death the day I was shut of yourself. [*Pointing to the door.*] Let you walk out through that door, I'm telling you, and let you not be passing this way if it's hungry you are, or wanting a bed.

TRAMP [*pointing to* MICHAEL]. Maybe himself would take her.

NORA. What would he do with me now?

TRAMP. Give you the half of a dry bed, and good food in your mouth.

DAN. Is it a fool you think him, stranger, or is it a fool you were born yourself? Let her walk out of that door, and let you go along with her stranger—if it's raining itself—for it's too much talk you have surely.

TRAMP [*going over to* NORA]. We'll be going now, lady of the house—the rain is falling but the air is kind, and maybe it'll be a grand morning by the grace of God.

NORA. What good is a grand morning when I'm destroyed surely, and I going out to get my death walking the roads?

TRAMP. You'll not be getting your death with myself, lady of the house, and I knowing all the ways a man can put food in his mouth. . . . We'll be going now, I'm telling you, and the time you'll be feeling the cold and the frost, and the great rain, and the sun again, and the south wind blowing in the glens, you'll not be sitting up on a wet ditch the way you're after sitting in this place, making yourself old with looking on each day and it passing you by. You'll be saying one time, 'It's a grand evening by the grace of God,' and another time, 'It's a wild night, God help us, but it'll pass surely.' You'll be saying—

DAN [goes over to them crying out impatiently]. Go out of that door, I'm telling you, and do your blathering below in the glen.

[NORA gathers a few things into her shawl.]

TRAMP [at the door]. Come along with me now, lady of the house, and it's not my blather you'll be hearing only, but you'll be hearing the herons crying out over the black lakes, and you'll be hearing the grouse, and the owls with them, and the larks and the big thrushes when the days are warm, and it's not from the like of them you'll be hearing a talk of getting old like Peggy Cavanagh, and losing the hair off you, and the light of your eyes, but it's fine songs you'll be hearing when the sun goes up, and there'll be no old fellow wheezing the like of a sick sheep close to your ear.

NORA. I'm thinking it's myself will be wheezing that time with lying down under the Heavens when the night is cold, but you've a fine bit of talk, stranger, and it's with yourself I'll go. [She goes towards the door, then turns to DAN.] You think it's a grand thing you're after doing with your letting on to be dead, but what is it at all? What way would a woman live in a lonesome place the like of this place, and she not making a talk with the men passing? And what way will yourself live from this day, with none to care you? What is it you'll have now but a black life, Daniel Burke, and it's not long, I'm telling you, till you'll be lying again under that sheet, and you dead surely.

[She goes out with THE TRAMP. MICHAEL is slinking after them, but DAN stops him.]

DAN. Sit down now and take a little taste of the stuff, Michael Dara, there's a great drouth on me, and the night is young.

MICHAEL [*coming back to the table*]. And it's very dry I am surely, with the fear of death you put on me, and I after driving mountain ewes since the turn of the day.

DAN [*throwing away his stick*]. I was thinking to strike you, Michael Dara, but you're a quiet man, God help you, and I don't mind you at all. [*He pours out two glasses of whiskey, and gives one to* MICHAEL.]

DAN. Your good health, Michael Dara.

MICHAEL. God reward you, Daniel Burke, and may you have a long life and a quiet life, and good health with it. [*They drink.*]

CURTAIN

THE TINKER'S WEDDING

A COMEDY IN TWO ACTS

(1902–1907)

PREFACE

THE drama is made serious—in the French sense of the word—not by the degree in which it is taken up with problems that are serious in themselves, but by the degree in which it gives the nourishment, not very easy to define, on which our imaginations live. We should not go to the theatre as we go to a chemist's, or a dram-shop, but as we go to a dinner, where the food we need is taken with pleasure and excitement. This was nearly always so in Spain and England and France when the drama was at its richest—the infancy and decay of the drama tend to be didactic—but in these days the playhouse is too often stocked with the drugs of many seedy problems, or with the absinthe or vermouth of the last musical comedy.

The drama, like the symphony, does not teach or prove anything. Analysts with their problems, and teachers with their systems, are soon as old-fashioned as the pharmacopoeia of Galen,—look at Ibsen and the Germans —but the best plays of Ben Jonson and Molière can no more go out of fashion than the blackberries on the hedges.

Of the things which nourish the imagination humour is one of the most needful, and it is dangerous to limit or destroy it. Baudelaire calls laughter the greatest sign of the Satanic element in man; and where a country loses its humour, as some towns in Ireland are doing, there will be morbidity of mind, as Baudelaire's mind was morbid.

In the greater part of Ireland, however, the whole people, from the tinkers to the clergy, have still a life, and view of life, that are rich and genial and humorous. I do not think that these country people, who have so much humour themselves, will mind being laughed at without malice, as the people in every country have been laughed at in their own comedies.

J. M. S.

December 2nd, 1907.

NOTE.—'The Tinker's Wedding' was first written a few years ago, about the time I was working at 'Riders to the Sea', and 'In the Shadow of the Glen'. I have re-written it since.

J. M. S.

PERSONS

MICHAEL BYRNE, a tinker
MARY BYRNE, an old woman, his mother
SARAH CASEY, a young tinker woman
A PRIEST

SCENE

A road-side near a village

ACT I

After nightfall. A fire of sticks is burning near the ditch a little to the right. MICHAEL *is working beside it. In the background, on the left, a sort of tent and ragged clothes drying on the hedge. On the right a chapel-gate.*

SARAH CASEY [*coming in on right, eagerly*]. We'll see his reverence this place, Michael Byrne, and he passing backward to his house to-night.

MICHAEL [*grimly*]. That'll be a sacred and a sainted joy!

SARAH [*sharply*]. It'll be small joy for yourself if you aren't ready with my wedding ring. [*She goes over to him.*] Is it near done this time, or what way is it at all?

MICHAEL. A poor way only, Sarah Casey, for it's the divil's job making a ring, and you'll be having my hands destroyed in a short while the way I'll not be able to make a tin can at all maybe at the dawn of day.

SARAH [*sitting down beside him and throwing sticks on the fire*]. If it's the divil's job, let you mind it, and leave your speeches that would choke a fool.

MICHAEL [*slowly and glumly*]. And it's you'll go talking of fools, Sarah Casey, when no man did ever hear a lying story even of your like unto this mortal day. You to be going beside me a great while, and rearing a lot of them, and then to be setting off with your talk of getting married, and your driving me to it, and I not asking it at all.

[SARAH *turns her back to him and arranges something in the ditch.*]

MICHAEL [*angrily*]. Can't you speak a word when I'm asking what is it ails you since the moon did change?

SARAH [*musingly*]. I'm thinking there isn't anything ails me, Michael Byrne; but the spring-time is a queer time, and it's queer thoughts maybe I do think at whiles.

MICHAEL. It's hard set you'd be to think queerer than welcome, Sarah Casey; but what will you gain dragging me to the priest this night, I'm saying, when it's new thoughts you'll be thinking at the dawn of day?

SARAH [*teasingly*]. It's at the dawn of day I do be thinking I'd have a right to be going off to the rich tinkers do be travelling from Tibradden to the Tara Hill; for it'd be a fine life to be driving with young Jaunting Jim, where there wouldn't be any big hills to break the back of you, with walking up and walking down.

MICHAEL [*with dismay*]. It's the like of that you do be thinking!

SARAH. The like of that, Michael Byrne, when there is a bit of sun in it, and a kind air, and a great smell coming from the thorn trees is above your head.

MICHAEL [*looks at her for a moment with horror, and then hands her the ring*]. Will that fit you now?

SARAH [*trying it on*]. It's making it tight you are, and the edges sharp on the tin.

MICHAEL [*looking at it carefully*]. It's the fat of your own finger, Sarah Casey; and isn't it a mad thing I'm saying again that you'd be asking marriage of me, or making a talk of going away from me, and you thriving and getting your good health by the grace of the Almighty God?

SARAH [*giving it back to him*]. Fix it now, and it'll do, if you're wary you don't squeeze it again.

MICHAEL [*moodily, working again*]. It's easy saying be wary; there's many things easy said, Sarah Casey, you'd wonder a fool even would be saying at all. [*He starts violently.*] The divil mend you, I'm scalded again!

SARAH [*scornfully*]. If you are, it's a clumsy man you are this night, Michael Byrne [*raising her voice*]; and let you make haste now, or herself will be coming with the porter.

MICHAEL [*defiantly, raising his voice*]. Let me make haste? I'll be making haste maybe to hit you a great clout; for I'm thinking it's the like of that you want. I'm thinking on the day I got you above at Rathvanna, and the way you began crying out and we coming down off the hill, crying out and saying, 'I'll go back to my ma,' and I'm thinking on the way I came behind you that time, and hit you a great clout in the lug, and how quiet and easy it was you came along with me from that hour to this present day.

SARAH [*standing up and throwing all her sticks into the fire*]. And a big fool I was too, maybe; but we'll be seeing Jaunting Jim to-morrow in Ballinaclash, and he after getting a great price for his white foal in the horse-fair of Wicklow, the way it'll be a great sight to see him squandering his share of gold, and he with a grand eye for a fine horse, and a grand eye for a woman.

MICHAEL [*working again with impatience*]. The divil do him good with the two of them.

SARAH [*kicking up the ashes with her foot*]. Ah, he's a great lad, I'm telling you, and it's proud and happy I'll be to see him, and he the first one called me the Beauty of Ballinacree, a fine name for a woman.

MICHAEL [*with contempt*]. It's the like of that name they do be putting on the horses they have below racing in Arklow. It's easy pleased you are, Sarah Casey, easy pleased with a big word, or the liar speaks it.

SARAH. Liar!

MICHAEL. Liar, surely.

SARAH [*indignantly*]. Liar, is it? Didn't you ever hear tell of the peelers followed me ten miles along the Glen Malure, and they talking love to me in the dark night, or of the children you'll meet coming from school and they saying one to the other, 'It's this day we seen Sarah Casey, the Beauty of Ballinacree, a great sight surely.'

MICHAEL. God help the lot of them!

SARAH. It's yourself you'll be calling God to help, in two weeks or three, when you'll be waking up in the dark night and thinking you see me coming with the sun on me, and I driving a high cart with Jaunting Jim going behind. It's lonesome and cold you'll be feeling the ditch where you'll be lying down that night, I'm telling you, and you hearing the old woman making a great noise in her sleep, and the bats squeaking in the trees.

MICHAEL. Whisht. I hear some one coming the road.

SARAH [*looking out right*]. It's some one coming forward from the doctor's door.

MICHAEL. It's often his reverence does be in there playing cards, or drinking a sup, or singing songs, until the dawn of day.

SARAH. It's a big boast of a man with a long step on him and a trumpeting voice. It's his reverence surely; and if you have the ring done, it's a great bargain we'll make now and he after drinking his glass.

MICHAEL [*going to her and giving her the ring*]. There's your ring, Sarah Casey; but I'm thinking he'll walk by and not stop to speak with the like of us at all.

SARAH [*tidying herself, in great excitement*]. Let you be sitting here and keeping a great blaze, the way he can look on my face; and let you seem to be working, for it's great love the like of him have to talk of work.

MICHAEL [*moodily, sitting down and beginning to work at a tin can*]. Great love surely.

SARAH [*eagerly*]. Make a great blaze now, Michael Byrne.

[*The* PRIEST *comes in on right; she comes forward in front of him.*]

SARAH [*in a very plausible voice*]. Good evening, your reverence. It's a grand fine night, by the grace of God.

PRIEST. The Lord have mercy on us! What kind of a living woman is it that you are at all?

SARAH. It's Sarah Casey I am, your reverence, the Beauty of Ballinacree, and it's Michael Byrne is below in the ditch.

PRIEST. A holy pair, surely! Let you get out of my way. [*He tries to pass by.*]

SARAH [*keeping in front of him*]. We are wanting a little word with your reverence.

PRIEST. I haven't a halfpenny at all. Leave the road I'm saying.

SARAH. It isn't a halfpenny we're asking, holy father; but we were thinking maybe we'd have a right to be getting married; and we were thinking it's yourself would marry us for not a halfpenny at all; for you're a kind man, your reverence, a kind man with the poor.

PRIEST [*with astonishment*]. Is it marry you for nothing at all?

SARAH. It is, your reverence; and we were thinking maybe you'd give us a little small bit of silver to pay for the ring.

PRIEST [*loudly*]. Let you hold your tongue; let you be quiet, Sarah Casey. I've no silver at all for the like of you; and if you want to be married, let you pay your pound. I'd do it for a pound only, and that's making it a sight cheaper than I'd make it for one of my own pairs is living here in the place.

SARAH. Where would the like of us get a pound, your reverence?

PRIEST. Wouldn't you easy get it with your selling asses, and making cans, and your stealing east and west in Wicklow and Wexford and the county Meath? [*He tries to pass her.*] Let you leave the road, and not be plaguing me more.

SARAH [*pleadingly, taking money from her pocket*]. Wouldn't you have a little mercy on us, your reverence? [*Holding out money.*] Wouldn't you marry us for a half a sovereign, and it a nice shiny one with a view on it of the living king's mamma?

PRIEST. If it's ten shillings you have, let you get ten more the same way, and I'll marry you then.

SARAH [*whining*]. It's two years we are getting that bit, your reverence, with our pence and our halfpence and an odd threepenny bit; and if you don't marry us now, himself and the old woman, who has a great drouth, will be drinking it to-morrow in the fair [*she puts her apron to her eyes, half sobbing*], and then I won't be married any time, and I'll be saying till I'm an old woman: 'It's a cruel and a wicked thing to be bred poor.'

PRIEST [*turning up towards the fire*]. Let you not be crying, Sarah Casey. It's a queer woman you are to be crying at the like of that, and you your whole life walking the roads.

SARAH [*sobbing*]. It's two years we are getting the gold, your reverence, and now you won't marry us for that bit, and we hard-working poor people do be making cans in the dark night, and blinding our eyes with the black smoke from the bits of twigs we do be burning.

[*An old woman is heard singing tipsily on the left.*]

PRIEST [*looking at the can* MICHAEL *is making*]. When will you have that can done, Michael Byrne?

MICHAEL. In a short space only, your reverence, for I'm putting the last dab of solder on the rim.

PRIEST. Let you get a crown along with the ten shillings and the gallon can, Sarah Casey, and I will wed you so.

MARY [*suddenly shouting behind, tipsily*]. Larry was a fine lad, I'm saying; Larry was a fine lad, Sarah Casey—

MICHAEL. Whisht, now, the two of you. There's my mother coming, and she'd have us destroyed if she heard the like of that talk the time she's been drinking her fill.

MARY [*comes in singing*]—
    And when we asked him what way he'd die,
        And he hanging unrepented,
    'Begob,' says Larry, 'that's all in my eye,
        By the clergy first invented.'

SARAH. Give me the jug now, or you'll have it spilt in the ditch.

MARY [*holding the jug with both her hands, in a stilted voice*]. Let you leave me easy, Sarah Casey. I won't spill it, I'm saying. God help you; are you thinking it's frothing full to the brim it is at this hour of the night, and I after carrying it in my two hands a long step from Jemmy Neill's?

MICHAEL [*anxiously*]. Is there a sup left at all?

SARAH [*looking into the jug*]. A little small sup only I'm thinking.

MARY [*sees the priest, and holds out jug towards him*]. God save your reverence. I'm after bringing down a smart drop; and let you drink it up now, for it's a middling drouthy man you are at all times, God forgive you, and this night is cruel dry. [*She tries to go towards him. SARAH holds her back.*]

PRIEST [*waving her away*]. Let you not be falling to the flames. Keep off, I'm saying.

MARY [*persuasively*]. Let you not be shy of us, your reverence. Aren't we all sinners, God help us! Drink a sup now, I'm telling you; and we won't let on a word about it till the Judgment Day. [*She takes up a tin mug, pours some porter into it, and gives it to him.*]

MARY [*singing, and holding the jug in her hand*]—

> A lonesome ditch in Ballygan
> The day you're beating a tenpenny can;
> A lonesome bank in Ballyduff
> The time . . . [*She breaks off.*]

It's a bad, wicked song, Sarah Casey; and let you put me down now in the ditch, and I won't sing it till himself will be gone; for it's bad enough he is, I'm thinking, without ourselves making him worse.

SARAH [*putting her down, to the* PRIEST, *half laughing*]. Don't mind her at all, your reverence. She's no shame the time she's a drop taken; and if it was the Holy Father from Rome was in it, she'd give him a little sup out of her mug, and say the same as she'd say to yourself.

MARY [*to the* PRIEST]. Let you drink it up, holy father. Let you drink it up, I'm saying, and not be letting on you wouldn't do the like of it, and you with a stack of pint bottles above, reaching the sky.

PRIEST [*with resignation*]. Well, here's to your good health, and God forgive us all. [*He drinks.*]

MARY. That's right now, your reverence, and the blessing of God be on you. Isn't it a grand thing to see you sitting down, with no pride in you, and drinking a sup with the like of us, and we the poorest, wretched, starving creatures you'd see any place on the earth?

PRIEST. If it's starving you are itself, I'm thinking it's well for the like of you that do be drinking when there's drouth on you, and lying down to sleep when your legs are stiff. [*He sighs gloomily.*] What would you do if it was the like of myself you were, saying Mass with your mouth dry, and running east and west for a sick call maybe, and hearing the rural people again and they saying their sins?

MARY [*with compassion*]. It's destroyed you must be hearing the sins of the rural people on a fine spring.

PRIEST [*with despondency*]. It's a hard life I'm telling you, a hard life, Mary Byrne; and there's the bishop coming in the morning, and he an old man, would have you destroyed if he seen a thing at all.

MARY [*with great sympathy*]. It'd break my heart to hear you talking and sighing the like of that, your reverence. [*She pats him on the knee.*] Let you rouse up, now, if it's a poor, single man you are itself, and I'll be singing you songs unto the dawn of day.

PRIEST [*interrupting her*]. What is it I want with your songs when it'd be better for the like of you, that'll soon die, to be down on your two knees saying prayers to the Almighty God?

MARY. If it's prayers I want, you'd have a right to say one yourself, holy father; for we don't have them at all, and I've heard tell a power of times it's that you're for. Say one now, your reverence; for I've heard a power of queer things and I walking the world, but there's one thing I never heard any time, and that's a real priest saying a prayer.

PRIEST. The Lord protect us!

MARY. It's no lie, holy father. I often heard the rural people making a queer noise and they going to rest; but who'd mind the like of them? And I'm thinking it should be great game to hear a scholar, the like of you, speaking Latin to the saints above.

PRIEST [*scandalized*]. Stop your talking, Mary Byrne; you're an old flagrant heathen, and I'll stay no more with the lot of you. [*He rises.*]

MARY [*catching hold of him*]. Stop till you say a prayer, your reverence; stop till you say a little prayer, I'm telling you, and I'll give you my blessing and the last sup from the jug.

PRIEST [*breaking away*]. Leave me go, Mary Byrne; for I never met your like for hard abominations the score and two years I'm living in the place.

MARY [*innocently*]. Is that the truth?

PRIEST. It is, then, and God have mercy on your soul.

[*The* PRIEST *goes towards the left, and* SARAH *follows him.*]

SARAH [*in a low voice*]. And what time will you do the thing I'm asking, holy father? for I'm thinking you'll do it surely, and not have me growing into an old wicked heathen like herself.

MARY [*calling out shrilly*]. Let you be walking back here, Sarah Casey, and not be talking whisper-talk with the like of him in the face of the Almighty God.

SARAH [*to the* PRIEST]. Do you hear her now, your reverence? Isn't it true, surely, she's an old, flagrant heathen, would destroy the world?

PRIEST [*to* SARAH, *moving off*]. Well, I'll be coming down early to the chapel, and let you come to me a while after you see me passing, and bring the bit of gold along with you, and the tin can. I'll marry you for them two, though it's a pitiful small sum; for I wouldn't be easy in my soul if I left you growing into an old, wicked heathen the like of her.

SARAH [*following him out*]. The blessing of the Almighty God be on you, holy father, and that He may reward and watch you from this present day.

MARY [*nudging* MICHAEL]. Did you see that, Michael Byrne? Didn't you hear me telling you she's flighty a while back since the change of the moon? With her fussing for marriage, and she making whisper-talk with one man or another man along by the road.

MICHAEL. Whisht now, or she'll knock the head of you the time she comes back.

MARY. Ah, it's a bad, wicked way the world is this night, if there's a fine air in it itself. You'd never have seen me, and I a young woman, making whisper-talk with the like of him, and he the fearfullest old fellow you'd see any place walking the world.

[SARAH *comes back quickly*.]

MARY [*calling out to her*]. What is it you're after whispering above with himself?

SARAH [*exultingly*]. Lie down, and leave us in peace. [*She whispers with* MICHAEL.]

MARY [*poking out her pipe with a straw, sings*]—
    She'd whisper with one, and she'd whisper with two—
[*She breaks off coughing*.] My singing voice is gone for this night, Sarah Casey. [*She lights her pipe*.] But if it's flighty you are itself, you're a grand handsome woman, the glory of tinkers, the pride of Wicklow, the Beauty of Ballinacree. I wouldn't have you lying down and you lonesome to sleep this night in a dark ditch when the spring is coming in the trees; so let you sit down there by the big bough, and I'll be telling you the finest story you'd hear any place from Dundalk to Ballinacree, with great queens in it, making themselves matches from the start to the end, and they with shiny silks on them the length of the day, and white shifts for the night.

C

MICHAEL [*standing up with the tin can in his hand*]. Let you go asleep, and not have us destroyed.

MARY [*lying back sleepily*]. Don't mind him, Sarah Casey. Sit down now, and I'll be telling you a story would be fit to tell a woman the like of you in the spring-time of the year.

SARAH [*taking the can from* MICHAEL, *and tying it up in a piece of sacking*]. That'll not be rusting now in the dews of night. I'll put it up in the ditch the way it will be handy in the morning; and now we've that done, Michael Byrne, I'll go along with you and welcome for Tim Flaherty's hens. [*She puts the can in the ditch.*]

MARY [*sleepily*]. I've a grand story of the great queens of Ireland with white necks on them the like of Sarah Casey, and fine arms would hit you a slap the way Sarah Casey would hit you.

SARAH [*beckoning on the left*]. Come along now, Michael, while she's falling asleep.

[*He goes towards left.* MARY *sees that they are going, starts up suddenly, and turns over on her hands and knees.*]

MARY [*piteously*]. Where is it you're going? Let you walk back here, and not be leaving me lonesome when the night is fine.

SARAH. Don't be waking the world with your talk when we're going up through the back wood to get two of Tim Flaherty's hens are roosting in the ash-tree above at the well.

MARY. And it's leaving me lone you are? Come back here, Sarah Casey. Come back here, I'm saying; or if it's off you must go, leave me the two little coppers you have, the way I can walk up in a short while, and get another pint for my sleep.

SARAH. It's too much you have taken. Let you stretch yourself out and take a long sleep; for isn't that the best thing any woman can do, and she an old drinking heathen like yourself.

[*She and* MICHAEL *go out left.*]

MARY [*standing up slowly*]. It's gone they are, and I with my feet that weak under me you'd knock me down with a rush, and my head with a noise in it the like of what you'd hear in a stream and it running between two rocks and rain falling. [*She goes over to the ditch where the can is tied in sacking, and takes it down.*] What good am I this night, God help me? What good are the grand stories I have when it's few would listen to an old woman, few but a girl maybe would be in great fear the time her hour was come, or a little child wouldn't be sleeping with the hunger on a cold night? [*She takes the can from the sacking, and fits in three empty bottles and straw in its place, and ties them up.*] Maybe the two of them have a good right to be walking out the little short while they'd be young; but if they have itself, they'll not keep Mary Byrne from her full pint when the night's fine, and there's a dry moon in the sky. [*She takes up the can, and puts the package back in the ditch.*] Jemmy Neill's a decent lad; and he'll give me a good drop for the can; and maybe if I keep near the peelers to-morrow for the first bit of the fair, herself won't strike me at all; and if she does itself, what's a little stroke on your head beside sitting lonesome on a fine night, hearing the dogs barking, and the bats squeaking, and you saying over, it's a short while only till you die. [*She goes out singing 'The night before Larry was stretched'.*]

CURTAIN

ACT II

The same. Early morning. SARAH *is washing her face in an old bucket; then plaits her hair.* MICHAEL *is tidying himself also.* MARY BYRNE *is asleep against the ditch.*

SARAH [*to* MICHAEL, *with pleased excitement*]. Go over, now, to the bundle beyond, and you'll find a kind of a red handkerchief to put upon your neck, and a green one for myself.

MICHAEL [*getting them*]. You're after spending more money on the like of them. Well, it's a power we're losing this time, and we not gaining a thing at all. [*With the handkerchiefs.*] Is it them two?

SARAH. It is, Michael. [*She takes one of them.*] Let you tackle that one round under your chin; and let you not forget to take your hat from your head when we go up into the church. I asked Biddy Flynn below, that's after marrying her second man, and she told me it's the like of that they do.

[MARY *yawns, and turns over in her sleep.*]

SARAH [*with anxiety*]. There she is waking up on us, and I thinking we'd have the job done before she'd know of it at all.

MICHAEL. She'll be crying out now, and making game of us, and saying it's fools we are surely.

SARAH. I'll send her to her sleep again, or get her out of it one way or another; for it'd be a bad case to have a divil's scholar the like of her turning the priest against us maybe with her godless talk.

MARY [*waking up, and looking at them with curiosity, blandly*]. That's fine things you have on you, Sarah Casey; and it's a great stir you're making this day, washing your face. I'm that used to the hammer, I wouldn't hear it at all, but washing is a rare thing, and you're after waking me up, and I having a great sleep in the sun. [*She looks around cautiously at the bundle in which she has hidden the bottles.*]

SARAH [*coaxingly*]. Let you stretch out again for a sleep, Mary Byrne, for it'll be a middling time yet before we go to the fair.

MARY [*with suspicion*]. That's a sweet tongue you have, Sarah Casey; but if sleep's a grand thing, it's a grand thing to be waking up a day the like of this, when there's a warm sun in it, and a kind air, and you'll hear the cuckoos singing and crying out on the top of the hills.

SARAH. If it's that gay you are, you'd have a right to walk down and see would you get a few halfpence from the rich men do be driving early to the fair.

MARY. When rich men do be driving early, it's queer tempers they have, the Lord forgive them; the way it's little but bad words and swearing out you'd get from them all.

SARAH [*losing her temper and breaking out fiercely*]. Then if you'll neither beg nor sleep, let you walk off from this place where you're not wanted, and not have us waiting for you maybe at the turn of day.

MARY [*rather uneasy, turning to* MICHAEL]. God help our spirits, Michael; there she is again rousing cranky from the break of dawn. Oh! isn't she a terror since the moon did change [*she gets up slowly*]? and I'd best be going forward to sell the gallon can. [*She goes over and takes up the bundle.*]

SARAH [*crying out angrily*]. Leave that down, Mary Byrne. Oh! aren't you the scorn of women to think that you'd have that drouth and roguery on you that you'd go drinking the can and the dew not dried from the grass?

MARY [*in a feigned tone of pacification, with the bundle still in her hand*]. It's not a drouth but a heartburn I have this day, Sarah Casey, so I'm going down to cool my gullet at the blessed well; and I'll sell the can to the parson's daughter below, a harmless poor creature would fill your hand with shillings for a brace of lies.

SARAH. Leave down the tin can, Mary Byrne, for I hear the drouth upon your tongue to-day.

MARY. There's not a drink-house from this place to the fair, Sarah Casey; the way you'll find me below with the full price, and not a farthing gone. [*She turns to go off left.*]

SARAH [*jumping up, and picking up the hammer threateningly*]. Put down that can, I'm saying.

MARY [*looking at her for a moment in terror, and putting down the bundle in the ditch*]. Is it raving mad you're going, Sarah Casey, and you the pride of women to destroy the world?

SARAH [*going up to her, and giving her a push off left*]. I'll show you if it's raving mad I am. Go on from this place, I'm saying, and be wary now.

MARY [*turning back after her*]. If I go, I'll be telling old and young you're a weathered heathen savage, Sarah Casey, the one did put down a head of the parson's cabbage to boil in the pot with your clothes [*the priest comes in behind her on the left, and listens*], and quenched the flaming candles on the throne of God the time your shadow fell within the pillars of the chapel door.

[SARAH *turns on her, and she springs round nearly into the* PRIEST's *arms. When she sees him, she claps her shawl over her mouth, and goes up towards the ditch, laughing to herself.*]

PRIEST [*going to* SARAH, *half terrified at the language that he has heard*]. Well, aren't you a fearful lot? I'm thinking it's only humbug you were making at the fall of night, and you won't need me at all.

SARAH [*with anger still in her voice*]. Humbug is it! would you be turning back upon your spoken promise in the face of God!

PRIEST [*dubiously*]. I'm thinking you were never christened, Sarah Casey; and it would be a queer job to go dealing Christian sacraments unto the like of you. [*Persuasively, feeling in his pocket.*] So it would be best, maybe, I'd give you a shilling for to drink my health, and let you walk on, and not trouble me at all.

SARAH. That's your talking, is it? If you don't stand to your spoken word, holy father, I'll make my own complaint to the mitred bishop in the face of all.

PRIEST. You'd do that!

SARAH. I would surely, holy father, if I walked to the city of Dublin with blood and blisters on my naked feet.

PRIEST [*uneasily scratching his ear*]. I wish this day was done, Sarah Casey; for I'm thinking it's a risky thing getting mixed in any matters with the like of you.

SARAH. Be hasty then, and you'll have us done with before you'd think at all.

PRIEST [*giving in*]. Well, maybe it's right you are, and let you come up to the chapel when you see me looking from the door. [*He goes up into the chapel.*]

SARAH [*calling after him*]. We will, and God preserve you, holy father.

MARY [*coming down to them, speaking with amazement and consternation, but without anger*]. Going to the chapel! It's at marriage you're fooling again, maybe? [SARAH *turns her back on her.*] It was for that you were washing your face, and you after sending me for porter at the fall of night the way I'd drink a good half from the jug? [*Going round in front of* SARAH.] Is it at marriage you're fooling again?

SARAH [*triumphantly*]. It is, Mary Byrne. I'll be married now in a short while; and from this day there will no one have a right to call me a dirty name and I selling cans in Wicklow or Wexford or the city of Dublin itself.

MARY [*turning to* MICHAEL]. And it's yourself is wedding her, Michael Byrne?

MICHAEL [*gloomily*]. It is, God spare us.

MARY [*looks at* SARAH *for a moment, and then bursts out into a laugh of derision*]. Well, she's a tight, hardy girl, and it's no lie; but I never knew till this day it was a black born fool I had for a son. You'll breed asses, I've heard them say, and poaching dogs, and horses'd go licking the wind, but it's a hard thing, God help me, to breed sense in a son.

MICHAEL [*gloomily*]. If I didn't marry her, she'd be walking off to Jaunting Jim maybe at the fall of night; and it's well yourself knows there isn't the like of her for getting money and selling songs to the men.

MARY. And you're thinking it's paying gold to his reverence would make a woman stop when she's a mind to go?

SARAH [*angrily*]. Let you not be destroying us with your talk when I've as good a right to a decent marriage as any speckled female does be sleeping in the black hovels above, would choke a mule.

MARY [*soothingly*]. It's as good a right you have surely, Sarah Casey, but what good will it do? Is it putting that ring on your finger will keep you from getting an aged woman and losing the fine face you have, or be easing your pains, when it's the grand ladies do be married in silk dresses, with rings of gold, that do pass any woman with their share of torment in the hour of birth, and do be paying the doctors in the city of Dublin a great price at that time, the like of what you'd pay for a good ass and a cart? [*She sits down.*]

SARAH [*puzzled*]. Is that the truth?

MARY [*pleased with the point she has made*]. Wouldn't any know it's the truth? Ah, it's few short years you are yet in the world, Sarah Casey, and it's little or nothing at all maybe you know about it.

SARAH [*vehement but uneasy*]. What is it yourself knows of the fine ladies when they wouldn't let the like of you go near to them at all?

MARY. If you do be drinking a little sup in one town and another town, it's soon you get great knowledge and a great sight into the world. You'll see men there, and women there, sitting up on the ends of barrels in the dark night, and they making great talk would soon have the like of you, Sarah Casey, as wise as a March hare.

MICHAEL [*to* SARAH]. That's the truth she's saying, and maybe if you've sense in you at all, you'd have a right still to leave your fooling, and not be wasting our gold.

SARAH [*decisively*]. If it's wise or fool I am, I've made a good bargain and I'll stand to it now.

MARY. What is it he's making you give?

MICHAEL. The ten shillings in gold, and the tin can is above tied in the sack.

MARY [*looking at the bundle with surprise and dread*]. The bit of gold and the tin can, is it?

MICHAEL. The half a sovereign, and the gallon can.

MARY [*scrambling to her feet quickly*]. Well, I think I'll be walking off the road to the fair the way you won't be destroying me going too fast on the hills. [*She goes a few steps towards the left, then turns and speaks to* SARAH *very persuasively.*] Let you not take the can from the sack, Sarah Casey; for the people is coming above would be making game of you, and pointing their fingers if they seen you do the like of that. Let you leave it safe in the bag, I'm saying, Sarah darling. It's that way will be best. [*She goes towards left, and pauses for a moment, looking about her with embarrassment.*]

MICHAEL [*in a low voice*]. What ails her at all?

SARAH [*anxiously*]. It's real wicked she does be when you hear her speaking as easy as that.

MARY [*to herself*]. I'd be safer in the chapel, I'm thinking; for if she caught me after on the road, maybe she would kill me then. [*She comes hobbling back towards the right.*]

SARAH. Where is it you're going? It isn't that way we'll be walking to the fair.

MARY. I'm going up into the chapel to give you my blessing and hear the priest saying his prayers. It's a lonesome road is running below to Greenane, and a woman would never know the things might happen her and she walking single in a lonesome place.

[*As she reaches the chapel-gate, the* PRIEST *comes to it in his surplice.*]

PRIEST [*crying out*]. Come along now. Is it the whole day you'd keep me here saying my prayers, and I getting my death with not a bit in my stomach, and my breakfast in ruins, and the Lord Bishop maybe driving on the road to-day?

SARAH. We're coming now, holy father.

PRIEST. Give me the bit of gold into my hand.

SARAH. It's here, holy father.

[*She gives it to him.* MICHAEL *takes the bundle from the ditch and brings it over, standing a little behind* SARAH. *He feels the bundle, and looks at* MARY *with a meaning look.*]

PRIEST [*looking at the gold*]. It's a good one I'm thinking wherever you got it. And where is the can?

SARAH [*taking the bundle*]. We have it here in a bit of clean sack, your reverence. We tied it up in the inside of that to keep it from rusting in the dews of night, and let you not open it now or you'll have the people making game of us and telling the story on us, east and west to the butt of the hills.

PRIEST [*taking the bundle*]. Give it here into my hand, Sarah Casey. What is it any person would think of a tinker making a can? [*He begins opening the bundle.*]

SARAH. It's a fine can, your reverence, for if it's poor simple people we are, it's fine cans we can make, and himself, God help him, is a great man surely at the trade.

[PRIEST *opens the bundle; the three empty bottles fall out.*]

SARAH. Glory to the saints of joy!

PRIEST. Did ever any man see the like of that? To think you'd be putting deceit on me, and telling lies to me, and I going to marry you for a little sum wouldn't marry a child.

SARAH [*crestfallen and astonished*]. It's the divil did it, your reverence, and I wouldn't tell you a lie. [*Raising her hands.*] May the Lord Almighty strike me dead if the divil isn't after hooshing the tin can from the bag.

PRIEST [*vehemently*]. Go along now, and don't be swearing your lies. Go along now, and let you not be thinking I'm big fool enough to believe the like of that, when it's after selling it you are or making a swap for drink of it, maybe, in the darkness of the night.

MARY [*in a peacemaking voice, putting her hand on the* PRIEST'*s left arm*]. She wouldn't do the like of that, your reverence, when she hasn't a decent standing drouth on her at all; and she's setting great store on her marriage the way you'd have a right to be taking her easy, and not minding the can. What differ would an empty can make with a fine, rich, hardy man the like of you?

SARAH [*imploringly*]. Marry us, your reverence, for the ten shillings in gold, and we'll make you a grand can in the evening—a can would be fit to carry water for the holy man of God. Marry us now and I'll be saying fine prayers for you, morning and night, if it'd be raining itself, and it'd be in two black pools I'd be setting my knees.

PRIEST [*loudly*]. It's a wicked, thieving, lying, scheming lot you are, the pack of you. Let you walk off now and take every stinking rag you have there from the ditch.

MARY [*putting her shawl over her head*]. Marry her, your reverence, for the love of God, for there'll be queer doings below if you send her off the like of that and she swearing crazy on the road.

SARAH [*angrily*]. It's the truth she's saying; for it's herself, I'm thinking, is after swapping the tin can for a pint, the time she was raging mad with the drouth, and ourselves above walking the hill.

MARY [*crying out with indignation*]. Have you no shame, Sarah Casey, to tell lies unto a holy man?

SARAH [*to* MARY, *working herself into a rage*]. It's making game of me you'd be, and putting a fool's head on me in the face of the world; but if you were thinking to be mighty cute walking off, or going up to hide in the church, I've got you this time, and you'll not run from me now. [*She seizes up one of the bottles.*]

MARY [*hiding behind the* PRIEST]. Keep her off, your reverence, keep her off for the love of the Almighty God. What at all would the Lord Bishop say if he found me here lying with my head broken across, or the two of yous maybe digging a bloody grave for me at the door of the church?

PRIEST [*waving* SARAH *off*]. Go along, Sarah Casey. Would you be doing murder at my feet? Go along from me now, and wasn't I a big fool to have to do with you when it's nothing but distraction and torment I get from the kindness of my heart?

SARAH [*shouting*]. I've bet a power of strong lads east and west through the world, and are you thinking I'd turn back from a priest? Leave the road now, or maybe I would strike yourself.

PRIEST. You would not, Sarah Casey. I've no fear for the lot of you; but let you walk off I'm saying, and not be coming where you've no business, and screeching tumult and murder at the doorway of the church.

SARAH. I'll not go a step till I have her head broke, or till I'm wed with himself. If you want to get shut of us, let you marry us now, for I'm thinking the ten shillings in gold is a good price for the like of you, and you near burst with the fat.

PRIEST. I wouldn't have you coming in on me and soiling my church; for there's nothing at all, I'm thinking, would keep the like of you from hell. [*He throws down the ten shillings on the ground.*] Gather up your gold now, and begone from my sight, for if ever I set an eye on you again you'll hear me telling the peelers who it was stole the black ass belonging to Philly O'Cullen, and whose hay it is the grey ass does be eating.

SARAH. You'd do that?

PRIEST. I would, surely.

SARAH. If you do, you'll be getting all the tinkers from Wicklow and Wexford, and the County Meath, to put up block tin in the place of glass to shield your windows where you do be looking out and blinking at the girls. It's hard set you'll be that time, I'm telling you, to fill the depth of your belly the long days of Lent; for we wouldn't leave a laying pullet in your yard at all.

PRIEST [*losing his temper finally*]. Go on, now, or I'll send the Lords of Justice a dated story of your villainies—burning, stealing, robbing, raping to this mortal day. Go on now, I'm saying, if you'd run from Kilmainham or the rope itself.

MICHAEL [*taking off his coat*]. Is it run from the like of you, holy father? Go up to your own shanty, or I'll beat you with the ass's reins till the world would hear you roaring from this place to the coast of Clare.

PRIEST. Is it lift your hand upon myself when the Lord would blight your members if you'd touch me now? Go on from this. [*He gives him a shove.*]

MICHAEL. Blight me is it? Take it then, your reverence, and God help you so. [*He runs at him with the reins.*]

PRIEST [*runs up to ditch, crying out*]. There are the peelers passing by the grace of God—hey, below!

MARY [*clapping her hand over his mouth*]. Knock him down on the road; they didn't hear him at all.

[MICHAEL *pulls him down.*]

SARAH. Gag his jaws.

MARY. Stuff the sacking in his teeth.

[*They gag him with the sack that had the can in it.*]

SARAH. Tie the bag around his head, and if the peelers come, we'll put him headfirst in the boghole is beyond the ditch.

[*They tie him up in some sacking.*]

MICHAEL [*to* MARY]. Keep him quiet, and the rags tight on him for fear he'd screech. [*He goes back to their camp.*] Hurry with the things, Sarah Casey. The peelers aren't coming this way, and maybe we'll get off from them now.

[*They bundle the things together in wild haste, the* PRIEST *wriggling and struggling about on the ground, with old* MARY *trying to keep him quiet.*]

MARY [*patting his head*]. Be quiet, your reverence. What is it ails you, with your wrigglings now? Is it choking maybe? [*She puts her hand under the sack, and feels his mouth, patting him on the back.*] It's only letting on you are, holy father, for your nose is blowing back and forward as easy as an east wind on an April day. [*In a soothing voice.*] There now, holy father, let you stay easy, I'm telling you, and learn a little sense and patience, the way you'll not be so airy again going to rob poor sinners of their scraps of gold. [*He gets quieter.*] That's a good boy you are now, your reverence, and let you not be uneasy, for we wouldn't hurt you at all. It's sick and sorry we are to tease you; but what did you want meddling with the like of us, when it's a long time we are going our own ways—father and son, and his son after him, or mother and daughter, and her own daughter again—and it's little need we ever had of going up into a church and swearing—I'm told there's swearing with it—a word no man would believe, or with drawing rings on our fingers, would be cutting our skins maybe when we'd be taking the ass from the shafts, and pulling the straps the time they'd be slippy with going around beneath the heavens in rains falling.

MICHAEL [*who has finished bundling up the things, comes over with* SARAH]. We're fixed now; and I have a mind to run him in a bog-hole the way he'll not be tattling to the peelers of our games to-day.

SARAH. You'd have a right too, I'm thinking.

MARY [*soothingly*]. Let you not be rough with him, Sarah Casey, and he after drinking his sup of porter with us at the fall of night. Maybe he'd swear a mighty oath he wouldn't harm us, and then we'd safer loose him; for if we went to drown him, they'd maybe hang the batch of us, man and child and woman, and the ass itself.

MICHAEL. What would he care for an oath?

MARY. Don't you know his like do live in terror of the wrath of God? [*Putting her mouth to the* PRIEST's *ear in the sacking.*] Would you swear an oath, holy father, to leave us in our freedom, and not talk at all? [PRIEST *nods in sacking.*] Didn't I tell you? Look at the poor fellow nodding his head off in the bias of the sacks. Strip them off from him, and he'll be easy now.

MICHAEL [*as if speaking to a horse*]. Hold up, holy father.

[*He pulls the sacking off, and shows the* PRIEST *with his hair on end. They free his mouth.*]

MARY. Hold him till he swears.

PRIEST [*in a faint voice*]. I swear surely. If you let me go in peace, I'll not inform against you or say a thing at all, and may God forgive me for giving heed unto your like to-day.

SARAH [*puts the ring on his finger*]. There's the ring, holy father, to keep you minding of your oath until the end of time; for my heart's scalded with your fooling; and it'll be a long day till I go making talk of marriage or the like of that.

MARY [*complacently, standing up slowly*]. She's vexed now, your reverence; and let you not mind her at all, for she's right surely, and it's little need we ever had of the like of you to get us our bit to eat, and our bit to drink, and our time of love when we were young men and women, and were fine to look at.

MICHAEL. Hurry on now. He's a great man to have kept us from fooling our gold; and we'll have a great time drinking that bit with the trampers on the green of Clash.

[*They gather up their things. The* PRIEST *stands up.*]

PRIEST [*lifting up his hand*]. I've sworn not to call the hand of man upon your crimes to-day; but I haven't sworn I wouldn't call the fire of heaven from the hand of the Almighty God. [*He begins saying a Latin malediction in a loud ecclesiastical voice.*]

MARY. There's an old villain.

ALL [*together*]. Run, run. Run for your lives.

[*They rush out, leaving the* PRIEST *master of the situation.*]

CURTAIN

THE WELL OF THE SAINTS

A PLAY IN THREE ACTS

(1903–1908)

PERSONS

MARTIN DOUL, a weather-beaten, blind beggar
MARY DOUL, his wife, a weather-beaten, ugly
    woman, blind also, nearly fifty
TIMMY, a middle-aged, almost elderly, but vigorous
    smith
MOLLY BYRNE, a fine-looking girl with fair hair
BRIDE, another handsome girl
MAT SIMON
THE SAINT, a wandering Friar
OTHER GIRLS AND MEN

SCENE

*Some lonely mountainous district on the east of Ireland,
one or more centuries ago*

*The first act is in the autumn; the second towards the end
of winter; and the third at the beginning of spring.*

ACT I

Roadside with big stones, etc. on the right; low loose wall at back with gap near centre; at left, ruined doorway of church with bushes beside it. MARTIN DOUL *and* MARY DOUL *grope in on left and pass over to stones on right, where they sit.*

MARY DOUL. What place are we now, Martin Doul?

MARTIN DOUL. Passing the gap.

MARY DOUL [*raising her head*]. The length of that! Well, the sun's coming warm this day if it's late autumn itself.

MARTIN DOUL [*putting out his hands in sun*]. What way wouldn't it be warm and it getting high up in the south? You were that length plaiting your yellow hair you have the morning lost on us, and the people are after passing to the fair of Clash.

MARY DOUL. It isn't going to the fair, the time they do be driving their cattle and they with a litter of pigs maybe squealing in their carts, they'd give us a thing at all. [*She sits down.*] It's well you know that, but you must be talking.

MARTIN DOUL [*sitting down beside her and beginning to shred rushes she gives him*]. If I didn't talk I'd be destroyed in a short while listening to the clack you do be making, for you've a queer cracked voice, the Lord have mercy on you, if it's fine to look on you are itself.

MARY DOUL. Who wouldn't have a cracked voice sitting out all the year in the rain falling? It's a bad life for the voice, Martin Doul, though I've heard tell there isn't anything like the wet south wind does be blowing upon us, for keeping a white beautiful skin—the like of my skin—on your neck and on your brows, and there isn't anything at all like a fine skin for putting splendour on a woman.

MARTIN DOUL [*teasingly, but with good-humour*]. I do be thinking odd times we don't know rightly what way you have your splendour, or asking myself, maybe, if you have it at all, for the time I was a young lad, and had fine sight, it was the ones with sweet voices were the best in face.

MARY DOUL. Let you not be making the like of that talk when you've heard Timmy the smith, and Mat Simon, and Patch Ruadh, and a

power besides saying fine things of my face, and you know rightly
it was 'the beautiful dark woman', they did call me in Ballinatone.

MARTIN DOUL [*as before*]. If it was itself I heard Molly Byrne saying
at the fall of night it was little more than a fright you were.

MARY DOUL [*sharply*]. She was jealous, God forgive her, because
Timmy the smith was after praising my hair—

MARTIN DOUL [*with mock irony*]. Jealous!

MARY DOUL. Ay, jealous, Martin Doul, and if she wasn't itself, the
young and silly do be always making game of them that's dark, and
they'd think it a fine thing if they had us deceived, the way we
wouldn't know we were so fine-looking at all. [*She puts her hand to
her face with a complacent gesture and smoothes her hair back with her
hands.*]

MARTIN DOUL [*a little plaintively*]. I do be thinking in the long nights
it'd be a grand thing if we could see ourselves for one hour, or a
minute itself, the way we'd know surely we were the finest man, and
the finest woman, of the seven counties of the east. . . [*bitterly*] and
then the seeing rabble below might be destroying their souls telling
bad lies, and we'd never heed a thing they'd say.

MARY DOUL. If you weren't a big fool you wouldn't heed them this
hour Martin Doul, for they're a bad lot those that have their sight,
and they do have great joy, the time they do be seeing a grand thing,
to let on they don't see it at all, and to be telling fools' lies, the like
of what Molly Byrne was telling to yourself.

MARTIN DOUL. If it's lies she does be telling she's a sweet beautiful
voice you'd never tire to be hearing, if it was only the pig she'd be
calling, or crying out in the long grass, maybe, after her hens. . . .
[*Speaking pensively.*] It should be a fine soft, rounded woman, I'm
thinking, would have a voice the like of that.

MARY DOUL [*sharply again, scandalized*]. Let you not be minding if it's
flat or rounded she is, for she's a flighty, foolish woman you'll hear
when you're off a long way, and she making a great noise and laughing at the well.

MARTIN DOUL. Isn't laughing a nice thing the time a woman's young?

MARY DOUL [*bitterly*]. A nice thing is it? A nice thing to hear a woman
making a loud braying laugh the like of that? Ah, she's a great one

for drawing the men, and you'll hear Timmy himself, the time he does be sitting in his forge, getting mighty fussy if she'll come walking from Grianan, the way you'll hear his breath going, and he wringing his hands.

MARTIN DOUL [*slightly piqued*]. I've heard him say a power of times, it's nothing at all she is when you see her at the side of you, and yet I never heard any man's breath getting uneasy the time he'd be looking on yourself.

MARY DOUL. I'm not the like of the girls do be running round on the roads, swinging their legs, and they with their necks out looking on the men . . . Ah, there's a power of villainy walking the world, Martin Doul, among them that do be gadding around, with their gaping eyes, and their sweet words, and they with no sense in them at all.

MARTIN DOUL [*sadly*]. It's the truth, maybe, and yet I'm told it's a grand thing to see a young girl walking the road.

MARY DOUL. You'd be as bad as the rest of them if you had your sight, and I did well surely, not to marry a seeing man —it's scores would have had me and welcome—for the seeing is a queer lot, and you'd never know the thing they'd do.

[*A moment's pause.*]

MARTIN DOUL [*listening*]. There's someone coming on the road.

MARY DOUL. Let you put the pith away out of their sight, or they'll be picking it out with the spying eyes they have, and saying it's rich we are, and not sparing us a thing at all.

[*They bundle away the rushes.* TIMMY THE SMITH *comes in on left.*]

MARTIN DOUL [*with a begging voice*]. Leave a bit of silver for blind Martin, your honour. Leave a bit of silver, or a penny copper itself, and we'll be praying the Lord to bless you and you going the way.

TIMMY [*stopping before them*]. And you letting on a while back you knew my step! [*He sits down.*]

MARTIN DOUL [*with his natural voice*]. I know it when Molly Byrne's walking in front, or when she's two perches, maybe, lagging behind, but it's few times I've heard you walking up the like of that, as if you'd met a thing wasn't right and you coming on the road.

TIMMY [*hot and breathless, wiping his face*]. You've good ears, God bless you, if you're a liar itself, for I'm after walking up in great haste from hearing wonders in the fair.

MARTIN [*rather contemptuously*]. You're always hearing queer wonderful things, and the lot of them nothing at all, but I'm thinking, this time, it's a strange thing surely, you'd be walking up before the turn of day, and not waiting below to look on them lepping, or dancing, or playing shows on the green of Clash.

TIMMY [*huffed*]. I was coming to tell you it's in this place there'd be a bigger wonder done in a short while [MARTIN DOUL *stops working and looks at him*], than was ever done on the green of Clash, or the width of Leinster itself, but you're thinking, maybe, you're too cute a little fellow to be minding me at all.

MARTIN DOUL [*amused but incredulous*]. There'll be wonders in this place is it?

TIMMY. Here at the crossing of the roads.

MARTIN DOUL. I never heard tell of anything to happen in this place since the night they killed the old fellow going home with his gold, the Lord have mercy on him, and threw down his corpse into the bog. Let them not be doing the like of that this night, for it's ourselves have a right to the crossing roads, and we don't want any of your bad tricks, or your wonders either, for it's wonder enough we are ourselves.

TIMMY. If I'd a mind I'd be telling you of a real wonder this day, and the way you'll be having a great joy, maybe, you're not thinking on at all.

MARTIN DOUL [*interested*]. Are they putting up a still behind in the rocks? It'd be a grand thing if I'd a sup handy the way I wouldn't be destroying myself groping up across the bogs in the rain falling.

TIMMY [*still moodily*]. It's not a still they're bringing or the like of it either.

MARY DOUL [*persuasively, to* TIMMY]. Maybe they're hanging a thief, above at the bit of a tree? I'm told it's a great sight to see a man hanging by his neck, but what joy would that be to ourselves, and we not seeing it at all?

TIMMY [*more pleasantly*]. They're hanging no one this day, Mary Doul, and yet with the help of God, you'll see a power hanged before you die.

MARY DOUL. Well you've queer humbugging talk. . . . What way would I see a power hanged, and I a dark woman since the seventh year of my age?

TIMMY. Did ever you hear tell of a place across a bit of the sea, where there is an island, and the grave of the four beautiful saints?

MARY DOUL. I've heard people have walked round from the west and they speaking of that.

TIMMY [*impressively*]. There's a green ferny well, I'm told, behind of that place, and if you put a drop of the water out of it, on the eyes of a blind man, you'll make him see as well as any person is walking the world.

MARTIN DOUL [*with excitement*]. Is that the truth, Timmy? I'm thinking you're telling a lie.

TIMMY [*gruffly*]. That's the truth, Martin Doul, and you may believe it now, for you're after believing a power of things weren't as likely at all.

MARY DOUL. Maybe we could send a young lad to bring us the water. I could wash a naggin bottle in the morning, and I'm thinking Patch Ruadh would go for it, if we gave him a good drink, and the bit of money we have hid in the thatch.

TIMMY. It'd be no good to be sending a sinful man the like of ourselves, for I'm told the holiness of the water does be getting soiled with the villainy of your heart, the time you'd be carrying it, and you looking round on the girls, maybe, or drinking a small sup at a still.

MARTIN DOUL [*with disappointment*]. It'd be a long terrible way to be walking ourselves, and I'm thinking that's a wonder will bring small joy to us at all.

TIMMY [*turning on him impatiently*]. What is it you want with your walking? It's as deaf as blind you're growing if you're not after hearing me say it's in this place the wonder would be done.

MARTIN DOUL [*with a flash of anger*]. If it is can't you open the big slobbering mouth you have and say what way it'll be done, and not be making blather till the fall of night.

TIMMY [*jumping up*]. I'll be going on now [MARY DOUL *rises*], and not wasting time talking civil talk with the like of you.

MARY DOUL [*standing up, disguising her impatience*]. Let you come here to me, Timmy, and not be minding him at all. [TIMMY *stops, and she gropes up to him and takes him by the coat.*] . . . You're not huffy with myself, and let you tell me the whole story and don't be fooling me more . . . Is it yourself has brought us the water?

TIMMY. It is not, surely.

MARY DOUL. Then tell us your wonder, Timmy . . . What person'll bring it at all?

TIMMY [*relenting*]. It's a fine holy man will bring it, a saint of the Almighty God.

MARY DOUL [*overawed*]. A saint is it?

TIMMY. Ay, a fine saint, who's going round through the churches of Ireland, with a long cloak on him, and naked feet, for he's brought a sup of the water slung at his side, and, with the like of him, any little drop is enough to cure the dying, or to make the blind see as clear as the grey hawks do be high up, on a still day, sailing the sky.

MARTIN DOUL [*feeling for his stick*]. What place is he, Timmy? I'll be walking to him now.

TIMMY. Let you stay quiet, Martin. He's straying around saying prayers at the churches and high crosses, between this place and the hills, and he with a great crowd going behind—for it's fine prayers he does be saying, and fasting with it, till he's as thin as one of the empty rushes you have there on your knee—then he'll be coming after to this place to cure the two of you, we're after telling him the way you are, and to say his prayers in the church.

MARTIN DOUL [*turning suddenly to* MARY DOUL]. And we'll be seeing ourselves this day. Oh, glory be to God, is it true surely?

MARY DOUL [*very pleased, to* TIMMY]. Maybe I'd have time to walk down and get the big shawl I have below, for I do look my best, I've heard them say, when I'm dressed up with that thing on my head.

TIMMY. You'd have time surely—

MARTIN DOUL [*listening*]. Whisht now . . . I hear people again coming by the stream.

TIMMY [*looking out left, puzzled*]. It's the young girls I left walking after the saint. . . . They're coming now [*goes up to entrance*] carrying things in their hands, and they walking as easy as you'd see a child walk, who'd have a dozen eggs hid in her bib.

MARTIN DOUL [*listening*]. That's Molly Byrne, I'm thinking.

[MOLLY BYRNE *and* BRIDE *come on left and cross to* MARTIN DOUL, *carrying water-can*, SAINT'*s bell, and cloak*.]

MOLLY [*volubly*]. God bless you, Martin. I've holy water here from the grave of the four saints of the west, will have you cured in a short while and seeing like ourselves—

TIMMY [*crosses to* MOLLY, *interrupting her*]. He's heard that, God help you. But where at all is the saint, and what way is he after trusting the holy water with the likes of you?

MOLLY BYRNE. He was afeard to go a far way with the clouds is coming beyond, so he's gone up now through the thick woods to say a prayer at the crosses of Grianan, and he's coming on this road to the church.

TIMMY [*still astonished*]. And he's after leaving the holy water with the two of you? It's a wonder, surely. [*Comes down left a little.*]

MOLLY BYRNE. The lads told him no person could carry them things through the briars, and steep, slippy-feeling rocks he'll be climbing above, so he looked round then, and gave the water, and his big cloak, and his bell to the two of us, for young girls, says he, are the cleanest holy people you'd see walking the world.

[MARY DOUL *goes near seat.*]

MARY DOUL [*sits down, laughing to herself*]. Well, the saint's a simple fellow, and it's no lie.

MARTIN DOUL [*leaning forward, holding out his hands*]. Let you give me the water in my hand, Molly Byrne, the way I'll know you have it surely.

MOLLY BYRNE [*giving it to him*]. Wonders is queer things, and maybe it'd cure you, and you holding it alone.

MARTIN DOUL [*looking round*]. It does not, Molly. I'm not seeing at all. [*He shakes the can.*] There's a small sup only. Well, isn't it a great wonder the little trifling thing would bring seeing to the blind, and be showing us the big women and the young girls, and all the fine things is walking the world. [*He feels for* MARY DOUL *and gives her the can.*]

MARY DOUL [*shaking it*]. Well, glory be to God—

MARTIN DOUL [*pointing to* BRIDE]. And what is it herself has, making sounds in her hand?

BRIDE [*crossing to* MARTIN DOUL]. It's the saint's bell, you'll hear him ringing out the time he'll be going up some place, to be saying his prayers.

[MARTIN DOUL *holds out his hands; she gives it to him.*]

MARTIN DOUL [*ringing it*]. It's a sweet, beautiful sound.

MARY DOUL. You'd know I'm thinking by the little silvery voice of it, a fasting holy man was after carrying it a great way at his side.

[BRIDE *crosses a little right behind* MARTIN DOUL.]

MOLLY BYRNE [*unfolding* SAINT's *cloak*]. Let you stand up now, Martin Doul, till I put his big cloak on you, the way we'd see how you'd look, and you a saint of the Almighty God.

MARTIN DOUL [*rises, comes forward centre, a little diffidently*]. I've heard the priests a power of times making great talk and praises of the beauty of the saints.

[MOLLY BYRNE *slips cloak round him.*]

TIMMY [*uneasily*]. You'd have a right to be leaving him alone, Molly. What would the saint say if he seen you making game with his cloak?

MOLLY BYRNE [*recklessly*]. How would he see us, and he saying prayers in the wood? [*She turns* MARTIN DOUL *round.*] Isn't that a fine holy-looking saint, Timmy the smith? [*Laughing foolishly.*] There's a grand handsome fellow, Mary Doul, and if you seen him now, you'd be as proud, I'm thinking, as the archangels below, fell out with the Almighty God.

MARY DOUL [*with quiet confidence going to* MARTIN DOUL *and feeling his cloak*]. It's proud we'll be this day, surely.

[MARTIN DOUL *is still ringing bell*.]

MOLLY BYRNE [*to* MARTIN DOUL]. Would you think well to be all your life walking round the like of that Martin Doul, and you bell-ringing with the saints of God?

MARY DOUL [*turning on her, fiercely*]. How would he be bell-ringing with the saints of God and he wedded with myself?

MARTIN DOUL. It's the truth she's saying, and if bell-ringing is a fine life, yet I'm thinking, maybe, it's better I am wedded with the beautiful dark woman of Ballinatone.

MOLLY BYRNE [*scornfully*]. You're thinking that, God help you, but it's little you know of her at all.

MARTIN DOUL. It's little surely, and I'm destroyed this day waiting to look upon her face.

TIMMY [*awkwardly*]. It's well you know the way she is, for the like of you do have great knowledge in the feeling of your hands.

MARTIN DOUL [*still feeling the cloak*]. We do maybe. Yet it's little I know of faces, or of fine beautiful cloaks, for it's few cloaks I've had my hand to, and few faces [*plaintively*], for the young girls is mighty shy, Timmy the smith, and it isn't much they heed me, though they do be saying I'm a handsome man.

MARY DOUL [*mockingly, with good-humour*]. Isn't it a queer thing the voice he puts on him, when you hear him talking of the skinny young-looking girls, and he married with a woman he's heard called the wonder of the western world?

TIMMY [*pityingly*]. The two of you will see a great wonder this day, and it's no lie.

MARTIN DOUL. I've heard tell her yellow hair, and her white skin, and her big eyes are a wonder, surely—

BRIDE [*who has looked out left*]. Here's the saint coming from the selvage of the wood . . . Strip the cloak from him, Molly, or he'll be seeing it now.

MOLLY BYRNE [*hastily to* BRIDE]. Take the bell and put herself by the stones. [*To* MARTIN DOUL.] Will you hold your head up till I loosen the cloak. [*She pulls off the cloak and throws it over her arm. Then she pushes* MARTIN DOUL *over and stands him beside* MARY DOUL.] Stand there now, quiet, and let you not be saying a word.

[*She and* BRIDE *stand a little on their left, demurely, with bell, etc., in their hands.*]

MARTIN DOUL [*nervously arranging his clothes*]. Will he mind the way we are, and we not tidied or washed cleanly at all?

MOLLY BYRNE. He'll not see what way you are. . . . He'd walk by the finest woman in Ireland, I'm thinking, and not trouble to raise his two eyes to look upon her face . . . Whisht!

[SAINT *comes on left, with crowd.*]

SAINT. Are these the two poor people?

TIMMY [*officiously*]. They are, holy father, they do be always sitting here at the crossing of the roads, asking a bit of copper from them that do pass, or stripping rushes for lights, and they not mournful at all, but talking out straight with a full voice, and making game with them that likes it.

SAINT [*to* MARTIN DOUL *and* MARY DOUL]. It's a hard life you've had not seeing sun or moon, or the holy priests itself praying to the Lord, but it's the like of you who are brave in a bad time will make a fine use of the gift of sight the Almighty God will bring to you to-day. [*He takes his cloak and puts it about him.*] It's on a bare starving rock that there's the grave of the four beauties of God, the way it's little wonder, I'm thinking, if it's with bare starving people the water should be used. [*He takes the water and bell and slings them round his shoulders.*] So it's to the like of yourselves I do be going, who are wrinkled and poor, a thing rich men would hardly look at at all, but would throw a coin to or a crust of bread.

MARTIN DOUL [*moving uneasily*]. When they look on herself who is a fine woman—

TIMMY [*shaking him*]. Whisht now, and be listening to the saint.

SAINT [*looks at them a moment, continues*] If it's raggy and dirty you are itself, I'm saying, the Almighty God isn't at all like the rich men of

Ireland; and, with the power of the water I'm after bringing in a little curagh into Cashla Bay, he'll have pity on you, and put sight into your eyes.

MARTIN DOUL [*taking off his hat*]. I'm ready now, holy father—

SAINT [*taking him by the hand*]. I'll cure you first, and then I'll come for your wife. We'll go up now into the church, for I must say a prayer to the Lord . . . [*To* MARY DOUL *as he moves off.*] And let you be making your mind still and saying praises in your heart, for it's a great wonderful thing when the power of the Lord of the world is brought down upon your like.

PEOPLE [*pressing after him*]. Come now till we watch.

BRIDE. Come, Timmy.

SAINT [*waving them back*]. Stay back where you are, for I'm not wanting a big crowd making whispers in the church. Stay back there, I'm saying, and you'd do well to be thinking on the way sin has brought blindness to the world, and to be saying a prayer for your own sakes against false prophets and heathens, and the words of women and smiths, and all knowledge that would soil the soul or the body of a man.

[PEOPLE *shrink back. He goes into church.* MARY DOUL *gropes half way towards the door and kneels near path.* PEOPLE *form a group at right.*]

TIMMY. Isn't it a fine, beautiful voice he has, and he a fine, brave man if it wasn't for the fasting?

BRIDE. Did you watch him moving his hands?

MOLLY BYRNE. It'd be a fine thing if some one in this place could pray the like of him, for I'm thinking the water from our own blessed well would do rightly if a man knew the way to be saying prayers, and then there'd be no call to be bringing water from that wild place, where, I'm told, there are no decent houses, or fine-looking people at all.

BRIDE [*who is looking in at door from right*]. Look at the great trembling Martin has shaking him, and he on his knees.

TIMMY [*anxiously*]. God help him. . . . What will he be doing when he sees his wife this day? I'm thinking it was bad work we did when we let on she was fine-looking, and not a wrinkled wizened hag the way she is.

MAT SIMON. Why would he be vexed, and we after giving him great joy and pride, the time he was dark?

MOLLY BYRNE [*sitting down in* MARY DOUL's *seat and tidying her hair*]. If it's vexed he is itself, he'll have other things now to think on as well as his wife, and what does any man care for a wife, when it's two weeks, or three, he is looking on her face?

MAT SIMON. That's the truth now, Molly, and it's more joy dark Martin got from the lies we told of that hag is kneeling by the path, than your own man will get from you, day or night, and he living at your side.

MOLLY BYRNE [*defiantly*]. Let you not be talking, Mat Simon, for it's not yourself will be my man, though you'd be crowing and singing fine songs if you'd that hope in you at all.

TIMMY [*shocked, to* MOLLY BYRNE]. Let you not be raising your voice when the saint's above at his prayers.

BRIDE [*crying out*]. Whisht. . . . Whisht. . . . I'm thinking he's cured.

MARTIN DOUL [*crying out in the church*]. Oh, glory be to God—

SAINT [*solemnly*]. Laus patri sit et filio cum spiritu paraclito
                  Qui suae dono gratiae miseratus est Hiberniae—

MARTIN DOUL [*ecstatically*]. Oh, glory be to God, I see now surely. . . . I see the walls of the church, and the green bits of ferns in them, and yourself, holy father, and the great width of the sky.

[*He runs out half foolish with joy, and comes past* MARY DOUL *as she scrambles to her feet, drawing a little away from her as he goes by.*]

TIMMY [*to the others*]. He doesn't know her at all.

[SAINT *comes out behind* MARTIN DOUL *and leads* MARY DOUL *into the church.* MARTIN DOUL *comes on to the* PEOPLE. *The Men are between him and the Girls. He verifies his position with his stick.*]

MARTIN DOUL [*crying out joyfully*]. That's Timmy, I know Timmy by the black of his head. . . . That's Mat Simon, I know Mat by the length of his legs. . . . That should be Patch Ruadh, with the gamey eyes in him, and the fiery hair. [*He sees* MOLLY BYRNE *on* MARY DOUL's *seat, and his voice changes completely.*] Oh, it was no lie they told me, Mary Doul. Oh, glory to God and the seven saints I didn't die and not see you at all. The blessing of God on the water, and the feet carried it round through the land. The blessing of God on this day, and them that brought me the saint, for it's grand hair you have [*she lowers her head, a little confused*], and soft skin, and eyes would make the saints, if they were dark awhile and seeing again, fall down out of the sky. [*He goes nearer to her.*] Hold up your head, Mary, the way I'll see it's richer I am than the great kings of the east. Hold up your head, I'm saying, for it's soon you'll be seeing me, and I not a bad one at all. [*He touches her and she starts up.*]

MOLLY BYRNE. Let you keep away from me, and not be soiling my chin.

[PEOPLE *laugh loudly.*]

MARTIN DOUL [*bewildered*]. It's Molly's voice you have. . . .

MOLLY BYRNE. Why wouldn't I have my own voice? Do you think I'm a ghost?

MARTIN DOUL. Which of you all is herself? [*He goes up to* BRIDE.] Is it you is Mary Doul? I'm thinking you're more the like of what they said. [*Peering at her.*] For you've yellow hair, and white skin, and it's the smell of my own turf is rising from your shawl. [*He catches her shawl.*]

BRIDE [*pulling away her shawl*]. I'm not your wife, and let you get out of my way.

[PEOPLE *laugh again.*]

MARTIN DOUL [*with misgiving, to another girl*]. Is it yourself it is? You're not so fine looking, but I'm thinking you'd do, with the grand nose you have, and your nice hands and your feet.

GIRL [*scornfully*]. I never seen any person that took me for blind, and a seeing woman, I'm thinking, would never wed the like of you.

[*She turns away, and the* PEOPLE *laugh once more, drawing back a little and leaving him on their left.*]

PEOPLE [*jeeringly*]. Try again, Martin, try again, you'll find her yet.

MARTIN DOUL [*passionately*]. Where is it you have her hidden away? Isn't it a black shame for a drove of pitiful beasts the like of you to be making game of me, and putting a fool's head on me the grand day of my life? Ah, you're thinking you're a fine lot, with your giggling, weeping eyes, a fine lot to be making game of myself, and the woman I've heard called the great wonder of the west. . . .

[*During this speech, which he gives with his back towards the church,* MARY DOUL *has come out with her sight cured, and come down towards the right with a silly simpering smile, till she is a little behind* MARTIN DOUL.]

MARY DOUL [*when he pauses*]. Which of you is Martin Doul?

MARTIN DOUL [*wheeling round*]. It's her voice surely. . . . [*They stare at each other blankly.*]

MOLLY BYRNE [*to* MARTIN DOUL]. Go up now and take her under the chin and be speaking the way you spoke to myself. . . .

MARTIN DOUL [*in a low voice, with intensity*]. If I speak now, I'll speak hard to the two of you. . . .

MOLLY BYRNE [*to* MARY DOUL]. You're not saying a word, Mary. What is it you think of himself, with the fat legs on him, and the little neck like a ram?

MARY DOUL. I'm thinking it's a poor thing when the Lord God gives you sight, and puts the like of that man in your way.

MARTIN DOUL. It's on your two knees you should be thanking the Lord God you're not looking on yourself, for if it was yourself you seen, you'd be running round in a short while like the old screeching madwoman is running round in the glen.

MARY DOUL [*beginning to realize herself*]. If I'm not so fine as some of them said, I have my hair, and my big eyes, and my white skin—

MARTIN DOUL [*breaking out into a passionate cry*]. Your hair, and your big eyes, is it? . . . I'm telling you there isn't a wisp on any grey mare on the ridge of the world isn't finer than the dirty twist on your head. There isn't two eyes in any starving sow, isn't finer than the eyes you were calling blue like the sea.

MARY DOUL [*interrupting him*]. It's the devil cured you this day with your talking of sows; it's the devil cured you this day, I'm saying, and drove you crazy with lies.

MARTIN DOUL. Isn't it yourself is after playing lies on me, ten years, in the day, and in the night, but what is that to you now the Lord God has given eyes to me, the way I see you an old, wizendy hag, was never fit to rear a child to me itself.

MARY DOUL. I wouldn't rear a crumpled whelp the like of you. It's many a woman is married with finer than yourself should be praising God if she's no child, and isn't loading the earth with things would make the heavens lonesome above, and they scaring the larks, and the crows, and the angels passing in the sky.

MARTIN DOUL. Go on now to be seeking a lonesome place where the earth can hide you away, go on now, I'm saying, or you'll be having men and women with their knees bled, and they screaming to God for a holy water would darken their sight, for there's no man but would liefer be blind a hundred years, or a thousand itself, than to be looking on your like.

MARY DOUL [*raising her stick*]. Maybe if I hit you a strong blow you'd be blind again, and having what you want—

[SAINT *is seen in church-door with his head bent in prayer.*]

MARTIN DOUL [*raising his stick and driving* MARY DOUL *back towards left*]. Let you keep off from me now if you wouldn't have me strike out the little handful of brains you have about on the road.

[*He is going to strike her, but* TIMMY *catches him by the arm.*]

TIMMY. Have you no shame to be making a great row and the saint above saying his prayers?

MARTIN DOUL. What is it I care for the like of him? [*Struggling to free himself.*] Let me hit her one good one for the love of the Almighty God, and I'll be quiet after till I die.

TIMMY [*shaking him*]. Will you whisht, I'm saying.

SAINT [*coming forward, centre*]. Are their minds troubled with joy, or is their sight uncertain the way it does often be the day a person is restored?

TIMMY. It's too certain their sight is, holy father, and they're after making a great fight, because they're a pair of pitiful shows.

SAINT [*coming between them*]. May the Lord who has given you sight send a little sense into your heads, the way it won't be on your two selves you'll be looking—on two pitiful sinners of the earth—but on the splendour of the Spirit of God, you'll see an odd time shining out through the big hills, and steep streams falling to the sea. For if it's on the like of that you do be thinking, you'll not be minding the faces of men, but you'll be saying prayers and great praises, till you'll be living the way the great saints do be living, with little but old sacks, and skin covering their bones. [*To* TIMMY.] Leave him go now, you're seeing he's quiet again. [TIMMY *frees* MARTIN DOUL.] And let you [SAINT *turns to* MARY DOUL] not be raising your voice, a bad thing in a woman, but let the lot of you, who have seen the power of the Lord, be thinking on it in the dark night, and be saying to yourselves it's great pity, and love he has, for the poor, starving people of Ireland. [*He gathers his cloak about him.*] And now the Lord send blessing to you all, for I am going on to Annagolan, where there is a deaf woman, and to Laragh where there are two men without sense, and to Glenassil where there are children, blind from their birth, and then I'm going to sleep this night in the bed of the holy Kevin, and to be praising God, and asking great blessing on you all. [*He bends his head.*]

CURTAIN

ACT II

Village roadside, on left the door of a forge, with broken wheels, etc., lying about. A well near centre, with board above it, and room to pass behind it. MARTIN DOUL *is sitting near forge, cutting sticks.*

TIMMY [*heard hammering inside forge, then calls*]. Let you make haste out there. . . . I'll be putting up new fires at the turn of day, and you haven't the half of them cut yet.

MARTIN DOUL [*gloomily*]. It's destroyed I'll be whacking your old thorns till the turn of day, and I with no food in my stomach would keep the life in a pig. [*He turns towards the door.*] Let you come out here and cut them yourself if you want them cut, for there's an hour every day when a man has a right to his rest.

TIMMY [*coming out, with a hammer, impatiently*]. Do you want me to be driving you off again to be walking the roads? There you are now, and I giving you your food, and a corner to sleep, and money with it, and to hear the talk of you, you'd think I was after beating you, or stealing your gold.

MARTIN DOUL. You'd do it handy, maybe, if I'd gold to steal.

TIMMY [*throws down hammer; picks up some of the sticks already cut, and throws them into door*]. There's no fear of your having gold, a lazy, basking fool the like of you.

MARTIN DOUL. No fear, maybe, and I here with yourself, for it's more I got a while since, and I sitting blinded in Grianan, than I get in this place, working hard, and destroying myself, the length of the day.

TIMMY [*stopping with amazement*]. Working hard? [*He goes over to him.*] I'll teach you to work hard, Martin Doul. Strip off your coat now, and put a tuck in your sleeves, and cut the lot of them, while I'd rake the ashes from the forge, or I'll not put up with you another hour itself.

MARTIN DOUL [*horrified*]. Would you have me getting my death sitting out in the black wintery air with no coat on me at all?

D

TIMMY [*with authority*]. Strip it off now, or walk down upon the road.

MARTIN DOUL [*bitterly*]. Oh, God help me! [*He begins taking off his coat.*] I've heard tell you stripped the sheet from your wife and you putting her down into the grave, and that there isn't the like of you for plucking your living ducks, the short days, and leaving them running round in their skins, in the great rains and the cold. [*He tucks up his sleeves.*] Ah, I've heard a power of queer things of yourself, and there isn't one of them I'll not believe from this day, and be telling to the boys.

TIMMY [*pulling over a big stick*]. Let you cut that now, and give me a rest from your talk, for I'm not heeding you at all.

MARTIN DOUL [*taking stick*]. That's a hard terrible stick, Timmy, and isn't it a poor thing to be cutting strong timber the like of that, when it's cold the bark is, and slippy with the frost of the air?

TIMMY [*gathering up another armful of sticks*]. What way wouldn't it be cold, and it freezing since the moon was changed? [*He goes into forge.*]

MARTIN DOUL [*querulously, as he cuts slowly*]. What way, indeed, Timmy? For it's a raw, beastly day we do have each day, till I do be thinking it's well for the blind don't be seeing the like of them grey clouds driving on the hill, and don't be looking on people with their noses red, the like of your nose, and their eyes weeping, and watering, the like of your eyes, God help you, Timmy the smith.

TIMMY [*seen blinking in doorway*]. Is it turning now you are against your sight?

MARTIN DOUL [*very miserably*]. It's a hard thing for a man to have his sight, and he living near to the like of you [*he cuts a stick, and throws it away*], or wed with a wife [*cuts a stick*], and I do be thinking it should be a hard thing for the Almighty God to be looking on the world bad days, and on men the like of yourself walking around on it, and they slipping each way in the muck.

TIMMY [*with pot-hooks which he taps on anvil*]. You'd have a right to be minding, Martin Doul, for it's a power the saint cured lose their sight after a while—it's well you know Mary Doul's dimming again—and I'm thinking the Lord if He hears you making that talk will have little pity left for you at all.

MARTIN DOUL. There's not a bit of fear of me losing my sight, and if it's a dark day itself it's too well I see every wicked wrinkle you have round by your eye.

TIMMY [*looking at him sharply*]. Dark day is it? The day's not dark since the clouds broke in the east.

MARTIN DOUL. Let you not be tormenting yourself trying to make me afeard. You told me a power of bad lies the time I was blind, and it's right now for you to stop, and be taking your rest [MARY DOUL *comes in unnoticed on right with a sack filled with green stuff on her arm*], for it's little ease or quiet any person would get if the big fools of Ireland weren't weary at times. [*He looks up and sees* MARY DOUL.] Oh, glory be to God, she's coming again. [*He begins to work busily with his back to her.*]

TIMMY [*amused, to* MARY DOUL, *as she is going by without looking at them*]. Look on him now, Mary Doul. You'd be a great one for keeping him steady at his work, for he's after idling, and blathering, to this hour from the dawn of day.

MARY DOUL [*stiffly*]. Of what is it you're speaking, Timmy the smith?

TIMMY [*laughing*]. Of himself, surely. Look on him there, and he with the shirt on him ripping from his back. You'd have a right to come round this night, I'm thinking, and put a stitch into his clothes, for it's long enough you are not speaking one to the other.

MARY DOUL. Let the two of you not torment me at all. [*She goes out left, with her head in the air.*]

MARTIN DOUL [*stops work and looks after her*]. Well, isn't it a queer thing she can't keep herself two days without looking on my face?

TIMMY [*jeeringly*]. Looking on your face is it? And she after going by with her head turned the way you'd see a sainted lady going where there'd be drunken people in the side ditch singing to themselves. [MARTIN DOUL *gets up and goes to corner of forge, and looks out left.*] Come back here and don't mind her at all. Come back here, I'm saying, you've no call to be spying behind her since she went off, and left you, in place of breaking her heart, trying to keep you in the decency of clothes and food.

MARTIN DOUL [*crying out indignantly*]. You know rightly, Timmy, it was myself drove her away.

TIMMY. That's a lie you're telling, yet it's little I care which one of you was driving the other, and let you walk back here I'm saying to your work.

MARTIN DOUL [*turning round*]. I'm coming, surely. [*He stops and looks out right, going a step or two towards centre.*]

TIMMY. On what is it you're gaping, Martin Doul?

MARTIN DOUL. There's a person walking above . . . It's Molly Byrne I'm thinking, coming down with her can.

TIMMY. If she is itself let you not be idling this day, or minding her at all, and let you hurry with them sticks, for I'll want you in a short while to be blowing in the forge.   [*He throws down pot-hooks.*]

MARTIN DOUL [*crying out*]. Is it roasting me now, you'd be? [*He turns back and sees pot-hooks; he takes them up.*] Pot-hooks? Is it over them you've been inside sneezing   and sweating since the dawn of day?

TIMMY [*resting himself on anvil, with satisfaction*] I'm making a power of things you do have when you're settling with a wife, Martin Doul, for I heard tell last night the saint'll be passing again in a short while, and I'd have him wed Molly with myself. . . . He'd do it, I've heard them say, for not a penny at all.

MARTIN DOUL [*lays down hooks and looks at him steadily*]. Molly'll be saying great praises now to the Almighty God and he giving her a fine stout hardy man the like of you.

TIMMY [*uneasily*]. And why wouldn't she, if she's a fine woman itself?

MARTIN DOUL [*looking up right*]. Why wouldn't she indeed, Timmy? . . . . The Almighty God's made a fine match in the two of you, for if you went marrying a woman was the like of yourself you'd be having the fearfullest little children, I'm thinking, was ever seen in the world.

TIMMY [*seriously offended*]. God forgive you, if you're an ugly man to be looking at, I'm thinking your tongue's worse than your view.

MARTIN DOUL [*hurt also*]. Isn't it destroyed with the cold I am, and if I'm ugly itself I never seen any one the like of you for dreepiness this day, Timmy the smith, and I'm thinking now herself's coming above you'd have a right to step up into your old shanty, and give a rub to your face, and not be sitting there with your bleary eyes, and your big nose, the like of an old scarecrow stuck down upon the road.

TIMMY [*looking up the road uneasily*]. She's no call to mind what way I look, and I after building a house with four rooms in it above on the hill. [*He stands up.*] But it's a queer thing the way yourself and Mary Doul are after setting every person in this place, and up beyond to Rathvanna, talking of nothing, and thinking of nothing, but the way they do be looking in the face. [*Going towards forge.*] It's the devil's work you're after doing with your talk of fine looks, and I'd do right, maybe, to step in, and wash the blackness from my eyes.

[*He goes into forge.* MARTIN DOUL *rubs his face furtively with the tail of his coat.* MOLLY BYRNE *comes on right with a water-can, and begins to fill it at the well.*]

MARTIN DOUL. God save you, Molly Byrne.

MOLLY BYRNE [*indifferently*]. God save you.

MARTIN DOUL. That's a dark, gloomy day, and the Lord have mercy on us all.

MOLLY BYRNE. Middling dark. . . .

MARTIN DOUL. It's a power of dirty days, and dark mornings, and shabby-looking fellows [*he makes a gesture over his shoulder*] we do have to be looking on when we have our sight, God help us, but there's one fine thing we have, to be looking on a grand, white, handsome girl, the like of you . . . and every time I set my eyes on you, I do be blessing the saints, and the holy water, and the power of the Lord Almighty in the heavens above.

MOLLY BYRNE. I've heard the priests say it isn't looking on a young girl would teach many to be saying their prayers. [*Baling water into her can with a cup.*]

MARTIN DOUL. It isn't many have been the way I was, hearing your voice speaking, and not seeing you at all.

MOLLY BYRNE. That should have been a queer time for an old wicked, coaxing fool to be sitting there with your eyes shut, and not seeing a sight of girl or woman passing the road.

MARTIN DOUL. If it was a queer time itself, it was great joy and pride I had, the time I'd hear your voice speaking and you passing to Grianan [*beginning to speak with plaintive intensity*], for it's of many a fine thing your voice would put a poor dark fellow in mind, and the day I'd hear it, it's of little else at all I would be thinking.

MOLLY BYRNE. I'll tell your wife if you talk to me the like of that. . . . You've heard, maybe, she's below picking nettles for the widow O'Flinn, who took great pity on her when she seen the two of you fighting, and yourself putting shame on her at the crossing of the roads.

MARTIN DOUL [*impatiently*]. Is there no living person can speak a score of words to me, or say 'God speed you', itself, without putting me in mind of the old woman, or that day either at Grianan?

MOLLY BYRNE [*with malice*]. I was thinking it should be a fine thing to put you in mind of the day you called the grand day of your life.

MARTIN DOUL. Grand day, is it? [*Plaintively again, throwing aside his work, and leaning towards her.*] Or a bad black day when I was roused up and found I was the like of the little children do be listening to the stories of an old woman, and do be dreaming after in the dark night that it's in grand houses of gold they are, with speckled horses to ride, and do be waking again, in a short while, and they destroyed with the cold, and the thatch dripping maybe, and the starved ass braying in the yard?

MOLLY BYRNE [*working indifferently*]. You've great romancing this day, Martin Doul. Was it up at the still you were at the fall of night?

MARTIN DOUL [*stands up, comes towards her, but stands at far—right— side of well*]. It was not, Molly Byrne, but lying down in a little rickety shed. . . . Lying down across a sop of straw, and I thinking I was seeing you walk, and hearing the sound of your step on a dry road, and hearing you again, and you laughing and making great talk in a high room with dry timber lining the roof. For it's a fine sound your voice has that time, and it's better I am, I'm thinking, lying down, the way a blind man does be lying, than to be sitting here in the grey light, taking hard words of Timmy the smith.

MOLLY BYRNE [*looking at him with interest*]. It's queer talk you have if it's a little, old, shabby stump of a man you are itself.

MARTIN DOUL. I'm not so old as you do hear them say.

MOLLY BYRNE. You're old, I'm thinking, to be talking that talk with a girl.

MARTIN DOUL [*despondingly*]. It's not a lie you're telling maybe, for it's long years I'm after losing from the world, feeling love, and talking love, with the old woman, and I fooled the whole while with the lies of Timmy the smith.

MOLLY BYRNE [*half invitingly*]. It's a fine way you're wanting to pay Timmy the smith. . . . And it's not his *lies* you're making love to this day, Martin Doul.

MARTIN DOUL. It is not, Molly, but with the good looks of yourself [*passing behind her and coming near her left*], for if it's old I am maybe I've heard tell there are lands beyond in Cahir Iveraghig and the Reeks of Cork with warm sun in them, and fine light in the sky. [*Bending towards her.*] And light's a grand thing for a man ever was blind, or a woman, with a fine neck, and a skin on her the like of you, the way we'd have a right to go off this day till we'd have a fine life passing abroad through them towns of the south, and we telling stories, maybe, or singing songs at the fairs.

MOLLY BYRNE [*turning round half amused, and looking him over from head to foot*]. Well isn't it a queer thing when your own wife's after leaving you because you're a pitiful show you'd talk the like of that to me?

MARTIN [*drawing back a little, hurt, but indignant*]. It's a queer thing maybe for all things is queer in the world. [*In a low voice with peculiar emphasis.*] But there's one thing I'm telling you, if she walked off away from me, it wasn't because of seeing me, and I no more than I am, but because I was looking on her with my two eyes, and she getting up, and eating her food, and combing her hair, and lying down for her sleep.

MOLLY [*interested, off her guard*]. Wouldn't any married man you'd have be doing the like of that?

MARTIN DOUL [*seizing the moment that he has her attention*]. I'm thinking by the mercy of God it's few sees anything but them is blind for a space. [*With excitement.*] It's few sees the old women rotting for the grave, and it's few sees the like of yourself [*he bends over her*], though it's shining you are, like a high lamp, would drag in the ships out of the sea.

MOLLY BYRNE [*shrinking away from him*]. Keep off from me, Martin Doul.

MARTIN DOUL [*quickly, with low, furious intensity. He puts his hand on her shoulder and shakes her*]. You'd do right, I'm saying, not to marry a man is after looking out a long while on the bad days of the world, for what way would the like of him have fit eyes to look on yourself, when you rise up in the morning and come out of the little door you have above in the lane, the time it'd be a fine thing if a man would be seeing, and losing his sight, the way he'd have your two eyes facing him, and he going the roads, and shining above him, and he looking in the sky, and springing up from the earth, the time he'd lower his head, in place of the muck that seeing men do meet all roads spread on the world.

MOLLY BYRNE [*who has listened half-mesmerized, starting away*]. It's the like of that talk you'd hear from a man would be losing his mind.

MARTIN DOUL [*going after her, passing to her right*]. It'd be little wonder if a man near the like of you would be losing his mind. Put down your can now, and come along with myself, for I'm seeing you this day, seeing you, maybe, the way no man has seen you in the world. [*He takes her by the arm and tries to pull her away softly to the right.*] Let you come on now, I'm saying, to the lands of Iveragh and the Reeks of Cork, where you won't set down the width of your two feet and not be crushing fine flowers, and making sweet smells in the air. . . .

MOLLY BYRNE [*laying down can; trying to free herself*]. Leave me go, Martin Doul. . . .   Leave me go, I'm saying!

MARTIN DOUL. Come along now, let you come on the little path through the trees.

MOLLY BYRNE [*crying out towards forge*]. Timmy. . . . Timmy the smith. . . . [TIMMY *comes out of forge, and* MARTIN DOUL *lets her go.* MOLLY BYRNE, *excited and breathless, pointing to* MARTIN DOUL.] Did ever you hear that them that loses their sight loses their sense along with it, Timmy the smith?

TIMMY [*suspicious, but uncertain*]. He's no sense, surely, and he'll be having himself driven off this day from where he's good sleeping, and feeding, and wages for his work.

MOLLY BYRNE [*as before*]. He's a bigger fool than that, Timmy. Look on him now, and tell me if that isn't a grand fellow to think he's only to open his mouth to have a fine woman, the like of me, running along by his heels.

[MARTIN DOUL *recoils towards centre, with his hand to his eyes;* MARY DOUL *is seen on left coming forward softly.*]

TIMMY [*with blank amazement*]. Oh, the blind is wicked people, and it's no lie. But he'll walk off this day and not be troubling us more. [*He walks back left and picks up* MARTIN DOUL's *coat and stick; some things fall out of coat pocket, which he gathers up again.*]

MARTIN DOUL [*turns round, sees* MARY DOUL, *whispers to* MOLLY BYRNE *with imploring agony*]. Let you not put shame on me, Molly, before herself and the smith. Let you not put shame on me and I after saying fine words to you, and dreaming . . . dreams . . . in the night. [*He hesitates, and looks round the sky.*] Is it a storm of thunder is coming, or the last end of the world? [*He staggers towards* MARY DOUL, *tripping slightly over tin can.*] The heavens is closing, I'm thinking, with darkness and great trouble passing in the sky. [*He reaches* MARY DOUL, *and seizes her with both his hands—with a frantic cry.*] Is it the darkness of thunder is coming, Mary Doul? Do you see me clearly with your eyes?

MARY DOUL [*snatches her arm away, and hits him with empty sack across the face*]. I see you a sight too clearly, and let you keep off from me now.

MOLLY BYRNE [*clapping her hands*]. That's right, Mary. That's the way to treat the like of him is after standing there at my feet and asking me to go off with him, till I'd grow an old wretched road woman the like of yourself.

MARY DOUL [*defiantly*]. When the skin shrinks on your chin, Molly Byrne, there won't be the like of you for a shrunk hag in the four quarters of Ireland. . . . It's a fine pair you'd be, surely!

[MARTIN DOUL *is standing at back right centre, with his back to the audience*].

TIMMY [*coming over to* MARY DOUL]. Is it no shame you have to let on she'd ever be the like of you?

MARY DOUL. It's them that's fat and flabby do be wrinkled young, and that whitish yellowy hair she has does be soon turning the like of a handful of thin grass you'd see rotting, where the wet lies, at the north of a sty. [*Turning to go out on right.*] Ah, isn't it a grand thing for the like of your make to be setting fools mad a short while, and then to be turning a thing will drive off the little children from your feet.

[*She goes out.* MARTIN DOUL *has come forward again, mastering himself, but uncertain.*]

TIMMY. Oh, God protect us, Molly, from the words of the blind. [*He throws down* MARTIN DOUL's *coat and stick.*] There's your old rubbish now, Martin Doul, and let you take it up, for it's all you have, and walk off through the world, and if ever I meet you coming again, if it's seeing or blind you are itself, I'll bring out the big hammer and hit you a welt with it will leave you easy till the judgement day.

MARTIN DOUL [*rousing himself with an effort*]. What call have you to talk the like of that with myself?

TIMMY [*pointing to* MOLLY BYRNE]. It's well you know what call I have. It's well you know a decent girl, I'm thinking to wed, has no right to have her heart scalded with hearing talk—and queer, bad talk, I'm thinking—from a raggy-looking fool the like of you.

MARTIN DOUL [*raising his voice*]. It's making game of you she is, for what seeing girl would marry with yourself? Look on him, Molly, look on him, I'm saying, for I'm seeing him still, and let you raise your voice, for the time is come, and bid him go up into his forge and be sitting there by himself, sneezing, and sweating, and he beating pot-hooks till the judgement day. [*He seizes her arm again.*]

MOLLY BYRNE. Keep him off from me, Timmy!

TIMMY [*pushing* MARTIN DOUL *aside*]. Would you have me strike you, Martin Doul? Go along now after your wife, who's a fit match for you, and leave Molly with myself.

MARTIN DOUL [*despairingly*]. Won't you raise your voice, Molly, and lay hell's long curse on his tongue?

MOLLY BYRNE [*on* TIMMY's *left*]. I'll be telling him it's destroyed I am with the sight of you and the sound of your voice. Go off now after your wife, and if she beats you again, let you go after the tinker girls is above running the hills, or down among the sluts of the town, and you'll learn one day, maybe, the way a man should speak with a well-reared civil girl the like of me. [*She takes* TIMMY *by the arm.*] Come up now into the forge till he'll be gone down a bit on the road, for it's near afeard I am of the wild look he has come in his eyes.

[*She goes into the forge.* TIMMY *stops in the doorway.*]

TIMMY. Let me not find you out here again, Martin Doul. [*He bares his arm.*] It's well you know Timmy the smith has great strength in his arm, and it's a power of things it has broken a sight harder than the old bone of your skull. [*He goes into the forge and pulls the door after him.*]

MARTIN DOUL [*stands a moment with his hand to his eyes*]. And that's the last thing I'm to set my sight on in the life of the world, the villainy of a woman and the bloody strength of a man. Oh, God, pity a poor blind fellow the way I am this day with no strength in me to do hurt to them at all. [*He begins groping about for a moment, then stops.*] Yet if I've no strength in me I've a voice left for my prayers, and may God blight them this day, and my own soul the same hour with them, the way I'll see them after, Molly Byrne and Timmy the smith, the two of them on a high bed, and they screeching in hell. . . . It'll be a grand thing that time to look on the two of them; and they twisting and roaring out, and twisting and roaring again, one day and the next day, and each day always and ever. It's not blind I'll be that time, and it won't be hell to me I'm thinking, but the like of Heaven itself, and it's fine care I'll be taking the Lord Almighty doesn't know. [*He turns to grope out.*]

CURTAIN

ACT III

Same as in first Act, but gap in centre has been filled with briars, or branches of some sort. MARY DOUL, *blind again, gropes her way in on left, and sits as before. She has a few rushes with her. It is an early spring day.*

MARY DOUL [*mournfully*]. Ah, God help me . . . God help me, the blackness wasn't so black at all the other time as it is this time, and it's destroyed I'll be now, and hard set to get my living working alone, when it's few are passing and the winds are cold. [*She begins shredding rushes.*] I'm thinking short days will be long days to me from this time, and I sitting here, not seeing a blink, or hearing a word, and no thought in my mind but long prayers that Martin Doul'll get his reward in a short while for the villainy of his heart. It's great jokes the people'll be making now, I'm thinking, and they passing me by, pointing their fingers, maybe, and asking what place is himself, the way it's no quiet or decency I'll have from this day till I'm an old woman with long white hair and it twisting from my brow. [*She fumbles with her hair, and then seems to hear something. Listens for a moment.*] There's a queer slouching step coming on the road. . . . God help me, he's coming surely.

[*She stays perfectly quiet.* MARTIN DOUL *gropes in on right, blind also.*]

MARTIN DOUL [*gloomily*]. The devil mend Mary Doul for putting lies on me, and letting on she was grand. The devil mend the old saint for letting me see it was lies. [*He sits down near her.*] The devil mend Timmy the smith for killing me with hard work, and keeping me with an empty windy stomach in me, in the day and in the night. Ten thousand devils mend the soul of Molly Byrne [MARY DOUL *nods her head with approval*] and the bad wicked souls is hidden in all the women of the world. [*He rocks himself, with his hand over his face.*] It's lonesome I'll be from this day, and if living people is a bad lot, yet Mary Doul herself, and she a dirty, wrinkled-looking hag, was better maybe to be sitting along with than no one at all. I'll be getting my death now, I'm thinking, sitting alone in the cold air, hearing the night coming, and the blackbirds flying round in the briars crying to themselves, the time you'll hear one cart getting off a long way in the east, and another cart getting off a long way in the west, and a dog barking maybe, and a little wind turning the sticks. [*He listens and sighs heavily.*] I'll be destroyed sitting alone and losing my senses this time the way I'm after losing my sight, for it'd make any person afeard to be sitting up hearing the sound of his breath [*he moves his feet on the stones*], and the noise of his feet, when it's a power of queer things do be stirring, little sticks breaking, and the grass moving [MARY DOUL *half sighs, and he turns on her in horror*] till you'd take your dying oath on sun and moon a thing was breathing on the stones. [*He listens towards her for a moment, then starts up nervously, and gropes about for his stick.*] I'll be going now, I'm thinking, but I'm not sure what place my stick's in, and I'm destroyed with terror and dread. [*He touches her hand as he is groping about and cries out.*] There's a thing with a cold living hand on it sitting up at my side. [*He turns to run away, but misses his path and stumbles in against the wall.*] My road is lost on me now! Oh, merciful God, set my foot on the path this day, and I'll be saying prayers morning and night, and not straining my ear after young girls, or doing any bad thing till I die—

MARY DOUL [*indignantly*]. Let you not be telling lies to the Almighty God.

MARTIN DOUL. Mary Doul is it? [*Recovering himself with immense relief.*] Is it Mary Doul, I'm saying?

MARY DOUL. There's a sweet tone in your voice I've not heard for a space. You're taking me for Molly Byrne, I'm thinking.

MARTIN DOUL [*coming towards her, wiping sweat from his face*]. Well, sight's a queer thing for upsetting a man. It's a queer thing to think I'd live to this day to be fearing the like of you, but if it's shaken I am for a short while, I'll soon be coming to myself.

MARY DOUL. You'll be grand then, and it's no lie.

MARTIN DOUL [*sitting down shyly, some way off*]. You've no call to be talking, for I've heard tell you're as blind as myself.

MARY DOUL. If I am I'm bearing in mind I'm married to a little dark stump of a fellow looks the fool of the world, and I'll be bearing in mind from this day the great hullabaloo he's after making from hearing a poor woman breathing quiet in her place.

MARTIN DOUL. And you'll be bearing in mind, I'm thinking, what you seen a while back when you looked down into a well, or a clear pool, maybe, when there was no wind stirring and a good light in the sky.

MARY DOUL. I'm minding that surely, for if I'm not the way the liars were saying below I seen a thing in them pools put joy and blessing in my heart. [*She puts her hand to her hair again.*]

MARTIN DOUL [*laughing ironically*]. Well! They were saying below I was losing my senses but I never went any day the length of that .... God help you, Mary Doul, if you're not a wonder for looks, you're the maddest female woman is walking the counties of the east.

MARY DOUL [*scornfully*]. You were saying all times you'd a great ear for hearing the lies in a word, a great ear, God help you, and you think you're using it now!

MARTIN DOUL. If it's not lies you're telling, would you have me think you're not a wrinkled poor woman is looking like three scores, maybe, or two scores and a half?

MARY DOUL. I would not, Martin. [*She leans forward earnestly.*] For when I seen myself in them pools, I seen my hair would be grey, or white maybe in a short while, and I seen with it that I'd a face would be a great wonder when it'll have soft white hair falling around it, the way when I'm an old woman there won't be the like of me surely in the seven counties of the east.

MARTIN DOUL [*with real admiration*]. You're a cute thinking woman, Mary Doul, and it's no lie.

MARY DOUL [*triumphantly*]. I am surely, and I'm telling you a beautiful white-haired woman is a grand thing to see, for I'm told when Kitty Bawn was selling poteen below, the young men itself would never tire to be looking in her face.

MARTIN DOUL [*taking off his hat and feeling his head, speaking with hesitation*]. Did you think to look, Mary Doul, would there be a whiteness the like of that coming upon me?

MARY DOUL [*with extreme contempt*]. On you, God help you? . . . In a short while you'll have a head on you as bald as an old turnip you'd see rolling round in the muck. You need never talk again of your fine looks, Martin Doul, for the day of that talk's gone for ever.

MARTIN DOUL. That's a hard word to be saying, for I was thinking if I'd a bit of comfort, the like of yourself, it's not far off we'd be from the good days went before, and that'd be a wonder surely. But I'll never rest easy, thinking you're a grey, beautiful woman, and myself a pitiful show.

MARY DOUL. I can't help your looks, Martin Doul. It wasn't myself made you with your rat's eyes, and your big ears, and your griseldy chin.

MARTIN DOUL [*rubs his chin ruefully, then beams with delight*]. There's one thing you've forgot, if you're a cute thinking woman itself!

MARY DOUL. Your slouching feet, is it? Or your hooky neck, or your two knees is black with knocking one on the other?

MARTIN DOUL [*with delighted scorn*]. There's talking for a cute woman! There's talking surely!

MARY DOUL [*puzzled at the joy of his voice*]. If you'd anything but lies to say you'd be talking yourself.

MARTIN DOUL [*bursting with excitement*]. I've this to say, Mary Doul. I'll be letting my beard grow in a short while— a beautiful, long, white, silken, streamy beard, you wouldn't see the like of in the eastern world. . . . Ah, a white beard's a grand thing on an old man, a grand thing for making the quality stop and be stretching out their hands with good silver or gold, and a beard's a thing you'll never have, so you may be holding your tongue.

MARY DOUL [*laughing cheerfully*]. Well, we're a great pair, surely, and it's great times we'll have yet, maybe, and great talking before we die.

MARTIN DOUL. Great times from this day, with the help of the Almighty God, for a priest itself would believe the lies of an old man would have a fine white beard growing on his chin.

MARY DOUL. There's the sound of one of them twittering yellow birds do be coming in the spring-time from beyond the sea, and there'll be a fine warmth now in the sun, and a sweetness in the air, the way it'll be a grand thing to be sitting here quiet and easy, smelling the things growing up, and budding from the earth.

MARTIN DOUL. I'm smelling the furze a while back sprouting on the hill, and if you'd hold your tongue you'd hear the lambs of Grianan, though it's near drowned their crying is with the full river making noises in the glen.

MARY DOUL [*listens*]. The lambs is bleating, surely, and there's cocks and laying hens making a fine stir a mile off on the face of the hill. [*She starts.*]

MARTIN DOUL. What's that is sounding in the west?

[*A faint sound of a bell is heard.*]

MARY DOUL. It's not the churches, for the wind's blowing from the sea.

MARTIN DOUL [*with dismay*]. It's the old saint, I'm thinking, ringing his bell.

MARY DOUL. The Lord protect us from the saints of God! [*They listen.*] He's coming this road, surely.

MARTIN DOUL [*tentatively*]. Will we be running off, Mary Doul?

MARY DOUL. What place would we run?

MARTIN DOUL. There's the little path going up through the sloughs. . . . If we reached the bank above, where the elders do be growing, no person would see a sight of us, if it was a hundred yeomen were passing itself, but I'm afeard after the time we were with our sight we'll not find our way to it at all.

MARY DOUL [*standing up*]. You'd find the way, surely. You're a grand man the world knows at finding your way if there was deep snow itself lying on the earth.

MARTIN DOUL [*taking her hand*]. Come a bit this way, it's here it begins. [*They grope about gap.*] There's a tree pulled into the gap, or a strange thing happened since I was passing it before.

MARY DOUL. Would we have a right to be crawling in below under the sticks?

MARTIN DOUL. It's hard set I am to know what would be right. And isn't it a poor thing to be blind when you can't run off itself, and you fearing to see?

MARY DOUL [*nearly in tears*]. It's a poor thing, God help us, and what good'll our grey hairs be itself, if we have our sight, the way we'll see them falling each day, and turning dirty in the rain?

[*The bell sounds near by.*]

MARTIN DOUL [*in despair*]. He's coming now, and we won't get off from him at all.

MARY DOUL. Could we hide in the bit of a briar is growing at the west butt of the church?

MARTIN DOUL. We'll try that, surely. [*He listens a moment.*] Let you make haste, I hear them trampling in the wood. [*They grope over to church.*]

MARY DOUL. It's the words of the young girls making a great stir in the trees. [*They find the bush.*] Here's the briar on my left, Martin; I'll go in first, I'm the big one, and I'm easy to see.

MARTIN DOUL [*turning his head anxiously*]. It's easy heard you are, and will you be holding your tongue?

MARY DOUL [*partly behind bush*]. Come in now beside of me. [*They kneel down, still clearly visible.*] Do you think can they see us now, Martin Doul?

MARTIN DOUL. I'm thinking they can't, but I'm hard set to know, for the lot of them young girls, the devil save them, have sharp terrible eyes, would pick out a poor man I'm thinking, and he lying below hid in his grave.

MARY DOUL. Let you not be whispering sin, Martin Doul, or maybe it's the finger of God they'd see pointing to ourselves.

MARTIN DOUL. It's yourself is speaking madness, Mary Doul, haven't you heard the saint say it's the wicked do be blind?

MARY DOUL. If it is you'd have a right to speak a big terrible word would make the water not cure us at all.

MARTIN DOUL. What way would I find a big terrible word, and I shook with the fear, and if I did itself, who'd know rightly if it's good words or bad would save us this day from himself?

MARY DOUL. They're coming. I hear their feet on the stones.

[SAINT *comes in on right with* TIMMY *and* MOLLY BYRNE *in holiday clothes, the others as before.*]

TIMMY. I've heard tell Martin Doul and Mary Doul were seen this day about on the road, holy father, and we were thinking you'd have pity on them and cure them again.

SAINT. I would, maybe, but where are they at all? I'll have little time left when I have the two of you wed in the church.

MAT SIMON [*at their seat*]. There are the rushes they do have lying round on the stones. It's not far off they'll be, surely.

MOLLY BYRNE [*pointing with astonishment*]. Look beyond, Timmy.

[*They all look over and see* MARTIN DOUL.]

TIMMY. Well, Martin's a lazy fellow to be lying in there at the height of the day. [*He goes over shouting.*] Let you get up out of that. You were near losing a great chance by your sleepiness this day, Martin Doul. . . . The two of them's in it, God help us all!

MARTIN DOUL [*scrambling up with* MARY DOUL]. What is it you want, Timmy, that you can't leave us in peace?

TIMMY. The saint's come to marry the two of us, and I'm after speaking a word for yourselves, the way he'll be curing you now, for if you're a foolish man itself, I do be pitying you, for I've a kind heart, when I think of you sitting dark again, and you after seeing a while, and working for your bread.

[MARTIN DOUL *takes* MARY DOUL's *hand and tries to grope his way off right, he has lost his hat, and they are both covered with dust, and grass seeds.*]

PEOPLE. You're going wrong. It's this way, Martin Doul.

[*They push him over in front of* SAINT *near centre*. MARTIN DOUL *and* MARY DOUL *stand with piteous hang-dog dejection.*]

SAINT. Let you not be afeard, for there's great pity with the Lord.

MARTIN DOUL. We aren't afeard, holy father.

SAINT. It's many a time those that are cured with the well of the four beauties of God lose their sight when a time is gone, but those I cure a second time go on seeing till the hour of death. [*He takes the cover from his can.*] I've a few drops only left of the water, but, with the help of God, it'll be enough for the two of you, and let you kneel down now upon the road.

[MARTIN DOUL *wheels round with* MARY DOUL *and tries to get away*].

SAINT. You can kneel down here, I'm saying, we'll not trouble this time going to the church.

TIMMY [*turning* MARTIN DOUL *round angrily*]. Are you going mad in your head, Martin Doul? It's here you're to kneel. Did you not hear his reverence, and he speaking to you now?

SAINT. Kneel down, I'm saying, the ground's dry at your feet.

MARTIN DOUL [*with distress*]. Let you go on your own way, holy father. We're not calling you at all.

SAINT. I'm not saying a word of penance, or fasting itself, so you've no call now to be fearing me, but let you kneel down till I give you your sight.

MARTIN DOUL [*more troubled*]. We're not asking our sight, holy father, and let you be walking on and leaving us in our peace at the crossing roads, for it's best we are this way, and we're not asking to see.

SAINT [*to the* PEOPLE]. Is his mind gone that he's no wish to be cured this day, and looking out on the wonders of the world?

MARTIN DOUL. It's wonders enough I seen in a short space for the life of one man only.

TIMMY. Is it he see wonders?

PATCH RUADH. He's making game.

MAT SIMON. He's maybe drunk, holy father.

SAINT [*severely*]. I never heard tell of any person wouldn't have great joy to be looking on the earth, and the image of the Lord is thrown upon men.

MARTIN DOUL [*raising his voice, by degrees*]. That's great sights, holy father. . . . What was it I seen my first day, but your own bleeding feet and they cut with the stones, and my last day, but the villainy of herself that you're wedding, God forgive you, with Timmy the smith. That was great sights maybe. . . . And wasn't it great sights seeing the roads when north winds would be driving and the skies would be harsh, and you'd see the horses and the asses and the dogs itself maybe with their heads hanging and they closing their eyes—

TIMMY. There's talking.

MAT SIMON. He's right maybe, it's lonesome living when the days are dark.

MOLLY BYRNE. He's not right. Let you speak up, holy father, and confound him now.

SAINT [*coming close to* MARTIN DOUL *and putting his hand on his shoulder.*] Did you never set eyes on the summer and the fine spring in the places where the holy men of Ireland have built up churches to the Lord, that you'd wish to be closed up and seeing no sight of the glittering seas, and the furze is opening above, will soon have the hills shining as if it was fine creels of gold they were, rising to the sky?

PATCH RUADH. That's it, holy father.

MAT SIMON. What have you now to say, Martin Doul?

MARTIN DOUL [*fiercely*]. Isn't it finer sights ourselves had a while since and we sitting dark smelling the sweet beautiful smells do be rising in the warm nights and hearing the swift flying things racing in the air [SAINT *draws back from him*], till we'd be looking up in our own minds into a grand sky, and seeing lakes, and broadening rivers, and hills are waiting for the spade and plough.

MAT SIMON [*roaring laughing*]. It's songs he's making now, holy father.

PATCH. It's mad he is.

MOLLY BYRNE. It's not, but lazy he is, holy father, and not wishing to work, for a while since he was all times longing and screeching for the light of day.

MARTIN DOUL [*turning on her*] . If I was, I seen my fill in a short while with the look of my wife, and of your own wicked grin, Molly Byrne, the time you're making game with a man.

MOLLY BYRNE. My grin, is it? Let you not mind him more, holy father, but leave him in darkness, if it's that is best fitting to the blackness of his heart.

TIMMY. Cure Mary Doul, your reverence, who is a quiet poor woman never said a hard word but when she'd be vexed with himself, or with the young girls do be making game of her below.

PEOPLE. That's it, cure Mary Doul your reverence.

SAINT. There is little use, maybe, talking to the like of him, but if you have any sense, Mary Doul, kneel down at my feet, and I'll bring the sight into your eyes.

MARTIN DOUL [*more defiantly*]. You will not, holy father! Would you have her looking on me, and saying hard words to me, till the hour of death?

SAINT [*severely*]. If she's wishing her sight it isn't the like of you'll stop her. [*To* MARY.] Kneel down, I'm saying.

MARY DOUL [*doubtfully*]. Let us be as we are, holy father, and then we'll be known again as the people is happy and blind, and we'll be having an easy time with no trouble to live, and we getting half-pence on the road.

MOLLY BYRNE. Let you not be raving. Kneel down and get your sight, and let himself be taking half-pence if he likes it best.

TIMMY. If it's choosing a wilful blindness you are, there isn't any one will give you a hap'worth of meal or be doing the little things you need to keep you at all living in the world.

MAT SIMON. If you had your sight you could be keeping a watch that no other woman came near to him at all.

MARY DOUL [*half persuaded*]. That's true, maybe. . . .

SAINT. Kneel down for I must be hastening with the marriage and going my own way before the fall of night.

PEOPLE [*all together*]. Kneel down, Mary! Kneel down when you're bid by the saint!

MARY DOUL [*looking uneasily towards* MARTIN DOUL]. Maybe it's right they are, and I will if you wish it, holy father. . . .

[*She kneels down.* SAINT *takes off his hat and gives it to someone near him. All the men take off their hats. He goes forward a step to take* MARTIN DOUL'*s hand away from* MARY DOUL.]

SAINT [*to* MARTIN DOUL]. Go aside now, we're not wanting you here.

MARTIN DOUL [*pushes him away roughly, and stands with his left hand on* MARY DOUL'*s shoulder*]. Keep off yourself, holy father, and let you not be taking my rest from me in the darkness of my wife. . . . What call have the like of you to be coming in where you're not wanted at all, and making a great mess with the holy water you have and the length of your prayers? [*Defiantly.*] Go on, I'm saying, and leave us this place on the road.

SAINT. If it was a seeing man I heard talking to me the like of that I'd put a black curse on him would weigh down his soul till it'd be falling to hell; but you're a poor blind sinner, God forgive you, and I don't mind you at all. [*He raises his can.*] Go aside now till I give the blessing to your wife, and if you won't go with your own will, there are those standing by will make you surely.

MARTIN DOUL [*pulling* MARY DOUL]. Make me, is it? Well, there's cruel hardship in the pity of your like, and what is it you want coming for to break our happiness and hour of rest. Let you rise up, Mary, against them and not heed them more.

SAINT [*imperiously to* PEOPLE]. Let you take that man and drive him down upon the road.

MAT SIMON. Come now, Martin, come on.

PATCH RUADH. Come off now from talking badness to the holy saint.

MARTIN DOUL [*throwing himself down on the ground clinging to* MARY DOUL]. I'll not come, I'm saying, and let you take his holy water to cure the blackness of your souls today.

MARY DOUL [*putting her arm round him*]. Leave him easy, holy father, when I'd liefer live dark all times beside him, than be seeing in new troubles now.

SAINT. You've taken your choice. Drag him away.

PEOPLE. That's it. Lift his head. [*They carry him to right.*]

MARTIN DOUL [*screaming*]. Make them leave me go, holy father. Make them leave me go, and let you have pity and forgive me for my heathen words, and you may cure her this day, holy father, and do anything that you will.

SAINT [*to* PEOPLE]. Let him be if his sense is come to him at all.

[*They put him down.*]

MARTIN DOUL [*shakes himself loose, feels for* MARY DOUL, *sinking his voice to a plausible whine*]. You may cure herself, surely, holy father, I wouldn't stop you at all—and it's great joy she'll have looking on your face—but let you cure myself along with her, the way I'll see when it's lies she's telling, and be looking out day and night upon the holy men of God. [*He kneels down a little before* MARY DOUL.]

SAINT [*speaking half to the* PEOPLE]. Men who are dark a long while and thinking over queer thoughts in their heads, aren't the like of simple men, who do be working every day, and praying, and living like ourselves, and with that it's my part to be showing a love to you would take pity on the worst that live. So if you've found a right mind at the last minute itself, I'll cure you, if the Lord will, and not be thinking of the hard, foolish words you're after saying this day to us all.

MARTIN DOUL [*listening eagerly*]. I'm waiting now, holy father.

SAINT [*with can in his hand, close to* MARTIN DOUL]. With the power of the water from the grave of the four beauties of God, with the power of this water, I'm saying, that I put upon your eyes— —

[*He raises can.* MARTIN DOUL *with a sudden movement strikes the can from* SAINT'*s hand and sends it rocketing across stage.*]

PEOPLE [*with a terrified murmur*]. Will you look what he's done. Oh, glory be to God. There's a villain surely.

MARTIN DOUL [*stands up triumphantly, and pulls* MARY DOUL *up*]. If I'm a poor dark sinner I've sharp ears, God help me, and it's well I heard the little splash of the water you had there in the can. Go on now, holy father, for if you're a fine saint itself, it's more sense is in a blind man, and more power maybe than you're thinking at all. Let you walk on now with your worn feet, and your welted knees, and your fasting, holy ways have left you with a big head on you and a thin pitiful arm.

PEOPLE. Go on from this.

[SAINT *looks at* MARTIN DOUL *for a moment severely, then turns away and picks up his can.*]

MARTIN DOUL. We're going surely, for if it's a right some of you have to be working and sweating the like of Timmy the smith, and a right some of you have to be fasting and praying and talking holy talk the like of yourself, I'm thinking it's a good right ourselves have to be sitting blind, hearing a soft wind turning round the little leaves of the spring and feeling the sun, and we not tormenting our souls with the sight of the grey days, and the holy men, and the dirty feet is trampling the world. [*He gropes towards his stone with* MARY DOUL.]

MAT SIMON. It'd be an unlucky fearful thing, I'm thinking, to have the like of that man living near us at all. Wouldn't he bring down a curse upon us, holy father, from the heavens of God?

SAINT [*tying his girdle*]. God has great mercy, but great wrath for them that sin.

PEOPLE [*all together*]. Go on now, Martin Doul. Go on from this place. Let you not be bringing great storms or droughts on us maybe from the power of the Lord. [*Some of them throw things at him.*]

MARTIN DOUL [*turning round defiantly and picking up his stick*]. Keep off now the yelping lot of you, or it's more than one maybe will get a bloody head on him from the welt of my stick. Keep off now, and let you not be afeard; for we're going on the two of us to the towns of the south, where the people will have kind voices maybe, and we won't know their bad looks or their villainy at all.

MARY DOUL [*despondingly*]. That's the truth, surely, and we'd have a right to be gone, if it's a long way itself, where you do have to be walking with a slough of wet on the one side and a slough of wet on the other, and you going a stony path with a north wind blowing behind.

MEN. Go on now. Go on from this place.

MARTIN DOUL. Keep off I'm saying. [*He takes* MARY DOUL's *hand again*.] Come along now and we'll be walking to the south, for we've seen too much of everyone in this place, and it's small joy we'd have living near them, or hearing the lies they do be telling from the grey of dawn till the night. [*They go.*]

TIMMY. There's a power of deep rivers with floods in them where you do have to be lepping the stones and you going to the south, so I'm thinking the two of them will be drowned together in a short while, surely.

SAINT. They have chosen their lot, and the Lord have mercy on their souls. [*He rings his bell.*] And let the two of you come up now into the church, Molly Byrne and Timmy the smith, till I make your marriage and put my blessing on you all.

[*He turns to the church, procession forms, and the curtain comes down, as they go slowly into the church.*]

CURTAIN

THE PLAYBOY OF THE WESTERN WORLD

A COMEDY IN THREE ACTS

(1905–1907)

PREFACE

IN writing *The Playboy of the Western World*, as in my other plays, I have used one or two words only, that I have not heard among the country people of Ireland, or spoken in my own nursery before I could read the newspapers. A certain number of the phrases I employ I have heard also from herds and fishermen along the coast from Kerry to Mayo, or from beggar-women and ballad-singers nearer Dublin; and I am glad to acknowledge how much I owe to the folk-imagination of these fine people. Anyone who has lived in real intimacy with the Irish peasantry will know that the wildest sayings and ideas in this play are tame indeed compared with the fancies one may hear in any little hill-side cabin in Geesala, or Carraroe, or Dingle Bay. All art is a collaboration; and there is little doubt that in the happy ages of literature striking and beautiful phrases were as ready to the story-teller's or the play-wright's hand as the rich cloaks and dresses of his time. It is probable that when the Elizabethan dramatist took his ink-horn and sat down to his work he used many phrases that he had just heard, as he sat at dinner, from his mother or his children. In Ireland those of us who know the people have the same privilege. When I was writing *The Shadow of the Glen*, some years ago, I got more aid than any learning could have given me, from a chink in the floor of the old Wicklow house where I was staying, that let me hear what was being said by the servant girls in the kitchen. This matter, I think, is of importance, for in countries where the imagination of the people, and the language they use, is rich and living, it is possible for a writer to be rich and copious in his words, and at the same time to give the reality which is the root of all poetry, in a comprehensive and natural form. In the modern literature of towns, however, richness is found only in sonnets, or prose poems, or in one or two elaborate books that are far away from the profound and common interests of life. One has, on one side, Mallarmé and Huysmans producing this literature; and on the other Ibsen and Zola dealing with the reality of life in joyless and pallid words. On the stage one must have reality, and one must have joy, and that is why the intellectual modern drama has failed, and people have grown sick of the false joy of the musical comedy, that has been given them in place of the rich joy found only in what is superb and wild in reality. In a good play every speech should be as fully flavoured as a nut or apple, and such speeches cannot be written by anyone who works among people who have shut their lips on poetry. In Ireland, for a few years more, we have a popular imagination that is fiery and magnificent, and tender; so that those of us who wish to write start with a chance that is not given to writers in places where the springtime of the local life has been forgotten, and the harvest is a memory only, and the straw has been turned into bricks.

J. M. S.

January 21st, 1907.

PERSONS

CHRISTOPHER MAHON

OLD MAHON, his father, a squatter

MICHAEL JAMES FLAHERTY (called MICHAEL JAMES), a publican

MARGARET FLAHERTY (called PEGEEN MIKE), his daughter

SHAWN KEOGH, her second cousin, a young farmer

PHILLY O'CULLEN,

JIMMY FARRELL,
}
small farmers

WIDOW QUIN

SARA TANSEY,

SUSAN BRADY,

HONOR BLAKE,
}
village girls

NELLY MCLAUGHLIN,

A BELLMAN

SOME PEASANTS

SCENE

The action takes place near a village, on a wild coast of Mayo. The first Act passes on a dark evening of autumn, the other two Acts on the following day.

ACT I

Country public house or shebeen, very rough and untidy. There is a sort of counter on the right with shelves, holding many bottles and jugs, just seen above it. Empty barrels stand near the counter. At back, a little to left of counter, there is a door into the open air; then, more to the left, there is a settle with shelves above it, with more jugs, and a table beneath a window. At the left there is a large open fire-place, with turf fire, and a small door into inner room. PEGEEN, a wild-looking but fine girl of about twenty, is writing at table. She is dressed in the usual peasant dress.

PEGEEN [*slowly, as she writes*]. Six yards of stuff for to make a yellow gown. A pair of lace boots with lengthy heels on them and brassy eyes. A hat is suited for a wedding-day. A fine tooth comb. To be sent with three barrels of porter in Jimmy Farrell's creel cart on the evening of the coming Fair to Mister Michael James Flaherty. With the best compliments of this season: Margaret Flaherty.

SHAWN KEOGH [*a fat and fair young man comes in down right centre as she signs and looks round awkwardly, when he sees she is alone*]. Where's himself?

PEGEEN [*without looking at him*]. He's coming. [*She directs letter.*] To Mister Sheamus Mulroy, Wine and Spirit Dealer, Castlebar.

SHAWN [*uneasily*]. I didn't see him on the road.

PEGEEN. How would you see him [*licks stamp and puts it on letter*] and it dark night this half an hour gone by?

SHAWN [*turning towards door again*]. I stood a while outside wondering would I have a right to pass on or to walk in and see you, Pegeen Mike [*comes to the fire*], and I could hear the cows breathing, and sighing in the stillness of the air, and not a step moving any place from this gate to the bridge.

PEGEEN [*putting letter in envelope*]. It's above at the cross-roads he is, meeting Philly O'Cullen and a couple more are going along with him to Kate Cassidy's wake.

E

SHAWN [*looking at her blankly*]. And he's going that length in the dark night?

PEGEEN [*impatiently*]. He is surely, and leaving me lonesome on the scruff of the hill. [*She gets up and puts envelope on dresser, then winds clock.*] Isn't it long the nights are now, Shawn Keogh, to be leaving a poor girl with her own self counting the hours to the dawn of day?

SHAWN [*with awkward humour*]. If it is, when we're wedded in a short while you'll have no call to complain, for I've little will to be walking off to wakes or weddings in the darkness of the night.

PEGEEN [*with rather scornful good humour*]. You're making mighty certain, Shaneen, that I'll wed you now.

SHAWN. Aren't we after making a good bargain, the way we're only waiting these days on Father Reilly's dispensation from the bishops or the Court of Rome.

PEGEEN [*looking at him teasingly, washing up at dresser*]. It's a wonder, Shaneen, the Holy Father'd be taking notice of the likes of you, for if I was him, I wouldn't bother with this place where you'll meet none but Red Linahan, has a squint in his eye, and Patcheen is lame in his heel, or the mad Mulrannies were driven from California and they lost in their wits. We're a queer lot these times to go troubling the Holy Father on his sacred seat.

SHAWN [*scandalized*]. If we are, we're as good this place as another, maybe, and as good these times as we were for ever.

PEGEEN [*with scorn*]. As good, is it? Where now will you meet the like of Daneen Sullivan knocked the eye from a peeler, or Marcus Quin, God rest him, got six months for maiming ewes, and he a great warrant to tell stories of holy Ireland till he'd have the old women shedding down tears about their feet. Where will you find the like of them, I'm saying?

SHAWN [*timidly*]. If you don't, it's a good job, maybe, for [*with peculiar emphasis on the words*] Father Reilly has small conceit to have that kind walking around and talking to the girls.

PEGEEN [*impatiently, throwing water from basin out of the door*]. Stop tormenting me with Father Reilly [*imitating his voice*], when I'm asking only what way I'll pass these twelve hours of dark, and not take my death with the fear. [*Looking out of door.*]

SHAWN [*timidly*]. Would I fetch you the Widow Quin, maybe.

PEGEEN. Is it the like of that murderer? You'll not, surely.

SHAWN [*going to her, soothingly*]. Then I'm thinking himself will stop along with you when he sees you taking on, for it'll be a long night and with great darkness, and I'm after feeling a kind of fellow above in the furzy ditch, groaning wicked like a maddening dog, the way it's good cause you have, maybe, to be fearing now.

PEGEEN [*turning on him sharply*]. What's that? Is it a man you seen?

SHAWN [*retreating*]. I couldn't see him at all, but I heard him groaning out and breaking his heart. It should have been a young man from his words speaking.

PEGEEN [*going after him*]. And you never went near to see was he hurted or what ailed him at all?

SHAWN. I did not, Pegeen Mike. It was a dark lonesome place to be hearing the like of him.

PEGEEN. Well, you're a daring fellow! And if they find his corpse stretched above in the dews of dawn, what'll you say then to the peelers or the Justice of the Peace?

SHAWN [*thunderstruck*]. I wasn't thinking of that. For the love of God, Pegeen Mike, don't let on I was speaking of him. Don't tell your father and the men is coming above, for if they heard that story they'd have great blabbing this night at the wake.

PEGEEN. I'll maybe tell them, and I'll maybe not.

SHAWN. They are coming at the door. Will you whisht, I'm saying.

PEGEEN. Whisht yourself.

[*She goes behind counter.* MICHAEL JAMES, *fat jovial publican, comes in down right centre followed by* PHILLY O'CULLEN, *who is thin and mistrusting, and* JIMMY FARRELL, *who is fat and amorous, about forty-five.*]

MEN [*together*]. God bless you. The blessing of God on this place.

PEGEEN. God bless you kindly.

MICHAEL [*to men, who go to the counter right*]. Sit down now, and take your rest. [*Crosses to* SHAWN *at the fire left.*] And how is it you are, Shawn Keogh? Are you coming over the sands to Kate Cassidy's wake?

SHAWN. I am not, Michael James. I'm going home the short-cut to my bed.

PEGEEN [*speaking across from counter*]. He's right too, and have you no shame, Michael James, to be quitting off for the whole night and leaving myself lonesome in the shop?

MICHAEL [*good-humouredly*]. Isn't it the same whether I go for the whole night or a part only? and I'm thinking it's a queer daughter you are if you'd have me crossing backward through the Stooks of the Dead Women, with a drop taken.

PEGEEN [*angrily*]. If I am a queer daughter, it's a queer father'd be leaving me lonesome these twelve hours of dark, and I piling the turf with the dogs barking, and the calves mooing, and my own teeth rattling with the fear.

JIMMY [*flatteringly*]. What is there to hurt you and you a fine, hardy girl would knock the head of any two men in the place.

PEGEEN [*working herself up*]. Isn't there the harvest boys with their tongues red for drink, and the ten tinkers is camped in the east glen, and the thousand militia—bad cess to them!—walking idle through the land? There's lots surely to hurt me, and I won't stop alone in it, let himself do what he will.

MICHAEL. If you're that afeard, let Shawn Keogh stop along with you. It's the will of God, I'm thinking, himself should be seeing to you now. [*They all turn on* SHAWN.]

SHAWN [*in horrified confusion*]. I would and welcome, Michael James; but I'm afeard of Father Reilly, and what at all would the Holy Father and the Cardinals of Rome be saying if they heard I did the like of that?

MICHAEL [*with contempt*]. God help you! Can't you sit in by the hearth with the light lit and herself beyond in the room? You'll do that surely, for I've heard tell there's a queer fellow above going mad or getting his death, maybe, in the gripe of the ditch, so she'd be safer this night with a person here.

SHAWN [*with plaintive despair*]. I'm afeard of Father Reilly, I'm saying. Let you not be tempting me and we near married itself.

PHILLY [*with cold contempt*]. Lock him in the west room. He'll stay then and have no sin to be telling to the priest.

MICHAEL [*to* SHAWN, *getting between him and the door*]. Go up now.

SHAWN [*at the top of his voice*]. Don't stop me, Michael James. Let me out of the door, I'm saying, for the love of the Almighty God. Let me out [*trying to dodge past him*]. Let me out of it and may God grant you His indulgence in the hour of need.

MICHAEL [*loudly*]. Stop your noising and sit down by the hearth. [*Gives him a push and goes to counter laughing.*]

SHAWN [*turning back, wringing his hands*]. Oh, Father Reilly and the saints of God, where will I hide myself today? Oh, St. Joseph and St. Patrick and St. Brigid and St. James, have mercy on me now! [*He turns round, sees door clear and makes a rush for it.*]

MICHAEL [*catching him by the coat-tail*]. You'd be going, is it?

SHAWN [*screaming*]. Leave me go, Michael James, leave me go, you old Pagan, leave me go or I'll get the curse of the priests on you, and of the scarlet-coated bishops of the courts of Rome. [*With a sudden movement he pulls himself out of his coat and disappears out of the door, leaving his coat in* MICHAEL'*s hands.*]

MICHAEL [*turning round, and holding up coat*]. Well, there's the coat of a Christian man. Oh, there's sainted glory this day in the lonesome west, and by the will of God I've got you a decent man, Pegeen, you'll have no call to be spying after if you've a score of young girls, maybe, weeding in your fields.

PEGEEN [*taking up the defence of her property*]. What right have you to be making game of a poor fellow for minding the priest when it's your own the fault is, not paying a penny pot-boy to stand along with me and give me courage in the doing of my work? [*She snaps the coat away from him, and goes behind counter with it.*]

MICHAEL [*taken aback*]. Where would I get a pot-boy? Would you have me send the bell-man screaming in the streets of Castlebar?

SHAWN [*opening the door a chink and putting in his head, in a small voice*]. Michael James!

MICHAEL [*imitating him*]. What ails you?

SHAWN. The queer dying fellow's beyond looking over the ditch. He's come up, I'm thinking, stealing your hens. [*Looks over his shoulder.*] God help me, he's following me now [*he runs into room*], and if he's heard what I said, he'll be having my life and I going home lonesome in the darkness of the night.

> [*For a perceptible moment they watch the door with curiosity. Someone coughs outside. Then* CHRISTY MAHON, *a slight young man, comes in, very tired and frightened and dirty.*]

CHRISTY [*in a small voice*]. God save all here!

MEN. God save you kindly.

CHRISTY [*going to counter*]. I'd trouble you for a glass of porter, woman of the house. [*He puts down coin.*]

PEGEEN [*serving him*]. You're one of the tinkers, young fellow, is beyond camped in the glen?

CHRISTY. I am not; but I'm destroyed walking.

MICHAEL [*patronizingly*]. Let you come up then to the fire. You're looking famished with the cold.

CHRISTY. God reward you. [*He takes up his glass, and goes a little way across to the left, then stops and looks about him.*] Is it often the polis do be coming into this place, master of the house?

MICHAEL. If you'd come in better hours, you'd have seen 'Licensed for the Sale of Beer and Spirits, to be consumed on the Premises,' written in white letters above the door, and what would the polis want spying on me, and not a decent house within four miles, the way every living Christian is a bona fide saving one widow alone?

CHRISTY [*with relief*]. It's a safe house, so. [*He goes over to the fire, sighing and moaning. Then he sits down putting his glass beside him and begins gnawing a turnip, too miserable to feel the others staring at him with curiosity.*]

MICHAEL [*going after him*]. Is it yourself is fearing the polis? You're wanting, maybe?

CHRISTY. There's many wanting.

MICHAEL. Many surely, with the broken harvest and the ended wars. [*He picks up some stockings etc. that are near the fire, and carries them away furtively.*] It should be larceny, I'm thinking?

CHRISTY [*dolefully*]. I had it in my mind it was a different word and a bigger.

PEGEEN. There's a queer lad! Were you never slapped in school, young fellow, that you don't know the name of your deed?

CHRISTY [*bashfully*]. I'm slow at learning, a middling scholar only.

MICHAEL. If you're a dunce itself, you'd have a right to know that larceny's robbing and stealing. Is it for the like of that you're wanting?

CHRISTY [*with a flash of family pride*]. And I the son of a strong farmer [*with a sudden qualm*], God rest his soul, could have bought up the whole of your old house a while since from the butt of his tail-pocket and not have missed the weight of it gone.

MICHAEL [*impressed*]. If it's not stealing, it's maybe something big.

CHRISTY [*flattered*]. Aye; it's maybe something big.

JIMMY. He's a wicked-looking young fellow. Maybe he followed after a young woman on a lonesome night.

CHRISTY [*shocked*]. Oh, the saints forbid, mister. I was all times a decent lad.

PHILLY [*turning on JIMMY*]. You're a silly man, Jimmy Farrell. He said his father was a farmer a while since, and there's himself now in a poor state. Maybe the land was grabbed from him, and he did what any decent man would do.

MICHAEL [*to CHRISTY, mysteriously*]. Was it bailiffs?

CHRISTY. The divil a one.

MICHAEL. Agents?

CHRISTY. The divil a one.

MICHAEL. Landlords?

CHRISTY [*peevishly*]. Ah, not at all, I'm saying. You'd see the like of them stories on any little paper of a Munster town. But I'm not calling to mind any person, gentle, simple, judge or jury, did the like of me.

[*They all draw nearer with delighted curiosity.*]

PHILLY. Well that lad's a puzzle-the-world.

JIMMY. He'd beat Dan Davies' Circus or the holy missioners making sermons on the villainy of man. Try him again, Philly.

PHILLY. Did you strike golden guineas out of solder, young fellow, or shilling coins itself?

CHRISTY. I did not mister, not sixpence nor a farthing coin.

JIMMY. Did you marry three wives maybe? I'm told there's a sprinkling have done that among the holy Luthers of the preaching North.

CHRISTY [*shyly*]. I never married with one, let alone with a couple or three.

PHILLY. Maybe he went fighting for the Boers, the like of the man beyond, was judged to be hanged, quartered, and drawn. Were you off east, young fellow, fighting bloody wars for Kruger and the freedom of the Boers?

CHRISTY. I never left my own parish till Tuesday was a week.

PEGEEN [*coming from counter*]. He's done nothing, so. [*To* CHRISTY.] If you didn't commit murder or a bad nasty thing, or false coining, or robbery, or butchery or the like of them, there isn't anything would be worth your troubling for to run from now. You did nothing at all.

CHRISTY [*his feelings hurt*]. That's an unkindly thing to be saying to a poor orphaned traveller, has a prison behind him, and hanging before, and hell's gap gaping below.

PEGEEN [*with a sign to the men to be quiet*]. You're only saying it. You did nothing at all. A soft lad the like of you wouldn't slit the windpipe of a screeching sow.

CHRISTY [*offended*]. You're not speaking the truth.

PEGEEN [*in mock rage*]. Not speaking the truth, is it? Would you have me knock the head of you with the butt of the broom?

CHRISTY [*twisting round on her with a sharp cry of horror*]. Don't strike me. . . . I killed my poor father, Tuesday was a week, for doing the like of that.

PEGEEN [*with blank amazement*]. Is it killed your father?

CHRISTY [*subsiding*]. With the help of God I did surely, and that the Holy Immaculate Mother may intercede for his soul.

PHILLY [*retreating with* JIMMY]. There's a daring fellow.

JIMMY. Oh, glory be to God!

MICHAEL [*with great respect*]. That was a hanging crime, mister honey. You should have had good reason for doing the like of that.

CHRISTY [*in a very reasonable tone*]. He was a dirty man, God forgive him, and he getting old and crusty, the way I couldn't put up with him at all.

PEGEEN. And you shot him dead?

CHRISTY [*shaking his head*]. I never used weapons. I've no licence, and I'm a law-fearing man.

MICHAEL. It was with a hilted knife maybe? I'm told, in the big world, it's bloody knives they use.

CHRISTY [*loudly, scandalized*]. Do you take me for a slaughter-boy?

PEGEEN. You never hanged him, the way Jimmy Farrell hanged his dog from the licence and had it screeching and wriggling three hours at the butt of a string, and himself swearing it was a dead dog, and the peelers swearing it had life?

CHRISTY. I did not then. I just riz the loy and let fall the edge of it on the ridge of his skull, and he went down at my feet like an empty sack, and never let a grunt or groan from him at all.

MICHAEL [*making a sign to* PEGEEN *to fill* CHRISTY's *glass*]. And what way weren't you hanged, mister? Did you bury him then?

CHRISTY [*considering*]. Aye. I buried him then. Wasn't I digging spuds in the field?

MICHAEL. And the peelers never followed after you the eleven days that you're out?

CHRISTY [*shaking his head*]. Never a one of them and I walking forward facing hog, dog, or divil on the highway of the road.

PHILLY [*nodding wisely*]. It's only with a common week-day kind of a murderer them lads would be trusting their carcase, and that man should be a great terror when his temper's roused.

MICHAEL. He should then. [*To* CHRISTY.] And where was it, mister honey, that you did the deed?

CHRISTY [*looking at him with suspicion*]. Oh, a distant place, master of the house, a windy corner of high distant hills.

PHILLY [*nodding with approval*]. He's a close man and he's right surely.

PEGEEN. That'd be a lad with the sense of Solomon to have for a pot-boy, Michael James, if it's the truth you're seeking one at all.

PHILLY. The peelers is fearing him, and if you'd that lad in the house there isn't one of them would come smelling around if the dogs itself were lapping poteen from the dung-pit of the yard.

JIMMY. Bravery's a treasure in a lonesome place, and a lad would kill his father, I'm thinking, would face a foxy divil with a pitchpike on the flags of hell.

PEGEEN. It's the truth they're saying, and if I'd that lad in the house, I wouldn't be fearing the loosèd khaki cut-throats, or the walking dead.

CHRISTY [*swelling with surprise and triumph*]. Well, glory be to God!

MICHAEL [*with deference*]. Would you think well to stop here and be pot-boy, mister honey, if we gave you good wages, and didn't destroy you with the weight of work?

SHAWN [*coming forward uneasily*]. That'd be a queer kind to bring into a decent quiet household with the like of Pegeen Mike.

PEGEEN [*very sharply*]. Will you whisht. Who's speaking to you?

SHAWN [*retreating*]. A bloody-handed murderer the like of. . . .

PEGEEN [*snapping at him*]. Whisht, I'm saying, we'll take no fooling from your like at all. [*To* CHRISTY *with a honeyed voice.*] And you, young fellow, you'd have a right to stop I'm thinking, for we'd do our all and utmost to content your needs.

CHRISTY [*overcome with wonder*]. And I'd be safe this place from the searching law?

MICHAEL. You would surely. If they're not fearing you itself, the peelers in this place is decent, droughty poor fellows, wouldn't touch a cur dog and not give warning in the dead of night.

PEGEEN [*very kindly and persuasively*]. Let you stop a short while anyhow. Aren't you destroyed walking with your feet in bleeding blisters, and your whole skin needing washing like a Wicklow sheep.

CHRISTY [*looking round with satisfaction*]. It's a nice room, and if it's not humbugging me you are, I'm thinking that I'll surely stay.

JIMMY [*jumps up*]. Now, by the grace of God, herself will be safe this night, with a man killed his father holding danger from the door, and let you come on, Michael James, or they'll have the best stuff drunk at the wake.

MICHAEL [*going to the door with* MEN]. And begging your pardon, mister, what name will we call you for we'd like to know.

CHRISTY. Christopher Mahon.

MICHAEL. Well, God bless you Christy, and a good rest till we meet again when the sun'll be rising to the noon of day.

CHRISTY. God bless you all.

MEN. God bless you. [*They go out except* SHAWN *who lingers at door.*]

SHAWN [*to* PEGEEN]. Are you wanting me to stop along with you and keep you from harm?

PEGEEN [*gruffly*]. Didn't you say you were fearing Father Reilly?

SHAWN. There'd be no harm staying now, I'm thinking, and himself in it too.

PEGEEN. You wouldn't stay when there was need for you, and let you step off nimble this time when there's none.

SHAWN. Didn't I say it was Father Reilly. . . .

PEGEEN. Go on then to Father Reilly [*in a jeering tone*], and let him put you in the holy brotherhoods and leave that lad to me.

SHAWN. If I meet the Widow Quin. . . .

PEGEEN. Go on, I'm saying, and don't be waking this place with your noise. [*She hustles him out and bolts door.*] That lad would wear the spirits from the saints of peace. [*Bustles about, then takes off her apron and pins it up in the window as a blind,* CHRISTY *watching her timidly. Then she comes to him and speaks with bland good humour.*] Let you stretch out now by the fire, young fellow. You should be destroyed travelling.

CHRISTY [*shyly again, drawing off his boots*]. I'm tired surely, walking wild eleven days and waking fearful in the night. [*He holds up one of his feet, feeling his blisters and looking at it with compassion.*]

PEGEEN [*standing beside him, watching him with delight*]. You should have had great people in your family, I'm thinking, with the little small feet you have, and you with a kind of a quality name, the like of what you'd find on the great powers and potentates of France and Spain.

CHRISTY [*with pride*]. We were great surely, with wide and windy acres of rich Munster land.

PEGEEN. Wasn't I telling you, and you a fine, handsome young fellow with a noble brow.

CHRISTY [*with a flash of delighted surprise*]. Is it me?

PEGEEN. Aye. Did you never hear that from the young girls where you come from in the west or south?

CHRISTY [*with venom*]. I did not then. . . . Oh, they're bloody liars in the naked parish where I grew a man.

PEGEEN. If they are itself, you've heard it these days, I'm thinking, and you walking the world telling out your story to young girls or old.

CHRISTY. I've told my story no place till this night, Pegeen Mike, and it's foolish I was here, maybe, to be talking free, but you're decent people, I'm thinking, and yourself a kindly woman, the way I wasn't fearing you at all.

PEGEEN [*filling a sack with straw, right*]. You've said the like of that, maybe, in every cot and cabin where you've met a young girl on your way.

CHRISTY [*going over to her, gradually raising his voice*]. I've said it nowhere till this night, I'm telling you, for I've seen none the like of you the eleven days I am walking the world, looking over a low ditch or a high ditch on my north or south, into stony scattered fields, or scribes of bog, where you'd see young limber girls, and fine prancing women making laughter with the men.

PEGEEN [*nodding with approval*]. If you weren't destroyed travelling you'd have as much talk and streeleen, I'm thinking, as Owen Roe O'Sullivan or the poets of the Dingle Bay, and I've heard all times it's the poets are your like, fine fiery fellows with great rages when their temper's roused.

CHRISTY [*drawing a little nearer to her*]. You've a power of rings, God bless you, and would there be any offence if I was asking are you single now?

PEGEEN. What would I want wedding so young?

CHRISTY [*with relief*]. We're alike, so.

PEGEEN [*putting sack on settle and beating it up*]. I never killed my father. I'd be afeard to do that, except I was the like of yourself with blind rages tearing me within, for I'm thinking you should have had great tussling when the end was come.

CHRISTY [*expanding with delight at the first confidential talk he has ever had with a woman*]. We had not then. It was a hard woman was come over the hill, and if he was always a crusty kind, when he'd a hard woman setting him on, not the divil himself or his four fathers could put up with him at all.

PEGEEN [*with curiosity*]. And isn't it a great wonder that one wasn't fearing you?

CHRISTY [*very confidentially*]. Up to the day I killed my father, there wasn't a person in Ireland knew the kind I was, and I there drinking, waking, eating, sleeping, a quiet, simple poor fellow with no man giving me heed.

PEGEEN [*getting a quilt out of cupboard and putting it on the sack*]. It was the girls were giving you heed maybe, and I'm thinking it's most conceit you'd have to be gaming with their like.

CHRISTY [*shaking his head, with simplicity*]. Not the girls itself, and I won't tell you a lie. There wasn't anyone heeding me in that place saving only the dumb beasts of the field. [*He sits down at fire.*]

PEGEEN [*with disappointment*]. And I thinking you should have been living the like of a king of Norway or the Eastern world. [*She comes and sits beside him after placing bread and mug of milk on the table.*]

CHRISTY [*laughing piteously*]. The like of a king, is it! And I after toiling, moiling, digging, dodging from the dawn till dusk with never a sight of joy or sport saving only when I'd be abroad in the dark night poaching rabbits on hills, for I was a divil to poach, God forgive me [*very naïvely*], and I near got six months for going with a dung-fork and stabbing a fish.

PEGEEN. And it's that you'd call sport is it, to be abroad in the darkness with yourself alone?

CHRISTY. I did, God help me, and there I'd be as happy as the sunshine of St. Martin's Day, watching the light passing the north or the patches of fog, till I'd hear a rabbit starting to screech and I'd go running in the furze. Then when I'd my full share I'd come walking down where you'd see the ducks and geese stretched sleeping on the highway of the road, and before I'd pass the dunghill, I'd hear himself snoring out, a loud lonesome snore he'd be making all times, the while he was sleeping, and he a man'd be raging all times the while he was waking, like a gaudy officer you'd hear cursing and damning and swearing oaths.

PEGEEN. Providence and Mercy, spare us all!

CHRISTY. It's that you'd say surely if you seen him and he after drinking for weeks, rising up in the red dawn, or before it maybe, and going out into the yard as naked as an ash tree in the moon of May, and shying clods again the visage of the stars till he'd put the fear of death into the banbhs and the screeching sows.

PEGEEN. I'd be well-nigh afeard of that lad myself, I'm thinking. And there was no one in it but the two of you alone?

CHRISTY. The divil a one, though he'd sons and daughters walking all great states and territories of the world, and not a one of them to this day would say their seven curses on him, and they rousing up to let a cough or sneeze, maybe, in the deadness of the night.

PEGEEN [*nodding her head*]. Well, you should have been a queer lot. . . . I never cursed my father the like of that though I'm twenty and more years of age.

CHRISTY. Then you'd have cursed mine, I'm telling you, and he a man never gave peace to any saving when he'd get two months or three, or be locked in the asylum for battering peelers or assaulting men [*with depression*], the way it was a bitter life he led me till I did up a Tuesday and halve his skull.

PEGEEN [*putting her hand on his shoulder*]. Well, you'll have peace in this place, Christy Mahon, and none to trouble you, and it's near time a fine lad the like of you should have your good share of the earth.

CHRISTY. It's time surely, and I a seemly fellow with great strength in me and bravery of. . . . [*Some one knocks.*]

CHRISTY [*clinging to* PEGEEN]. Oh, glory! it's late for knocking, and this last while I'm in terror of the peelers, and the walking dead. . . . [*Knocking again.*]

PEGEEN. Who's there?

VOICE [*outside*]. Me.

PEGEEN. Who's me?

VOICE. The Widow Quin.

PEGEEN [*jumping up and giving him the bread and milk*]. Go on now with your supper, and let on to be sleepy, for if she found you were such a warrant to talk, she'd be stringing gabble till the dawn of day.

[CHRISTY *takes bread and sits shyly with his back to the door.*]

PEGEEN [*opening door, with temper*]. What ails you, or what is it you're wanting at this hour of the night?

WIDOW QUIN [*coming in a step and peering at* CHRISTY]. I'm after meeting Shawn Keogh and Father Reilly below, who told me of your curiosity man, and they fearing by this time he was maybe roaring, romping on your hands with drink.

PEGEEN [*pointing to* CHRISTY]. Look now, is he roaring, and he stretched out drowsy with his supper, and his mug of milk. Walk down and tell that to Father Reilly and to Shaneen Keogh.

WIDOW QUIN [*coming forward*]. I'll not see them again, for I've their word to lead that lad forward for to lodge with me.

PEGEEN [*in blank amazement*]. This night, is it?

WIDOW QUIN [*going over*]. This night. 'It isn't fitting,' says the priesteen, 'to have his likeness lodging with an orphaned girl.' [*To* CHRISTY.] God save you, mister!

CHRISTY [*shyly*]. God save you kindly.

WIDOW QUIN [*looking at him with half-amused curiosity*]. Well, aren't you a little smiling fellow? It should have been great and bitter torments did rouse your spirits to a deed of blood.

CHRISTY [*doubtfully*]. It should, maybe.

WIDOW QUIN. It's more than 'maybe' I'm saying, and it'd soften my heart to see you sitting so simple with your cup and cake, and you fitter to be saying your catechism than slaying your da.

PEGEEN [*at counter, washing glasses*]. There's talking when any'd see he's fit to be holding his head high with the wonders of the world. Walk on from this, for I'll not have him tormented and he destroyed travelling since Tuesday was a week.

WIDOW QUIN [*peaceably*]. We'll be walking surely when his supper's done, and you'll find we're great company, young fellow, when it's of the like of you and me you'd hear the penny poets singing in an August Fair.

CHRISTY [*innocently*]. Did you kill your father?

PEGEEN [*contemptuously*]. She did not. She hit himself with a worn pick, and the rusted poison did corrode his blood the way he never overed it and died after. That was a sneaky kind of murder did win small glory with the boys itself. [*She crosses to* CHRISTY's *left.*]

WIDOW QUIN [*with good-humour*]. If it didn't, maybe all knows a widow woman has buried her children and destroyed her man is a wiser comrade for a young lad than a girl the like of you who'd go helter-skeltering after any man would let you a wink upon the road.

PEGEEN [*breaking out into wild rage*]. And you'll say that, Widow Quin, and you gasping with the rage you had racing the hill beyond to look on his face.

WIDOW QUIN [*laughing derisively*]. Me, is it! Well, Father Reilly has cuteness to divide you now. [*She pulls* CHRISTY *up.*] There's great temptation in a man did slay his da, and we'd best be going, young fellow; so rise up and come with me.

PEGEEN [*seizing his arm*]. He'll not stir. He's pot-boy in this place and I'll not have him stolen off and kidnabbed while himself's abroad.

WIDOW QUIN. It'd be a crazy pot-boy'd lodge him in the shebeen where he works by day, so you'd have a right to come on, young fellow, till you see my little houseen, a perch off on the rising hill.

PEGEEN. Wait till morning, Christy Mahon, wait till you lay eyes on her leaky thatch is growing more pasture for her buck goat than her square of fields, and she without a tramp itself to keep in order her place at all.

WIDOW QUIN. When you see me contriving in my little gardens, Christy Mahon, you'll swear the Lord God formed me to be living lone and that there isn't my match in Mayo for thatching or mowing or shearing a sheep.

PEGEEN [*with noisy scorn*]. It's true the Lord God formed you to contrive indeed! Doesn't the world know you reared a black ram at your own breast, so that the Lord Bishop of Connaught felt the elements of a Christian, and he eating it after in a kidney stew? Doesn't the world know you've been seen shaving the foxy skipper from France for a threepenny bit and a sop of grass tobacco would wring the liver from a mountain goat you'd meet lepping the hills?

WIDOW QUIN [*with amusement*]. Do you hear her now, young fellow? Do you hear the way she'll be rating at your own self when a week is by?

PEGEEN [*to* CHRISTY]. Don't heed her. Tell her to go on into her pigsty and not plague us here.

WIDOW QUIN. I'm going; but he'll come with me.

PEGEEN [*shaking him*]. Are you dumb, young fellow?

CHRISTY [*timidly to* WIDOW QUIN]. God increase you; but I'm pot-boy in this place, and it's here I'd liefer stay.

PEGEEN [*triumphantly*]. Now you've heard him, and go on from this.

WIDOW QUIN [*looking round the room*]. It's lonesome this hour crossing the hill, and if he won't come along with me, I'd have a right maybe to stop this night with yourselves. Let me stretch out on the settle, Pegeen Mike, and himself can lie by the hearth.

PEGEEN [*short and fiercely*]. Faith I won't. Quit off or I will send you now.

WIDOW QUIN [*gathering her shawl up*]. Well, it's a terror to be aged a score! [*To* CHRISTY.] God bless you now, young fellow, and let you be wary, or there's right torment will await you here if you go romancing with her like, and she waiting only, as they bade me say, on a sheep-skin parchment to be wed with Shawn Keogh of Killa-keen. [*She goes out.*]

CHRISTY [*going to* PEGEEN, *as she bolts door*]. What's that she's after saying?

PEGEEN. Lies and blather, you've no call to mind. Well isn't Shawn Keogh an impudent fellow to send up spying on me? Wait till I lay hands on him. Let him wait, I'm saying.

CHRISTY. And you're not wedding him at all?

PEGEEN. I wouldn't wed him if a bishop came walking for to join us here.

CHRISTY. That God in glory may be thanked for that.

PEGEEN. There's your bed now. I've put a quilt upon you I'm after quilting a while since with my own two hands, and you'd best stretch out now for your sleep, and may God give you a good rest till I call you in the morning when the cocks will crow.

CHRISTY [*as she goes to inner room*]. May God and Mary and St. Patrick bless you and reward you for your kindly talk. [*She shuts the door behind her. He settles his bed slowly, feeling the quilt with immense satisfaction.*] Well it's a clean bed and soft with it, and it's great luck and company I've won me in the end of time—two fine women fighting for the likes of me—, till I'm thinking this night wasn't I a foolish fellow not to kill my father in the years gone by.

CURTAIN

ACT II

Scene as before. Brilliant morning light. CHRISTY, *looking bright and cheerful, is cleaning a girl's boot.*

CHRISTY [*to himself, counting jugs on dresser*]. Half a hundred beyond. Ten there. A score that's above. Eighty jugs. Six cups and a broken one. Two plates. A power of glasses. Bottles, a school-master'd be hard set to count, and enough in them, I'm thinking, to drunken all the wealth and wisdom of the County Clare. [*He puts down the boot carefully.*] There's her boots now, nice and decent for her evening use, and isn't it grand brushes she has? [*He puts them down and goes by degrees to the looking-glass.*] Well, this'd be a fine place to be my whole life talking out with swearing Christians in place of my old dogs and cat, and I stalking around, smoking my pipe and drinking my fill, and never a day's work but drawing a cork an odd time, or wiping a glass, or rinsing out a shiny tumbler for a decent man. [*He takes the looking-glass from the wall and puts it on the back of a chair; then sits down in front of it and begins washing his face.*] Didn't I know rightly I was handsome, though it was the divil's own mirror we had beyond, would twist a squint across an angel's brow, and I'll be growing fine from this day, the way I'll have a soft lovely skin on me and won't be the like of the clumsy young fellows do be ploughing all times in the earth and dung. [*He starts.*] Is she coming again? [*He looks out.*] Stranger girls. God help me, where'll I hide myself away and my long neck naked to the world. [*He looks out.*] I'd best go to the room maybe till I'm dressed again.

[*He gathers up his coat and the looking-glass, and runs into the inner room. The door is pushed open, and* SUSAN BRADY *looks in, and knocks on door.*]

SUSAN. There's nobody in it. [*Knocks again.*]

NELLY [*pushing her in and following her, with* HONOR BLAKE *and* SARA TANSEY]. It'd be early for them both to be out walking the hill.

SUSAN. I'm thinking Shawn Keogh was making game of us and there's no such man in it at all.

HONOR [*pointing to straw and quilt*]. Look at that. He's been sleeping there in the night. Well, it'll be a hard case if he's gone off now, the way we'll never set our eyes on a man killed his father, and we after rising early and destroying ourselves running fast on the hill.

NELLY. Are you thinking them's his boots?

SARA [*taking them up*]. If they are, there should be his father's track on them. Did you never read in the papers the way murdered men do bleed and drip?

SUSAN. Is that blood there, Sara Tansey?

SARA [*smelling it*]. That's bog water, I'm thinking, but it's his own they are surely, for I never seen the like of them for whity mud, and red mud, and turf on them, and the fine sands of the sea. That man's been walking, I'm telling you. [*She goes down right, putting on one of his boots.*]

SUSAN [*going to window*]. Maybe he's stolen off to Belmullet with the boots of Michael James, and you'd have a right so to follow after him, Sara Tansey, and you the one yoked the ass cart and drove ten miles to set your eyes on the man bit the yellow lady's nostril on the northern shore. [*She looks out.*]

SARA [*running to window, with one boot on*]. Don't be talking, and we fooled to-day. [*Putting on other boot.*] There's a pair do fit me well, and I'll be keeping them for walking to the priest, when you'd be ashamed this place, going up winter and summer with nothing worth while to confess at all.

HONOR [*who has been listening at inner door*]. Whisht! there's some one inside the room. [*She pushes door a chink open.*] It's a man.

[SARA *kicks off boots and puts them where they were. They all stand in a line looking through chink.*]

SARA. I'll call him. Mister! Mister! [*He puts in his head.*] Is Pegeen within?

CHRISTY [*coming in as meek as a mouse, with the looking-glass held behind his back.*] She's above on the cnuceen, seeking the nanny goats, the way she'd have a sup of goat's milk for to colour my tea.

SARA. And asking your pardon, is it you's the man killed his father?

CHRISTY [*sidling toward the nail where the glass was hanging*]. I am, God help me!

SARA [*taking eggs she has brought*]. Then my thousand welcomes to you, and I've run up with a brace of duck's eggs for your food to-day. Pegeen's ducks is no use, but these are the real rich sort. Hold out your hand and you'll see it's no lie I'm telling you.

CHRISTY [*coming forward shyly, and holding out his left hand*]. They're a great and weighty size.

SUSAN. And I run up with a pat of butter, for it'd be a poor thing to have you eating your spuds dry, and you after running a great way since you did destroy your da.

CHRISTY. Thank you kindly.

HONOR. And I brought you a little cut of a cake, for you should have a thin stomach on you, and you that length walking the world.

NELLY. And I brought you a little laying pullet—boiled and all she is—was crushed at the fall of night by the curate's car. Feel the fat of that breast, Mister.

CHRISTY. It's bursting, surely. [*He feels it with the back of his left hand, in which he holds the presents.*]

SARA. Will you pinch it? Is your right hand too sacred for to use at all? [*She slips round behind him.*] It's a glass he has. Well I never seen to this day, a man with a looking-glass held to his back. Them that kills their fathers is a vain lot surely.

[GIRLS *giggle.*]

CHRISTY [*smiling innocently and piling presents on glass*]. I'm very thankful to you all to-day. . . .

WIDOW QUIN [*coming in quickly, at door*]. Sara Tansey, Susan Brady, Honor Blake! What in glory has you here at this hour of day?

GIRLS [*giggling*]. That's the man killed his father.

WIDOW QUIN.[*coming to them*]. I know well it's the man; and I'm after putting him down in the sports below for racing, lepping, pitching, and the Lord knows what.

SARA [*exuberantly*]. That's right, Widow Quin. I'll bet my dowry that he'll lick the world.

WIDOW QUIN. If you will, you'd have a right to have him fresh and nourished in place of nursing a feast. [*Taking presents.*] Are you fasting or fed, young fellow?

CHRISTY. Fasting, if you please.

WIDOW QUIN [*loudly*]. Well, you're the lot. Stir up now and give him his breakfast. [*To* CHRISTY.] Come here to me [*she puts him on bench beside her while the* GIRLS *make tea and get his breakfast*] and let you tell us your story before Pegeen will come, in place of grinning your ears off like the moon of May.

CHRISTY [*beginning to be pleased*]. It's a long story you'd be destroyed listening.

WIDOW QUIN. Don't be letting on to be shy, a fine, gamey, treacherous lad the like of you. Was it in your house beyond you cracked his skull?

CHRISTY [*shy, but flattered*]. It was not. We were digging spuds in his cold, sloping, stony divil's patch of a field.

WIDOW QUIN. And you went asking money of him, or making talk of getting a wife would drive him from his farm?

CHRISTY. I did not, then; but there I was, digging and digging, and 'You squinting idiot,' says he, 'let you walk down now and tell the priest you'll wed the Widow Casey in a score of days.'

WIDOW QUIN. And what kind was she?

CHRISTY [*with horror*]. A walking terror from beyond the hills, and she two score and five years, and two hundredweights and five pounds in the weighing scales, with a limping leg on her, and a blinded eye, and she a woman of noted misbehaviour with the old and young. [*He begins gnawing a chicken leg.*]

GIRLS [*clustering round him, serving him*]. Glory be!

WIDOW QUIN. And what did he want driving you to wed with her? [*She takes a bit of the chicken.*]

CHRISTY [*eating with growing satisfaction*]. He was letting on I was wanting a protector from the harshness of the world, and he without a thought the whole while but how he'd have her hut to live in and her gold to drink.

WIDOW QUIN. There's maybe worse than a dry hearth and a widow woman and your glass at night. So you hit him then?

CHRISTY [*getting almost excited*]. I did not. 'I won't wed her,' says I, 'when all know she did suckle me for six weeks when I came into the world, and she a hag this day with a tongue on her has the crows and seabirds scattered, the way they wouldn't cast a shadow on her garden with the dread of her curse.'

WIDOW QUIN [*teasingly*]. That one should be right company!

SARA [*eagerly*]. Don't mind her. Did you kill him then?

CHRISTY. 'She's too good for the like of you,' says he, 'and go on now or I'll flatten you out like a crawling beast has passed under a dray.' 'You will not if I can help it,' says I. 'Go on,' says he, 'or I'll have the divil making garters of your limbs to-night.' 'You will not if I can help it,' says I. [*He sits bolt up, brandishing his mug.*]

SARA. You were right surely.

CHRISTY [*impressively*]. With that the sun came out between the cloud and the hill, and it shining green in my face. 'God have mercy on your soul,' says he, lifting a scythe; 'or on your own,' says I, raising the loy.

SUSAN. That's a grand story.

HONOR. He tells it lovely.

CHRISTY [*flattered and confident, waving bone*]. He gave a drive with the scythe, and I gave a lep to the east. Then I turned around with my back to the north, and I hit a blow on the ridge of his skull, laid him stretched out, and he split to the knob of his gullet. [*He raises the chicken bone to his Adam's apple.*]

GIRLS [*together*]. Well, you're a marvel! Oh, God bless you! You're the lad surely!

SUSAN. I'm thinking the Lord God sent him this road to make a second husband to the Widow Quin, and she with a great yearning to be wedded though all dread her here. Lift him on her knee, Sara Tansey.

WIDOW QUIN. Don't tease him.

SARA [*going over to dresser and counter very quickly, and getting two glasses and porter*]. You're heroes surely, and let you drink a supeen with your arms linked like the outlandish lovers in the sailor's song. [*She links their arms and gives them the glasses.*] There now. Drink a health to the wonders of the western world, the pirates, preachers, poteen-makers, with the jobbing jockies, parching peelers, and the juries fill their stomachs selling judgments of the English law. [*Brandishing the bottle.*]

WIDOW QUIN. That's a right toast, Sara Tansey. Now Christy.

[*They drink with their arms linked, he drinking with his left hand, she with her right. As they are drinking,* PEGEEN MIKE *comes in with a milk can and stands aghast. They all spring away from* CHRISTY. *He goes down left.* WIDOW QUIN *remains seated.*]

PEGEEN [*angrily*]. What is it you're wanting [*to* SARA]?

SARA [*twisting her apron*]. An ounce of tobacco.

PEGEEN. Have you tuppence?

SARA. I've forgotten my purse.

PEGEEN. Then you'd best be getting it and not be fooling us here. [*To the* WIDOW QUIN, *with more elaborate scorn.*] And what is it you're wanting, Widow Quin?

WIDOW QUIN [*insolently*]. A penn'orth of starch.

PEGEEN [*breaking out*]. And you without a white shift or a shirt in your whole family since the drying of the flood. I've no starch for the like of you, and let you walk on now to Killamuck.

WIDOW QUIN [*turning to* CHRISTY, *as she goes out with the* GIRLS]. Well, you're mighty huffy this day, Pegeen Mike, and you young fellow, let you not forget the sports and racing when the noon is by. [*They go out.*]

PEGEEN [*imperiously*]. Fling out that rubbish and put them cups away. [CHRISTY *tidies away in great haste.*] Shove in the bench by the wall. [*He does so.*] And hang that glass on the nail. What disturbed it at all?

CHRISTY [*very meekly*]. I was making myself decent only, and this a fine country for young lovely girls.

PEGEEN [*sharply*]. Whisht your talking of girls. [*Goes to counter right.*]

CHRISTY. Wouldn't any wish to be decent in a place. . . .

PEGEEN. Whisht, I'm saying.

CHRISTY [*looks at her face for a moment with great misgivings, then as a last effort, takes up a loy, and goes towards her, with feigned assurance*]. It was with a loy the like of that I killed my father.

PEGEEN [*still sharply*]. You've told me that story six times since the dawn of day.

CHRISTY [*reproachfully*]. It's a queer thing you wouldn't care to be hearing it and them girls after walking four miles to be listening to me now.

PEGEEN [*turning round astonished*]. Four miles!

CHRISTY [*apologetically*]. Didn't himself say there were only bona fides living in the place?

PEGEEN. It's bona fides by the road they are, but that lot come over the river lepping the stones. It's not three perches when you go like that and I was down this morning looking on the papers the post-boy does have in his bag [*with meaning and emphasis*], for there was great news this day, Christopher Mahon. [*She goes into room left.*]

CHRISTY [*suspiciously*]. Is it news of my murder?

PEGEEN [*inside*]. Murder indeed!

CHRISTY [*loudly*]. A murdered da?

PEGEEN [*coming in again and crossing right*]. There was not, but a story filled half a page of the hanging of a man. Ah, that should be a fearful end, young fellow, and it worst of all for a man destroyed his da, for the like of him would get small mercies, and when it's dead he is, they'd put him in a narrow grave, with cheap sacking wrapping him round, and pour down quicklime on his head, the way you'd see a woman pouring any frish-frash from a cup.

CHRISTY [*very miserably*]. Oh, God help me. Are you thinking I'm safe? You were saying at the fall of night, I was shut of jeopardy and I here with yourselves.

PEGEEN [*severely*]. You'll be shut of jeopardy no place if you go talking with a pack of wild girls the like of them, do be walking abroad with the peelers, talking whispers at the fall of night.

CHRISTY [*with terror*]. And you're thinking they'd tell?

PEGEEN [*with mock sympathy*]. Who knows, God help you.

CHRISTY [*loudly*]. What joy would they have to bring hanging to the likes of me?

PEGEEN. It's queer joys they have, and who knows the thing they'd do, if it'd make the green stones cry itself to think of you swaying and swiggling at the butt of a rope, and you with a fine, stout neck, God bless you! the way you'd be a half an hour, in great anguish, getting your death.

CHRISTY [*getting his boots and putting them on*]. If there's that terror of them, it'd be best, maybe, I went on wandering like Esau or Cain and Abel on the sides of Neifin or the Erris Plain.

PEGEEN [*beginning to play with him*]. It would, maybe, for I've heard the Circuit Judges this place is a heartless crew.

CHRISTY [*bitterly*]. It's more than judges this place is a heartless crew. [*Looking up at her.*] And isn't it a poor thing to be starting again and I a lonesome fellow will be looking out on women and girls the way the needy fallen spirits do be looking on the Lord?

PEGEEN. What call have you to be that lonesome when there's poor girls walking Mayo in their thousands now?

CHRISTY [*grimly*]. It's well you know what call I have. It's well you know it's a lonesome thing to be passing small towns with the lights shining sideways when the night is down, or going in strange places with a dog nosing before you and a dog nosing behind, or drawn to the cities where you'd hear a voice kissing and talking deep love in every shadow of the ditch, and you passing on with an empty hungry stomach failing from your heart.

PEGEEN. I'm thinking you're an odd man, Christy Mahon. The oddest walking fellow I ever set my eyes on to this hour to-day.

CHRISTY. What would any be but odd men and they living lonesome in the world?

PEGEEN. I'm not odd, and I'm my whole life with my father only.

CHRISTY [*with infinite admiration*]. How would a lovely handsome woman the like of you be lonesome when all men should be thronging around to hear the sweetness of your voice, and the little infant children should be pestering your steps I'm thinking, and you walking the roads.

PEGEEN. I'm hard set to know what way a coaxing fellow the like of yourself should be lonesome either.

CHRISTY. Coaxing!

PEGEEN. Would you have me think a man never talked with the girls would have the words you've spoken to-day? It's only letting on you are to be lonesome, the way you'd get around me now.

CHRISTY. I wish to God I was letting on; but I was lonesome all times and born lonesome, I'm thinking, as the moon of dawn. [*Going to door.*]

PEGEEN [*puzzled by his talk*]. Well, it's a story I'm not understanding at all why you'd be worse than another, Christy Mahon, and you a fine lad with the great savagery to destroy your da.

CHRISTY. It's little I'm understanding myself, saving only that my heart's scalded this day, and I going off stretching out the earth between us, the way I'll not be waking near you another dawn of the year till the two of us do arise to hope or judgment with the saints of God, and now I'd best be going with my wattle in my hand, for hanging is a poor thing [*turning to go*], and it's little welcome only is left me in this house to-day.

PEGEEN [*sharply*]. Christy! [*He turns round.*] Come here to me. [*He goes towards her.*] Lay down that switch and throw some sods on the fire. You're pot-boy in this place, and I'll not have you mitch off from us now.

CHRISTY. You were saying I'd be hanged if I stay.

PEGEEN [*quite kindly at last*]. I'm after going down and reading the fearful crimes of Ireland for two weeks or three, and there wasn't a word of your murder. [*Getting up and going over to the counter.*] They've likely not found the body. You're safe so with ourselves.

CHRISTY [*astonished, slowly*]. It's making game of me you were [*following her with fearful joy*], and I can stay so, working at your side, and I not lonesome from this mortal day.

PEGEEN. What's to hinder you staying, except the widow woman or the young girls would inveigle you off?

CHRISTY [*with rapture*]. And I'll have your words from this day filling my ears, and that look is come upon you meeting my two eyes, and I watching you loafing around in the warm sun, or rinsing your ankles when the night is come.

PEGEEN [*kindly, but a little embarrassed*]. I'm thinking you'll be a loyal young lad to have working around, and if you vexed me a while since with your leaguing with the girls, I wouldn't give a thraneen for a lad hadn't a mighty spirit in him and a gamey heart.

[SHAWN KEOGH *runs in carrying a cleeve on his back, followed by the* WIDOW QUIN.]

SHAWN [*to* PEGEEN]. I was passing below and I seen your mountainy sheep eating cabbages in Jimmy's field. Run up or they'll be bursting surely.

PEGEEN. Oh, God mend them! [*She puts a shawl over her head and runs out.*]

CHRISTY [*looking from one to the other, still in high spirits*]. I'd best go to her aid maybe. I'm handy with ewes.

WIDOW QUIN [*closing the door*]. She can do that much, and there is Shaneen has long speeches for to tell you now. [*She sits down with an amused smile.*]

SHAWN [*taking something from his pocket and offering it to* CHRISTY]. Do you see that, Mister?

CHRISTY [*looking at it*]. The half of a ticket to the Western States!

SHAWN [*trembling with anxiety*]. I'll give it to you and my new hat [*pulling it out of hamper*]; and my breeches with the double seat [*pulling it out*]; and my new coat is woven from the blackest shearings for three miles around [*giving him the coat*]; I'll give you the whole of them and my blessing and the blessing of Father Reilly itself, maybe, if you'll quit from this and leave us in the peace we had till last night at the fall of dark.

CHRISTY [*with a new arrogance*]. And for what is it you're wanting to get shut of me?

SHAWN [*looking to the* WIDOW *for help*]. I'm a poor scholar with middling faculties to coin a lie, so I'll tell you the truth, Christy Mahon. I'm wedding with Pegeen beyond, and I don't think well of having a clever fearless man the like of you dwelling in her house.

CHRISTY [*almost pugnaciously*]. And you'd be using bribery for to banish me?

SHAWN [*in an imploring voice*]. Let you not take it badly, mister honey, isn't beyond the best place for you where you'll have golden chains and shiny coats and you riding upon hunters with the ladies of the land. [*He makes an eager sign to the* WIDOW QUIN *to come to help him.*]

WIDOW QUIN [*coming over*]. It's true for him, and you'd best quit off and not have that poor girl setting her mind on you, for there's Shaneen thinks she wouldn't suit you though all is saying that she'll wed you now.

[CHRISTY *beams with delight.*]

SHAWN [*in terrified earnest*]. She wouldn't suit you, and she with the divil's own temper the way you'd be strangling one another in a score of days. [*He makes the movement of strangling with his hands.*] It's the like of me only that she's fit for, a quiet simple fellow wouldn't raise a hand upon her if she scratched itself.

WIDOW QUIN [*putting* SHAWN'*s hat on* CHRISTY]. Fit them clothes on you anyhow, young fellow, and he'd maybe loan them to you for the sports. [*Pushing him towards inner door.*] Fit them on and you can give your answer when you have them tried.

CHRISTY [*beaming, delighted with the clothes*]. I will then, I'd like herself to see me in them tweeds and hat. [*He goes into room and shuts the door.*]

SHAWN [*in great anxiety*]. He'd like herself to see them! He'll not leave us, Widow Quin. He's a score of divils in him, the way it's well nigh certain he will wed Pegeen.

WIDOW QUIN [*jeeringly*]. It's true all girls are fond of courage and do hate the like of you.

SHAWN [*walking about in desperation*]. Oh, Widow Quin, what'll I be doing now? I'd inform again him, but he'd burst from Kilmain-ham and he'd be sure and certain to destroy me. If I wasn't so God-fearing, I'd near have courage to come behind him and run a pike into his side. Oh, it's a hard case to be an orphan and not to have your father that you're used to, and you'd easy kill and make your-self a hero in the sight of all. [*Coming up to her.*] Oh, Widow Quin, will you find me some contrivance when I've promised you a ewe?

WIDOW QUIN. A ewe's a small thing, but what would you give me if I did wed him and did save you so?

SHAWN [*with astonishment*]. You!

WIDOW QUIN. Aye. Would you give me the red cow you have and the mountainy ram, and the right of way across your rye path, and a load of dung at Michaelmas, and turbary upon the western hill?

SHAWN [*radiant with hope*]. I would surely, and I'd give you the wedding-ring I have, and the loan of the new suit, the way you'd have him decent on the wedding-day. I'd give you two kids for your dinner and a gallon of poteen, and I'd call the piper on the long car to your wedding from Crossmolina or from Ballina. I'd give you. . .

WIDOW QUIN. That'll do, so, and let you whisht, for he's coming now again.

[CHRISTY *comes in very natty in the new clothes.* WIDOW QUIN *goes to him admiringly.*]

WIDOW QUIN. If you seen yourself now, I'm thinking you'd be too proud to speak to us at all, and it'd be a pity surely to have your like sailing from Mayo to the Western World.

CHRISTY [*as proud as a peacock*]. I'm not going. If this is a poor place itself, I'll make myself contented to be lodging here.

[WIDOW QUIN *makes a sign to* SHAWN *to leave them.*]

SHAWN. Well, I'm going measuring the race-course while the tide is low, so I'll leave you the garments and my blessing for the sports to-day. God bless you! [*He wriggles out.*]

WIDOW QUIN [*admiring* CHRISTY]. Well you're mighty spruce, young fellow. Sit down now while you're quiet till you talk with me.

CHRISTY [*swaggering*]. I'm going abroad on the hillside for to seek Pegeen.

WIDOW QUIN. You'll have time and plenty for to seek Pegeen, and you heard me saying at the fall of night the two of us should be great company.

CHRISTY. From this out I'll have no want of company when all sorts is bringing me their food and clothing [*he swaggers to the door, tightening his belt*], the way they'd set their eyes upon a gallant orphan cleft his father with one blow to the breeches belt. [*He opens door, then staggers back.*] Saints of glory! Holy angels from the throne of light!

WIDOW QUIN [*going over*]. What ails you?

CHRISTY. It's the walking spirit of my murdered da!

WIDOW QUIN [*looking out*]. Is it that tramper?

CHRISTY [*wildly*]. Where'll I hide my poor body from that ghost of hell?

[*The door is pushed open, and* OLD MAHON *appears on threshold.* CHRISTY *darts in behind door* .]

WIDOW QUIN [*in great amusement*]. God save you, my poor man.

MAHON [*gruffly*]. Did you see a young lad passing this way in the early morning or the fall of night?

WIDOW QUIN. You're a queer kind to walk in not saluting at all.

MAHON. Did you see the young lad?

WIDOW QUIN [*stiffly*]. What kind was he?

MAHON. An ugly young streeler with a murderous gob on him and a little switch in his hand. I met a tramper seen him coming this way at the fall of night.

WIDOW QUIN. There's harvest hundreds do be passing these days for the Sligo boat. For what is it you're wanting him, my poor man?

MAHON. I want to destroy him for breaking the head on me with the clout of a loy. [*He takes off a big hat, and shows his head in a mass of bandages and plaster, with some pride.*] It was he did that, and amn't I a great wonder to think I've traced him ten days with that rent in my crown?

WIDOW QUIN [*taking his head in both hands and examining it with extreme delight*]. That was a great blow. And who hit you? A robber maybe?

MAHON. It was my own son hit me, and he the divil a robber or anything else but a dirty, stuttering lout.

WIDOW QUIN [*letting go his skull and wiping her hands in her apron*]. You'd best be wary of a mortified scalp, I think they call it, lepping around with that wound in the splendour of the sun. It was a bad blow surely, and you should have vexed him fearful to make him strike that gash in his da.

MAHON. Is it me?

WIDOW QUIN [*amusing herself*]. Aye. And isn't it a great shame when the old and hardened do torment the young?

MAHON [*raging*]. Torment him is it? And I after holding out with the patience of a martyred saint, till there's nothing but destruction on me and I'm driven out in my old age with none to aid me?

WIDOW QUIN [*greatly amused*]. It's a sacred wonder the way that wickedness will spoil a man.

MAHON. My wickedness, is it? Amn't I after saying it is himself has me destroyed, and he a lier on walls, a talker of folly, a man you'd see stretched the half of the day in the brown ferns with his belly to the sun.

WIDOW QUIN. Not working at all?

MAHON. The divil a work, or if he did itself, you'd see him raising up a haystack like the stalk of a rush or driving our last cow till he broke her leg at the hip, and when he wasn't at that he'd be fooling over

F

little birds he had—finches and felts—or making mugs at his own self in the bit of a glass we had hung on the wall.

WIDOW QUIN [*looking at* CHRISTY]. What way was he so foolish? It was running wild after the girls maybe?

MAHON [*with a shout of derision*]. Running wild, is it? If he seen a red petticoat coming swinging over the hill, he'd be off to hide in the sticks, and you'd see him shooting out his sheep's eyes between the little twigs and leaves, and his two ears rising like a hare looking out through a gap. Girls indeed!

WIDOW QUIN. It was drink maybe?

MAHON. And he a poor fellow would get drunk on the smell of a pint! He'd a queer rotten stomach, I'm telling you, and when I gave him three pulls from my pipe a while since, he was taken with contortions till I had to send him in the ass cart to the females' nurse.

WIDOW QUIN [*clasping her hands*]. Well, I never till this day heard tell of a man the like of that.

MAHON. I'd take a mighty oath you didn't surely, and wasn't he the laughing joke of every female woman where four baronies meet, the way the girls would stop their weeding if they seen him coming the road to let a roar at him, and call him the looney of Mahon's.

WIDOW QUIN. I'd give the world and all to see the like of him. What kind was he?

MAHON. A small low fellow.

WIDOW QUIN. And dark?

MAHON. Dark and dirty.

WIDOW QUIN [*considering*]. I'm thinking I seen him.

MAHON [*eagerly*]. An ugly young blackguard?

WIDOW QUIN. A hideous, fearful villain, and the spit of you.

MAHON. What way is he fled?

WIDOW QUIN. Gone over the hills to catch a coasting steamer to the north or south.

MAHON. Could I pull up on him now?

WIDOW QUIN. If you'll cross the sands below where the tide is out, you'll be in it as soon as himself, for he had to go round ten miles by the top of the bay. [*She points from the door.*] Strike down by the head beyond and then follow on the roadway to the north and east.

[MAHON *goes abruptly.*]

WIDOW QUIN [*shouting after him*]. Let you give him a good vengeance when you come up with him, but don't put yourself in the power of the law, for it'd be a poor thing to see a judge in his black cap reading out his sentence on a civil warrior the like of you. [*She swings the door to and looks at* CHRISTY, *who is cowering in terror, for a moment, then she bursts into a laugh.*] Well, you're the walking playboy of the western world, and that's the poor man you had divided to his breeches belt.

CHRISTY [*looking out; then, to her*]. What'll Pegeen say when she hears that story? What'll she be saying to me now?

WIDOW QUIN. She'll knock the head of you, I'm thinking, and drive you from the door. God help her to be taking you for a wonder, and you a little schemer making up a story you destroyed your da.

CHRISTY [*turning to the door, nearly speechless with rage, half to himself*]. To be letting on he was dead, and coming back to his life, and following me like an old weazel tracing a rat, and coming in here laying desolation between my own self and the fine women of Ireland, and he a kind of carcase that you'd fling upon the sea. . . .

WIDOW QUIN [*more soberly*]. There's talking for a man's one only son.

CHRISTY [*breaking out*]. His one son, is it? May I meet him with one tooth and it aching, and one eye to be seeing seven and seventy divils in the twists of the road, and one old timber leg on him to limp into the scalding grave. [*Looking out.*] There he is now crossing the strands, and that the Lord God would send a high wave to wash him from the world.

WIDOW QUIN [*scandalized*]. Have you no shame? [*Putting her hand on his shoulder and turning him round.*] What ails you? Near crying, is it?

CHRISTY [*in despair and grief*]. Amn't I after seeing the love-light of the star of knowledge shining from her brow, and hearing words would put you thinking on the holy Brigid speaking to the infant saints, and now she'll be turning again, and speaking hard words to me, like an old woman with a spavindy ass she'd have, urging on a hill.

WIDOW QUIN. There's poetry talk for a girl you'd see itching and scratching, and she with a stale stink of poteen on her from selling in the shop.

CHRISTY [*impatiently*]. It's her like is fitted to be handling merchandise in the heavens above, and what'll I be doing now, I ask you, and I a kind of wonder was jilted by the heavens when a day was by.

[*There is a distant noise of girls' voices.* WIDOW QUIN *looks from window and comes to him, hurriedly.*]

WIDOW QUIN. You'll be doing like myself, I'm thinking, when I did destroy my man, for I'm above many's the day, odd times in great spirits, abroad in the sunshine, darning a stocking or stitching a shift, and odd times again looking out on the schooners, hookers, trawlers is sailing the sea, and I thinking on the gallant hairy fellows are drifting beyond, and myself long years living alone.

CHRISTY [*interested*]. You're like me, so.

WIDOW QUIN. I am your like, and it's for that I'm taking a fancy to you, and I with my little houseen above where there'd be myself to tend you, and none to ask were you a murderer or what at all.

CHRISTY. And what would I be doing if I left Pegeen?

WIDOW QUIN. I've nice jobs you could be doing, gathering shells to make a whitewash for our hut within, building up a little goosehouse, or stretching a new skin on an old curagh I have, and if my hut is far from all sides, it's there you'll meet the wisest old men, I tell you, at the corner of my wheel, and it's there yourself and me will have great times whispering and hugging . . .

VOICES [*outside, calling far away*]. Christy! Christy Mahon! Christy!

CHRISTY. Is it Pegeen Mike?

WIDOW QUIN. It's the young girls, I'm thinking, coming to bring you to the sports below, and what is it you'll have me to tell them now?

CHRISTY. Aid me for to win Pegeen. It's herself only that I'm seeking now. [WIDOW QUIN *gets up and goes to window.*] Aid me for to win her, and I'll be asking God to stretch a hand to you in the hour of death, and lead you short cuts through the Meadows of Ease, and up the floor of Heaven to the Footstool of the Virgin's Son.

WIDOW QUIN. There's praying!

VOICES [*nearer*]. Christy! Christy Mahon!

CHRISTY [*with agitation*]. They're coming. Will you swear to aid and save me for the love of Christ?

WIDOW QUIN [*looks at him for a moment*]. If I aid you, will you swear to give me a right of way I want, and a mountainy ram, and a load of dung at Michaelmas, the time that you'll be master here?

CHRISTY. I will, by the elements and stars of night.

WIDOW QUIN. Then we'll not say a word of the old fellow, the way Pegeen won't know your story till the end of time.

CHRISTY. And if he chances to return again?

WIDOW QUIN. We'll swear he's a maniac and not your da. I could take an oath I seen him raving on the sands to-day.

[GIRLS *run in.*]

SUSAN. Come on to the sports below. Pegeen says you're to come.

SARA TANSEY. The lepping's beginning, and we've a jockey's suit to fit upon you for the mule race on the sands below.

HONOR. Come on, will you.

CHRISTY. I will then if Pegeen's beyond.

SARA. She's in the boreen making game of Shaneen Keogh.

CHRISTY. Then I'll be going to her now. [*He runs out, followed by the* GIRLS.]

WIDOW QUIN. Well, if the worst comes in the end of all, it'll be great game to see there's none to pity him but a widow woman, the like of me, has buried her children and destroyed her man. [*She goes out.*]

CURTAIN

ACT III

Scene, as before. Later in the day. JIMMY *comes in, slightly drunk.*

JIMMY [*calls*]. Pegeen! [*Crosses to inner door.*] Pegeen Mike! [*Comes back again into the room.*] Pegeen! [PHILLY *comes in in the same state.*] [*To* PHILLY.] Did you see herself?

PHILLY. I did not; but I sent Shawn Keogh with the ass cart for to bear him home. [*Trying cupboards which are locked.*] Well, isn't he a nasty man to get into such staggers at a morning wake, and isn't herself the divil's daughter for locking, and she so fussy after that young gaffer, you might take your death with drought and none to heed you.

JIMMY. It's little wonder she'd be fussy, and he after bringing bankrupt ruin on the roulette man, and the trick-o'-the-loop man, and breaking the nose of the cockshot-man, and winning all in the sports below, racing, lepping, dancing, and the Lord knows what! He's right luck, I'm telling you.

PHILLY. If he has he'll be rightly hobbled yet, and he not able to say ten words without making a brag of the way he killed his father and the great blow he hit with the loy.

JIMMY. A man can't hang by his own informing, and his father should be rotten by now.

[OLD MAHON *passes window slowly.*]

PHILLY. Supposing a man's digging spuds in that field with a long spade, and supposing he flings up the two halves of that skull, what'll be said then in the papers and the courts of law?

JIMMY. They'd say it was an old Dane, maybe, was drowned in the flood. [OLD MAHON *comes in and sits down near door listening.*] Did you never hear tell of the skulls they have in the city of Dublin, ranged out like blue jugs in a cabin of Connaught?

PHILLY. And you believe that?

JIMMY [*pugnaciously*]. Didn't a lad see them and he after coming from harvesting in the Liverpool boat? 'They have them there,' says he, 'making a show of the great people there was one time walking the world. White skulls and black skulls and yellow skulls, and some with full teeth and some haven't only but one.'

PHILLY. It was no lie, maybe, for when I was a young lad, there was a graveyard beyond the house with the remnants of a man who had thighs as long as your arm. He was a horrid man, I'm telling you, and there was many a fine Sunday I'd put him together for fun, and he with shiny bones you wouldn't meet the like of these days in the cities of the world.

MAHON [*getting up*]. You wouldn't is it? Lay your eyes on that skull, and tell me where and when there was another the like of it, is splintered only from the blow of a loy.

PHILLY. Glory be to God! And who hit you at all?

MAHON [*triumphantly*]. It was my own son hit me. Would you believe that?

JIMMY. Well there's wonders hidden in the heart of man!

PHILLY [*suspiciously*]. And what way was it done?

MAHON [*wandering about the room*]. I'm after walking hundreds and long scores of miles, winning clean beds and the fill of my belly four times in the day, and I doing nothing but telling stories of that naked truth. [*He comes to them a little aggressively.*] Give me a supeen and I'll tell you now.

[WIDOW QUIN *comes in and stands aghast behind him. He is facing* JIMMY *and* PHILLY, *who are on the left.*]

JIMMY. Ask herself beyond. She's the stuff hidden in her shawl.

WIDOW QUIN [*coming to* MAHON *quickly*]. You here, is it? You didn't go far at all?

MAHON. I seen the coasting steamer passing, and I got a drought upon me and a cramping leg, so I said, 'The divil go along with him,' and turned again. [*Looking under her shawl.*] And let you give me a supeen, for I'm destroyed travelling since Tuesday was a week.

WIDOW QUIN [*getting a glass, in a cajoling tone*]. Sit down then by the fire and take your ease for a space. You've a right to be destroyed indeed, with your walking, and fighting, and facing the sun [*giving *him poteen from a stone jar she has brought in*]. There now is a drink for you, and may it be to your happiness and length of life.

MAHON [*taking glass greedily, and sitting down by fire*]. God increase you!

WIDOW QUIN [*taking MEN to the right stealthily*]. Do you know what? That man's raving from his wound to-day, for I met him a while since telling a rambling tale of a tinker had him destroyed. Then he heard of Christy's deed, and he up and says it was his son had cracked his skull. Oh, isn't madness a fright, for he'll go killing someone yet and he thinking it's the man has struck him so!

JIMMY [*entirely convinced*]. It's a fright surely. I knew a party was kicked in the head by a red mare, and he went killing horses a great while, till he eat the insides of a clock and died after.

PHILLY [*with suspicion*]. Did he see Christy?

WIDOW QUIN. He didn't. [*With a warning gesture.*] Let you not be putting him in mind of him, or you'll be likely summoned if there's murder done. [*Looking round at MAHON.*] Whisht! He's listening. Wait now till you hear me taking him easy and unravelling all. [*She goes to MAHON.*] And what way are you feeling, Mister? Are you in contentment now?

MAHON [*slightly emotional from his drink*]. I'm poorly only, for it's a hard story the way I'm left to-day, when it was I did tend him from his hour of birth, and he a dunce never reached his second book, the way he'd come from school, many's the day, with his legs lamed under him, and he blackened with his beatings like a tinker's ass. It's a hard story, I'm saying, the way some do have their next and nighest raising up a hand of murder on them, and some is lonesome getting their death with lamentation in the dead of night.

WIDOW QUIN [*not knowing what to say*]. To hear you talking so quiet, who'd know you were the same fellow we seen pass to-day?

MAHON. I'm the same surely. The wrack and ruin of three score years; and it's a terror to live that length, I tell you, and to have your sons going to the 'dogs against you, and you wore out scolding them, and skelping them, and God knows what.

PHILLY [*to JIMMY*]. He's not raving. [*To WIDOW QUIN.*] Will you ask him what kind was his son?

WIDOW QUIN [*to* MAHON, *with a peculiar look*]. Was your son that hit you a lad of one year and a score maybe, a great hand at racing and lepping and licking the world?

MAHON [*turning on her with a roar of rage*]. Didn't you hear me say he was the fool of men, the way from this out he'll know the orphan's lot with old and young making game of him and they swearing, raging, kicking at him like a mangy cur.

[*A great burst of cheering outside, some way off.*]

MAHON [*putting his hands to his ears*]. What in the name of God do they want roaring below?

WIDOW QUIN [*with the shade of a smile*]. They're cheering a young lad, the champion playboy of the western world.

[*More cheering.*]

MAHON [*going to window*]. It'd split my heart to hear them, and I with pulses in my brain-pan for a week gone by. Is it racing they are?

JIMMY [*looking from door*]. It is then. They are mounting him for the mule race will be run upon the sands. That's the playboy on the winkered mule.

MAHON [*puzzled*]. That lad, is it? If you said it was a fool he was, I'd have laid a mighty oath he was the likeness of my wandering son. [PHILLY *nods at* JIMMY. MAHON, *uneasily, putting his hand to his head.*] Faith, I'm thinking I'll go walking for to view the race.

WIDOW QUIN [*stopping him, sharply*]. You will not. You'd best take the road to Belmullet, and not be dilly-dallying in this place where there isn't a spot you could sleep.

PHILLY [*coming forward*]. Don't mind her. Mount there on the bench and you'll have a view of the whole. They're hurrying before the tide will rise, and it'd be near over if you went down the pathway through the crags below.

MAHON [*mounts on bench*, WIDOW QUIN *beside him*]. That's a right view again the edge of the sea. They're coming now from the point. He's leading. Who is he at all?

WIDOW QUIN. He's the champion of the world I tell you, and there isn't a hap'orth isn't falling lucky to his hands to-day.

PHILLY [*looking out, interested in the race*]. Look at that. They're pressing him now.

JIMMY. He'll win it yet.

PHILLY. Take your time, Jimmy Farrell. It's too soon to say.

WIDOW QUIN [*shouting*]. Watch him taking the gate. There's riding.

JIMMY [*cheering*]. More power to the young lad!

MAHON. He's passing the third.

JIMMY. He'll lick them yet.

WIDOW QUIN. He'd lick them if he was running races with a score itself.

MAHON. Look at the mule he has kicking the stars.

WIDOW QUIN. There was a lep! [*Catching hold of* MAHON *in her excitement*.] He's fallen! He's mounted again! Faith, he's passing them all!

JIMMY. Look at him skelping her!

PHILLY. And the mountain girls hooshing him on!

JIMMY. It's the last turn! The post's cleared for them now!

MAHON. Look at the narrow place. He'll be into the bogs! [*With a yell.*] Good rider! He's through it again!

JIMMY. He's neck and neck!

MAHON. Good boy to him! Flames, but he's in!

[*Great cheering, in which all join.*]

MAHON [*with hesitation*]. What's that? They're raising him up. They're coming this way. [*With a roar of rage and astonishment.*] It's Christy! by the stars of God! I'd know his way of spitting and he astride the moon. [*He jumps down and makes a run for the door, but* WIDOW QUIN *catches him and pulls him back.*]

WIDOW QUIN. Stay quiet, will you. That's not your son. [*To* JIMMY.] Stop him, or you'll get a month for the abetting of manslaughter and be fined as well.

JIMMY. I'll hold him.

MAHON [*struggling*]. Let me out! Let me out the lot of you! till I have my vengeance on his head to-day.

WIDOW QUIN [*shaking him, vehemently*]. That's not your son. That's a man is going to make a marriage with the daughter of this house, a place with fine trade, with a licence, and with poteen too.

MAHON [*amazed*]. That man marrying a decent and a moneyed girl! Is it mad yous are? Is it in a crazy-house for females that I'm landed now?

WIDOW QUIN. It's mad yourself is with the blow upon your head. That lad is the wonder of the western world.

MAHON. I seen it's my son.

WIDOW QUIN. You seen that you're mad. [*Cheering outside.*] Do you hear them cheering him in the zig-zags of the road? Aren't you after saying that your son's a fool, and how would they be cheering a true idiot born?

MAHON [*getting distressed*]. It's maybe out of reason that man's himself. [*Cheering again.*] There's none surely will go cheering him. Oh, I'm raving with a madness that would fright the world. [*He sits down with his hand to his head.*] There was one time I seen ten scarlet divils letting on they'd cork my spirit in a gallon can; and one time I seen rats as big as badgers sucking the life blood from the butt of my lug; but I never till this day confused that dribbling idiot with a likely man. I'm destroyed surely.

WIDOW QUIN. And who'd wonder when it's your brain-pan that is gaping now?

MAHON. Then the blight of the sacred drought upon myself and him, for I never went mad to this day, and I not three weeks with the Limerick girls drinking myself silly and parlatic from the dusk to dawn. [*To* WIDOW QUIN, *suddenly.*] Is my visage astray?

WIDOW QUIN. It is then. You're a sniggering maniac, a child could see.

MAHON [*getting up more cheerfully*]. Then I'd best be going to the Union beyond, and there'll be a welcome before me, I tell you [*with great pride*], and I a terrible and fearful case, the way that there I was one time screeching in a straitened waistcoat with seven doctors writing out my sayings in a printed book. Would you believe that?

WIDOW QUIN. If you're a wonder itself, you'd best be hasty, for them lads caught a maniac one time and pelted the poor creature till he ran out raving and foaming and was drowned in the sea.

MAHON [*with philosophy*]. It's true mankind is the divil when your head's astray. Let me out now and I'll slip down the boreen and not see them so.

WIDOW QUIN [*showing him out*]. That's it. Run to the right, and not a one will see.

[*He runs off.*]

PHILLY [*wisely*]. You're at some gaming, Widow Quin; but I'll walk after him and give him his dinner and a time to rest, and I'll see then if he's raving or as sane as you.

WIDOW QUIN [*annoyed*]. If you go near that lad, let you be wary of your head, I'm saying. Didn't you hear him telling he was crazed at times?

PHILLY. I heard him telling a power; and I'm thinking we'll have right sport, before night will fall. [*He goes out.*]

JIMMY. Well, Philly's a conceited and foolish man. How could that madman have his senses and his brain-pan slit? I'll go after them and see him turn on Philly now.

[*He goes;* WIDOW QUIN *hides poteen behind counter. Then hubbub outside.*]

VOICES. There you are! Good jumper! Grand lepper! Darlint boy! He's the racer! Bear him on, will you!

[CHRISTY *comes in, in Jockey's dress, with* PEGEEN MIKE, SARA, *and other* GIRLS, *and* MEN.]

PEGEEN [*to* CROWD]. Go on now and don't destroy him and he drenching with sweat. Go along, I'm saying, and have your tug-of-warring till he's dried his skin.

CROWD. Here's his prizes! A bagpipes! A fiddle was played by a poet in the years gone by! A flat and three-thorned blackthorn would lick the scholars out of Dublin town!

CHRISTY [*taking prizes from the* MEN]. Thank you kindly, the lot of you. But you'd say it was little only I did this day if you'd seen me a while since striking my one single blow.

TOWN CRIER [*outside, ringing a bell*]. Take notice, last event of this day! Tug-of-warring on the green below! Come on, the lot of you! Great achievements for all Mayo men!

PEGEEN. Go on, and leave him for to rest and dry. Go on, I tell you, for he'll do no more. [*She hustles* CROWD *out;* WIDOW QUIN *following them.*]

MEN [*going*]. Come on then. Good luck for the while!

PEGEEN [*radiantly, wiping his face with her shawl*]. Well you're the lad, and you'll have great times from this out when you could win that wealth of prizes, and you sweating in the heat of noon!

CHRISTY [*looking at her with delight*]. I'll have great times if I win the crowning prize I'm seeking now, and that's your promise that you'll wed me in a fortnight, when our banns is called.

PEGEEN [*backing away from him*]. You've right daring to go ask me that, when all knows you'll be starting to some girl in your own townland, when your father's rotten in four months, or five.

CHRISTY [*indignantly*]. Starting from you, is it! [*He follows her.*] I will not then, and when the airs is warming in four months or five, it's then yourself and me should be pacing Neifin in the dews of night, the times sweet smells do be rising, and you'd see a little shiny new moon maybe sinking on the hills.

PEGEEN [*looking at him playfully*]. And it's that kind of a poacher's love you'd make, Christy Mahon, on the sides of Neifin, when the night is down?

CHRISTY. It's little you'll think if my love's a poacher's or an earl's itself when you'll feel my two hands stretched around you, and I squeezing kisses on your puckered lips till I'd feel a kind of pity for the Lord God is all ages sitting lonesome in his golden chair.

PEGEEN. That'll be right fun, Christy Mahon, and any girl would walk her heart out before she'd meet a young man was your like for eloquence or talk at all.

CHRISTY [*encouraged*]. Let you wait to hear me talking till we're astray in Erris when Good Friday's by, drinking a sup from a well, and making mighty kisses with our wetted mouths, or gaming in a gap of sunshine with yourself stretched back unto your necklace in the flowers of the earth.

PEGEEN [*in a lower voice, moved by his tone*]. I'd be nice so, is it?

CHRISTY [*with rapture*]. If the mitred bishops seen you that time, they'd be the like of the holy prophets, I'm thinking, do be straining the bars of Paradise to lay eyes on the Lady Helen of Troy, and she abroad pacing back and forward with a nosegay in her golden shawl.

PEGEEN [*with real tenderness*]. And what is it I have, Christy Mahon, to make me fitting entertainment for the like of you that has such poet's talking, and such bravery of heart?

CHRISTY [*in a low voice*]. Isn't there the light of seven heavens in your heart alone, the way you'll be an angel's lamp to me from this out, and I abroad in the darkness spearing salmons in the Owen or the Carrowmore.

PEGEEN. If I was your wife, I'd be along with you those nights, Christy Mahon, the way you'd see I was a great hand at coaxing bailiffs, or coining funny nicknames for the stars of night.

CHRISTY. You, is it! Taking your death in the hailstones or the fogs of dawn.

PEGEEN. Yourself and me would shelter easy in a narrow bush, [*with a qualm of dread*] but we're only talking maybe, for this would be a poor thatched place to hold a fine lad is the like of you.

CHRISTY [*putting his arm round her*]. If I wasn't a good Christian, it's on my naked knees I'd be saying my prayers and paters to every jackstraw you have roofing your head, and every stony pebble is paving the laneway to your door.

PEGEEN [*radiantly*]. If that's the truth, I'll be burning candles from this out to the miracles of God have brought you from the south to-day, and I with my gowns bought ready the way that I can wed you, and not wait at all.

CHRISTY. It's miracles and that's the truth. Me there toiling a long while, and walking a long while, not knowing at all I was drawing all times nearer to this holy day.

PEGEEN. And myself a girl was tempted often to go sailing the seas till I'd marry a Jew-man with ten kegs of gold, and I not knowing at all there was the like of you drawing nearer like the stars of God.

CHRISTY. And to think I'm long years hearing women talking that talk to all bloody fools, and this the first time I've heard the like of your voice talking sweetly for my own delight.

PEGEEN. And to think it's me is talking sweetly, Christy Mahon, and I the fright of seven townlands for my biting tongue. Well the heart's a wonder, and I'm thinking there won't be our like in Mayo for gallant lovers from this hour to-day. [*Drunken singing is heard outside.*] There's my father coming from the wake, and when he's had his sleep we'll tell him, for he's peaceful then. [*They separate.*]

MICHAEL [*singing outside*]—

> The jailor and the turnkey
>   They quickly ran us down,
> And brought us back as prisoners
>   Once more to Cavan town.

[*He comes in supported by* SHAWN.]

> There we lay bewailing
>   All in a prison bound. . . .

[*He sees* CHRISTY. *Goes and shakes him drunkenly by the hand, while* PEGEEN *and* SHAWN *talk on the left.*]

MICHAEL [*to* CHRISTY]. The blessing of God and the holy angels on your head, young fellow. I hear tell you're after winning all in the sports below; and wasn't it a shame I didn't bear you along with me to Kate Cassidy's wake, a fine, stout lad, the like of you, for you'd never see the match of it for flows of drink, the way when we sunk her bones at noonday in her narrow grave, there were five men, aye, and six men, stretched out retching speechless on the holy stones.

CHRISTY [*uneasily, watching* PEGEEN]. Is that the truth?

MICHAEL. It is then, and aren't you a louty schemer to go burying your poor father unbeknownst when you'd a right to throw him on the crupper of a Kerry mule and drive him westwards, like holy Joseph in the days gone by, the way we could have given him a decent burial and not have him rotting beyond and not a Christian drinking a smart drop to the glory of his soul.

CHRISTY [*gruffly*]. It's well enough he's lying for the likes of him.

MICHAEL [*slapping him on the back*]. Well, aren't you a hardened slayer? It'll be a poor thing for the household man where you go sniffing for a female wife; and [*pointing to* SHAWN] look beyond at that shy and decent Christian I have chosen for my daughter's hand, and I after getting the gilded dispensation this day for to wed them now.

CHRISTY. And you'll be wedding them this day, is it?

MICHAEL [*drawing himself up*]. Aye. Are you thinking, if I'm drunk itself I'd leave my daughter living single with a little frisky rascal is the like of you?

PEGEEN [*breaking away from* SHAWN]. Is it the truth the dispensation's come?

MICHAEL [*triumphantly*]. Father Reilly's after reading it in gallous Latin, and 'It's come in the nick of time,' says he; 'so I'll wed them in a hurry, dreading that young gaffer who'd capsize the stars.'

PEGEEN [*fiercely*]. He's missed his nick of time, for it's that lad, Christy Mahon, that I'm wedding now.

MICHAEL [*loudly, with horror*]. You'd be making him a son to me and he wet and crusted with his father's blood?

PEGEEN. Aye. Wouldn't it be a bitter thing for a girl to go marrying the like of Shaneen, and he a middling kind of a scarecrow with no savagery or fine words in him at all?

MICHAEL [*gasping and sinking on a chair*]. Oh, aren't you a heathen daughter to go shaking the fat of my heart, and I swamped and drownded with the weight of drink? Would you have them turning on me the way that I'd be roaring to the dawn of day with the wind upon my heart? Have you not a word to aid me, Shaneen? Are you not jealous at all?

SHAWN [*in great misery*]. I'd be afeard to be jealous of a man did slay his da.

PEGEEN. Well, it'd be a poor thing to go marrying your like. I'm seeing there's a world of peril for an orphan girl, and isn't it a great blessing I didn't wed you, before himself came walking from the west or south.

SHAWN. It's a queer story you'd go picking a dirty tramp up from the highways of the world.

PEGEEN [*playfully*]. And you think you're a likely beau to go straying along with, the shiny Sundays of the opening year, when it's sooner on a bullock's liver you'd put a poor girl thinking than on the lily or the rose.

SHAWN. And have you no mind of my weight of passion, and the holy dispensation, and the drift of heifers I am giving, and the golden ring?

PEGEEN. I'm thinking you're too fine for the like of me, Shawn Keogh of Killakeen, and let you go off till you'd find a radiant lady with droves of bullocks on the plains of Meath, and herself bedizened in the diamond jewelleries of Pharaoh's ma. That'd be your match, Shaneen. So God save you now! [*She retreats behind* CHRISTY.]

SHAWN. Won't you hear me telling you. . . .

CHRISTY [*with ferocity*]. Take yourself from this, young fellow, or I'll maybe add a murder to my deeds to-day.

MICHAEL [*springing up with a shriek*]. Murder is it? Is it mad yous are? Would you go making murder in this place, and it piled with poteen for our drink to-night? Go on to the foreshore if it's fighting you want, where the rising tide will wash all traces from the memory of man. [*Pushing* SHAWN *towards* CHRISTY.]

SHAWN [*shaking himself free, and getting behind* MICHAEL]. I'll not fight him, Michael James. I'd liefer live a bachelor simmering in passions to the end of time, than face a lepping savage the like of him has descended from the Lord knows where. Strike him yourself, Michael James, or you'll lose my drift of heifers and my blue bull from Sneem.

MICHAEL. Is it me fight him, when it's father-slaying he's bred to now? [*Pushing* SHAWN.] Go on you fool and fight him now.

SHAWN [*coming forward a little*]. Will I strike him with my hand?

MICHAEL. Take the loy is on your western side.

SHAWN. I'd be afeard of the gallows if I struck with that.

CHRISTY [*taking up the loy*]. Then I'll make you face the gallows or quit off from this. [SHAWN *flies out of the door.*]

CHRISTY. Well, fine weather be after him, [*going to* MICHAEL, *coaxingly*] and I'm thinking you wouldn't wish to have that quaking blackguard in your house at all. Let you give us your blessing and hear her swear her faith to me, for I'm mounted on the spring-tide of the stars of luck the way it'll be good for any to have me in the house.

PEGEEN [*at the other side of* MICHAEL]. Bless us now, for I swear to God I'll wed him, and I'll not renege.

MICHAEL [*standing up in the centre, holding on to both of them*]. It's the will of God, I'm thinking, that all should win an easy or a cruel end, and it's the will of God that all should rear up lengthy families for the nurture of the earth. What's a single man, I ask you, eating a bit in one house and drinking a sup in another, and he with no place of his own, like an old braying jackass strayed upon the rocks? [*To* CHRISTY.] It's many would be in dread to bring your like into their house for to end them maybe with a sudden end; but I'm a decent man of Ireland, and I'd liefer face the grave untimely and I seeing a score of grandsons growing up little gallant swearers by the name of God, than go peopling my bedside with puny weeds the like of what you'd breed, I'm thinking, out of Shaneen Keogh. [*He joins their hands.*] A daring fellow is the jewel of the world, and a man did split his father's middle with a single clout should have the bravery of ten, so may God and Mary and St. Patrick bless you, and increase you from this mortal day.

CHRISTY and PEGEEN. Amen, O Lord!

[*Hubbub outside.* OLD MAHON *rushes in, followed by all the* CROWD *and* WIDOW QUIN. *He makes a rush at* CHRISTY, *knocks him down, and begins to beat him.*]

PEGEEN [*dragging back his arm*]. Stop that, will you. Who are you at all?

MAHON. His father, God forgive me!

PEGEEN [*drawing back*]. Is it rose from the dead?

MAHON. Do you think I look so easy quenched with the tap of a loy? [*Beats* CHRISTY *again.*]

PEGEEN [*glaring at* CHRISTY]. And it's lies you told, letting on you had him slitted, and you nothing at all.

CHRISTY [*catching* MAHON'*s stick*]. He's not my father. He's a raving maniac would scare the world. [*Pointing to* WIDOW QUIN.] Herself knows it is true.

CROWD. You're fooling Pegeen! The Widow Quin seen him this day and you likely knew! You're a liar!

CHRISTY [*dumbfounded*]. It's himself was a liar, lying stretched out with an open head on him, letting on he was dead.

MAHON. Weren't you off racing the hills before I got my breath with the start I had seeing you turn on me at all?

PEGEEN. And to think of the coaxing glory we had given him, and he after doing nothing but hitting a soft blow and chasing northward in a sweat of fear. Quit off from this.

CHRISTY [*piteously*]. You've seen my doings this day, and let you save me from the old man; for why would you be in such a scorch of haste to spur me to destruction now?

PEGEEN. It's there your treachery is spurring me, till I'm hard set to think you're the one I'm after lacing in my heart-strings half-an-hour gone by. [*To* MAHON.] Take him on from this, for I think bad the world should see me raging for a Munster liar and the fool of men.

MAHON. Rise up now to retribution, and come on with me.

CROWD [*jeeringly*]. There's the playboy! There's the lad thought he'd rule the roost in Mayo. Slate him now, Mister.

CHRISTY [*getting up in shy terror*]. What is it drives you to torment me here, when I'd ask the thunders of the might of God to blast me if I ever did hurt to any saving only that one single blow.

MAHON [*loudly*]. If you didn't, you're a poor good-for-nothing, and isn't it by the like of you the sins of the whole world are committed?

CHRISTY [*raising his hands*]. In the name of the Almighty God . . . .

MAHON. Leave troubling the Lord God. Would you have him sending down droughts, and fevers, and the old hen and the cholera morbus?

CHRISTY [*to* WIDOW QUIN]. Will you come between us and protect me now?

WIDOW QUIN. I've tried a lot, God help me! and my share is done.

CHRISTY [*looking round in desperation*]. And I must go back into my torment is it, or run off like a vagabond straying through the Unions with the dusts of August making mudstains in the gullet of my throat, or the winds of March blowing on me till I'd take an oath I felt them making whistles of my ribs within.

SARA. Ask Pegeen to aid you. Her like does often change.

CHRISTY. I will not then, for there's torment in the splendour of her like and she a girl any moon of midnight would take pride to meet, facing southwards on the heaths of Keel. But what did I want crawling forward to scorch my understanding at her flaming brow?

PEGEEN [*to* MAHON, *vehemently, fearing she will break into tears*]. Take him on from this or I'll set the young lads to destroy him here.

MAHON [*going to him, shaking his stick*]. Come on now if you wouldn't have the company to see you skelped.

PEGEEN [*half laughing, through her tears*]. That's it, now the world will see him pandied, and he an ugly liar was playing off the hero and the fright of men!

CHRISTY [*to* MAHON, *very sharply*]. Leave me go!

CROWD. That's it. Now Christy. If them two set fighting, it will lick the world.

MAHON [*making a grab at* CHRISTY]. Come here to me.

CHRISTY [*more threateningly*]. Leave me go, I'm saying.

MAHON. I will maybe when your legs is limping, and your back is blue.

CROWD. Keep it up, the two of you. I'll back the old one. Now the playboy.

CHRISTY [*in low and intense voice*]. Shut your yelling, for if you're after making a mighty man of me this day by the power of a lie, you're setting me now to think if it's a poor thing to be lonesome, it's worse maybe go mixing with the fools of earth.

[MAHON *makes a movement towards him.*]

CHRISTY [*almost shouting*]. Keep off . . . lest I do show a blow unto the lot of you would set the guardian angels winking in the clouds above. [*He swings round with a sudden rapid movement and picks up a loy.*]

CROWD [*half frightened, half amused*]. He's going mad! Mind yourselves! Run from the idiot!

CHRISTY. If I am an idiot, I'm after hearing my voice this day saying words would raise the topknot on a poet in a merchant's town. I've won your racing and your lepping and . . . .

MAHON. Shut your gullet and come on with me.

CHRISTY. I'm going but I'll stretch you first.

[*He runs at* OLD MAHON *with the loy, chases him out of the door, followed by* CROWD *and* WIDOW QUIN. *There is a great noise outside, then a yell, and dead silence for a moment.* CHRISTY *comes in, half dazed, and goes to fire.*]

WIDOW QUIN [*coming in, hurriedly, and going to him*]. They're turning again you. Come on or you'll be hanged indeed.

CHRISTY. I'm thinking from this out, Pegeen'll be giving me praises the same as in the hours gone by.

WIDOW QUIN [*impatiently*]. Come by the back-door. I'd think bad to have you stifled on the gallows tree.

CHRISTY [*indignantly*]. I will not then. What good'd be my life-time if I left Pegeen?

WIDOW QUIN. Come on and you'll be no worse than you were last night; and you with a double murder this time to be telling to the girls.

CHRISTY. I'll not leave Pegeen Mike.

WIDOW QUIN [*impatiently*]. Isn't there the match of her in every parish public, from Binghamstown unto the plain of Meath? Come on, I tell you, and I'll find you finer sweethearts at each waning moon.

CHRISTY. It's Pegeen I'm seeking only, and what'd I care if you brought me a drift of chosen females, standing in their shifts itself maybe, from this place to the Eastern World.

SARA [*runs in, pulling off one of her petticoats*]. They're going to hang him. [*Holding out petticoat and shawl.*] Fit these upon him and let him run off to the east.

WIDOW QUIN. He's raving now; but we'll fit them on him and I'll take him in the ferry to the Achill boat.

CHRISTY [*struggling feebly*]. Leave me go, will you, when I'm thinking of my luck to-day, for she will wed me surely and I a proven hero in the end of all. [*They try to fasten petticoat round him.*]

WIDOW QUIN. Take his left hand and we'll pull him now. Come on, young fellow.

CHRISTY [*suddenly starting up*]. You'll be taking me from her? You're jealous, is it, of her wedding me? Go on from this. [*He snatches up a stool, and threatens them with it.*]

WIDOW QUIN [*going*]. It's in the mad-house they should put him not in jail at all. We'll go by the back-door to call the doctor and we'll save him so.

[*She goes out, with* SARA, *through inner room.* MEN *crowd in the doorway.* CHRISTY *sits down again by the fire.*]

MICHAEL [*in a terrified whisper*]. Is the old lad killed surely?

PHILLY. I'm after feeling the last gasps quitting his heart. [*They peer in at* CHRISTY.]

MICHAEL [*with a rope*]. Look at the way he is. Twist a hangman's knot on it and slip it over his head while he's not minding at all.

PHILLY. Let you take it, Shaneen. You're the soberest of all that's here.

SHAWN. Is it me to go near him, and he the wickedest and worst with me? Let you take it, Pegeen Mike.

PEGEEN. Come on, so. [*She goes forward with the others, and they drop the double hitch over his head.*]

CHRISTY. What ails you?

SHAWN [*triumphantly, as they pull the rope tight on his arms*]. Come on to the peelers till they stretch you now.

CHRISTY. Me!

MICHAEL. If we took pity on you, the Lord God would maybe bring us ruin from the law to-day, so you'd best come easy, for hanging is an easy and a speedy end.

CHRISTY. I'll not stir. [*To* PEGEEN.] And what is it you'll say to me and I after doing it this time in the face of all?

PEGEEN. I'll say a strange man is a marvel with his mighty talk; but what's a squabble in your back-yard and the blow of a loy, have taught me that there's a great gap between a gallous story and a dirty deed. [*To* MEN.] Take him on from this, or the lot of us will be likely put on trial for his deed to-day.

CHRISTY [*with horror in his voice*]. And it's yourself will send me off to have a horny-fingered hangman hitching his bloody slip-knots at the butt of my ear?

MEN [*pulling rope*]. Come on, will you?

[*He is pulled down on the floor.*]

CHRISTY [*twisting his legs round the table*]. Cut the rope, Pegeen, and I'll quit the lot of you and live from this out like the madmen of Keel, eating muck and green weeds on the faces of the cliffs.

PEGEEN. And leave us to hang, is it, for a saucy liar, the like of you? [*To* MEN.] Take him on out from this.

SHAWN. Pull a twist on his neck, and squeeze him so.

PHILLY. Twist yourself. Sure he cannot hurt you, if you keep your distance from his teeth alone.

SHAWN. I'm afeard of him. [*To* PEGEEN.] Lift a lighted sod will you and scorch his leg.

PEGEEN [*blowing the fire with a bellows*]. Leave go now young fellow or I'll scorch your shins.

CHRISTY. You're blowing for to torture me? [*His voice rising and growing stronger.*] That's your kind, is it? Then let the lot of you be wary, for if I've to face the gallows I'll have a gay march down, I tell you, and shed the blood of some of you before I die.

SHAWN [*in terror*]. Keep a good hold, Philly. Be wary for the love of God, for I'm thinking he would liefest wreak his pains on me.

CHRISTY [*almost gaily*]. If I do lay my hands on you, it's the way you'll be at the fall of night hanging as a scarecrow for the fowls of hell. Ah, you'll have a gallous jaunt I'm saying, coaching out through Limbo with my father's ghost.

SHAWN [*to* PEGEEN]. Make haste, will you. Oh, isn't he a holy terror, and isn't it true for Father Reilly that all drink's a curse that has the lot of you so shaky and uncertain now.

CHRISTY. If I can wring a neck among you, I'll have a royal judgment looking on the trembling jury in the courts of law. And won't there be crying out in Mayo the day I'm stretched upon the rope with ladies in their silks and satins snivelling in their lacy kerchiefs, and they rhyming songs and ballads on the terror of my fate? [*He squirms round on the floor and bites* SHAWN's *leg*.]

SHAWN [*shrieking*]. My leg's bit on me! He's the like of a mad dog, I'm thinking, the way that I will surely die.

CHRISTY [*delighted with himself*]. You will then, the way you can shake out hell's flags of welcome for my coming in two weeks or three, for I'm thinking Satan hasn't many have killed their da in Kerry and in Mayo too.

[OLD MAHON *comes in behind on all fours and looks on unnoticed.*]

MEN [*to* PEGEEN]. Bring the sod, will you.

PEGEEN [*coming over*]. God help him so. [*Burns his leg.*]

CHRISTY [*kicking and screaming*]. Oh, glory be to God!

[*He kicks loose from the table, and they all drag him towards the door.*]

JIMMY [*seeing* OLD MAHON]. Will you look what's come in?

[*They all drop* CHRISTY *and run left.*]

CHRISTY [*scrambling on his knees face to face with* OLD MAHON]. Are you coming to be killed a third time or what ails you now?

MAHON. For what is it they have you tied?

CHRISTY. They're taking me to the peelers to have me hanged for slaying you.

MICHAEL [*apologetically*]. It is the will of God that all should guard their little cabins from the treachery of law and what would my daughter be doing if I was ruined or was hanged itself?

MAHON [*grimly, loosening* CHRISTY]. It's little I care if you put a bag on her back and went picking cockles till the hour of death; but my son and myself will be going our own way and we'll have great times from this out telling stories of the villainy of Mayo and the fools is here. [*To* CHRISTY, *who is freed.*] Come on now.

CHRISTY. Go with you, is it! I will then, like a gallant captain with his heathen slave. Go on now and I'll see you from this day stewing my oatmeal and washing my spuds, for I'm master of all fights from now. [*Pushing* MAHON.] Go on, I'm saying.

MAHON. Is it me?

CHRISTY. Not a word out of you. Go on from this.

MAHON [*walking out and looking back at* CHRISTY *over his shoulder*]. Glory be to God! [*With a broad smile.*] I am crazy again! [*Goes.*]

CHRISTY. Ten thousand blessings upon all that's here, for you've turned me a likely gaffer in the end of all, the way I'll go romancing through a romping lifetime from this hour to the dawning of the judgment day. [*He goes out.*]

MICHAEL. By the will of God, we'll have peace now for our drinks. Will you draw the porter, Pegeen?

SHAWN [*going up to her*]. It's a miracle Father Reilly can wed us in the end of all, and we'll have none to trouble us when his vicious bite is healed.

PEGEEN [*hitting him a box on the ear*]. Quit my sight. [*Putting her shawl over her head and breaking out into wild lamentations.*] Oh my grief, I've lost him surely. I've lost the only playboy of the western world.

CURTAIN

DEIRDRE OF THE SORROWS[1]

A PLAY IN THREE ACTS

(1907–1909)

[1] The following draft of an essay was written by Synge during the early stages of his work on *Deirdre of the Sorrows*, and might have served as the basis for a preface to the completed play:

Historical or Peasant Drama 18/3/07

The moment the sense of historical truth awoke in Europe, historical fiction became impossible. For a time it seemed otherwise. Antiquarian writers, fools now exploded. Old writers (Elizabethan Louis XIV) saw historical personages as living contemporaries. Now it is impossible to use our own language or feeling with perfect sincerity for personages we know to have been different from ourselves. Hence Hist. Fiction insincere. It is possible to use a national tradition a century or more old which is still alive in the soul of the people see Walter Scott. But any one who is familiar with Elizabethan writings will not tolerate Kenilworth or Westward Ho. Promessi Sposi(?) To us now as *readers* the old literature itself is so priceless we look with disgust at imitations of it. As creators? It is impossible to use a legend [such] as Faust which from the outset defies historical reality— in the making up of an absolutely modern work. [That] is only to be done possibly in verse, as our modern spoken prose cannot be put into the mouths of antique persons. On stage this is so most of all. In thinking over the poems of the last century that one reads with most pleasure how many are historical? Browning, Rossetti. For my own part I only care for personal lyrical modern poetry and little of that, but I am possibly exceptional. That is why lyrical poetry is now the only poetry. The real world is mostly unpoetical, fiction even in poetry is not totally sincere hence failure of modern poetry. This is to be taken with all reserve, there is always the poet's dream which makes itself a sort of world. When it is kept a dream is this possible on the stage? I think not. Maeterlinck, Pelleas and Melisande? Is the drama—as a beautiful thing a lost art? The drama of swords is. Few of us except soldiers have seen swords in use, to drag them out on the stage is babyish. They are so rustic for us with the association of pseudo-antique fiction and drama. For the present the only possible beauty in drama is peasant drama, for the future we must await the making of life beautiful again before we can have beautiful drama. You cannot gather grapes of chimney pots.

PREFACE TO *DEIRDRE OF THE SORROWS*
by W. B. YEATS

IT was Synge's practice to write many complete versions of a play, distinguishing them with letters, and running half through the alphabet before he finished. He read me a version of this play the year before his death, and would have made several more always altering and enriching. He felt that the story, as he had told it, required a grotesque element mixed into its lyrical melancholy to give contrast and create an impression of solidity, and had begun this mixing with the character of Owen, who would have had some part in the first act also, where he was to have entered Lavarcham's cottage with Conchubor. Conchubor would have taken a knife from his belt to cut himself free from threads of silk that caught in brooch or pin as he leant over Deirdre's embroidery frame, and forgotten this knife behind him. Owen was to have found it and stolen it. Synge asked that either I or Lady Gregory should write some few words to make this possible, but after writing in a passage we were little satisfied and thought it better to have the play performed, as it is printed here, with no word of ours. When Owen killed himself in the second act, he was to have done it with Conchubor's knife. He did not speak to me of any other alteration, but it is probable that he would have altered till the structure had become as strong and varied as in his other plays; and had he lived to do that, 'Deirdre of the Sorrows' would have been his masterwork, so much beauty is there in its course, and such wild nobleness in its end, and so poignant is an emotion and wisdom that were his own preparation for death.

W. B. Yeats. April, 1910

PERSONS

LAVARCHAM, a wise woman and servant of Conchubor, about fifty

OLD WOMAN, cook and Deirdre's foster-mother

CONCHUBOR, High King of Ulster, about sixty

FERGUS, Conchubor's friend and warrior of the Red Branch of Ulster

DEIRDRE

NAISI, son of Usna, Deirdre's lover

AINNLE } brothers to Naisi, with him heroes of
ARDAN }   the Red Branch

OWEN, Conchubor's spy

TWO SOLDIERS

SCENE

The first Act takes place in Lavarcham's house on Slieve Fuadh; the second Act in a wood outside the tent of Deirdre and Naisi in Alban; the third Act in a tent below Emain Macha.

ACT I

LAVARCHAM's *house on Slieve Fuadh. There is a door to the inner room on the left, and a door to the open air on the right. Window at back and a frame with a half-finished piece of tapestry; a high chair of state centre stage with a stool near it. There are also a large press and heavy oak chest near the back wall. The place is neat and clean but bare.* LAVARCHAM, *a woman of fifty, is working at tapestry frame.* OLD WOMAN *comes in from left.*

OLD WOMAN. She hasn't come yet is it, and it falling to the night?

LAVARCHAM. She has not. [*Concealing her anxiety.*] It's dark with the clouds are coming from the west and south, but it isn't later than the common.

OLD WOMAN. It's later surely, and I hear tell the Sons of Usna, Naisi and his brothers, are above chasing hares for two days or three, and the same a while since when the moon was full.

LAVARCHAM [*more anxiously*]. The gods send they don't set eyes on her [*with a sign of helplessness*] ... yet if they do, itself, it wasn't *my* wish brought them or could send them away.

OLD WOMAN [*reprovingly*]. If it was not, you'd do well to keep a check on her, and she turning a woman that was meant to be a queen.

LAVARCHAM. Who'd check her like was made to have her pleasure only, the way if there were no warnings told about her you'd see troubles coming when an old king is taking her, and she without a thought but for her beauty and to be straying the hills.

OLD WOMAN. The gods help the lot of us. . . . Shouldn't she be well pleased getting the like of Conchubor, and he middling settled in his years itself? I don't know what he wanted putting her this wild place to be breaking her in, or putting myself to be roasting her suppers, and she with no patience for her food at all. [*She looks out.*]

LAVARCHAM. Is she coming from the glen?

OLD WOMAN. She is not. But whisht . . . there's two men leaving the furze. . . . [*Crying out.*] It's Conchubor and Fergus along with him! Conchubor'll be in a blue stew this night and herself abroad.

LAVARCHAM [*settling room hastily*]. Are they close by?

OLD WOMAN. Crossing the stream, and there's herself on the hillside with a load of twigs. Will I run out and put her in order before they'll set eyes on her at all?

LAVARCHAM. You will not. Would you have him see you, and he a man would be jealous of a hawk would fly between her and the rising sun. [*She looks out.*] Go up to the hearth and be as busy as if you hadn't seen them at all.

OLD WOMAN [*sitting down to polish vessels*]. There'll be trouble this night, for he should be in his tempers from the way he's stepping out, and he swinging his hands.

LAVARCHAM [*wearied with the whole matter*]. It'd be best of all maybe if he got in tempers with herself, and made an end quickly, for I'm in a poor way between the pair of them. [*Going back to tapestry frame.*] There they are now at the door.

[CONCHUBOR *and* FERGUS *come in.*]

CONCHUBOR and FERGUS. The gods save you.

LAVARCHAM [*getting up and curtseying*]. The gods save and keep you kindly, and stand between you and all harm forever.

CONCHUBOR [*looking around*]. Where is Deirdre?

LAVARCHAM [*trying to speak with indifference*]. Abroad upon Slieve Fuadh. She does be all times straying around picking flowers or nuts, or sticks itself, but so long as she's gathering new life I've a right not to heed her, I'm thinking, and she taking her will.

[FERGUS *talks to* OLD WOMAN.]

CONCHUBOR [*stiffly*]. A night with thunder coming is no night to be abroad.

LAVARCHAM [*more uneasily*]. She's used to every track and pathway and the lightning itself wouldn't let down its flame to singe the beauty of her like.

FERGUS [*cheerfully*]. She's right Conchubor, and let you sit down and take your ease [*he takes a wallet from under his cloak*] . . . and I'll count out what we've brought, and put it in the presses within.

[*He goes into the inner room with* OLD WOMAN.]

CONCHUBOR [*sitting down and looking about*]. Where are the mats and hangings and the silver skillets I sent up for Deirdre?

LAVARCHAM. The mats and hangings are in this press, Conchubor. She wouldn't wish to be soiling them, she said, running out and in with mud and grasses on her feet, and it raining since the night of Samhain. The silver skillets and the golden cups, we have beyond locked in the chest.

CONCHUBOR. Bring them out and use them from this day.

LAVARCHAM. We'll do it, Conchubor.

CONCHUBOR [*getting up and going to frame*]. Is this hers?

LAVARCHAM [*pleased to speak of it*]. It is, Conchubor. All say there isn't her match at fancying figures and throwing purple upon crimson, and she edging them all times with her greens and gold.

CONCHUBOR [*a little uneasily*]. Is she keeping wise and busy since I passed before, and growing ready for her life in Emain?

LAVARCHAM [*drily*]. That's questions will give small pleasure to yourself or me. . . . [*She sits on a stool and faces him, making up her mind to speak out.*] If it's the truth I'll tell you, she's growing too wise to marry a big king and she a score only. Let you not be taking it bad, Conchubor, but you'll get little good seeing her this night, for with all my talking it's wilfuller she's growing these two months or three.

CONCHUBOR [*severely, but relieved things are no worse*]. Isn't it a poor thing that you're doing so little to school her to meet what is to come?

LAVARCHAM. I'm after serving you two score of years, and I'll tell you this night, Conchubor, she's little call to mind an old woman when she has the birds to school her, and the pools in the rivers where she goes bathing in the sun. I'll tell you if you seen her that time, with her white skin, and her red lips, and the blue water and

G

the ferns about her, you'd know maybe, and you greedy itself, it wasn't for your like she was born at all.

CONCHUBOR. It's little I heed for what she was born; she'll be my comrade surely. [*He examines her workbox.*]

LAVARCHAM [*sinking into sadness again*]. I'm in dread, so, they were right saying she'd bring destruction on the world, for it's a poor thing when you see a settled man putting the love he has for a young child, and the love he has for a full woman, on a girl the like of her, and it's a poor thing, Conchubor, to see a High King the way you are this day, prying after her needles and numbering her lines of thread.

CONCHUBOR [*getting up*]. Let you not be talking too far and you old itself. [*Walks across the room and back.*] . . . Does she know the troubles are foretold?

LAVARCHAM [*in the tone of the earlier talk*]. I'm after telling her one time and another but I'd do as well speaking to a lamb of ten weeks and it racing the hills. . . . It's not the dread of death or troubles that would tame her like.

CONCHUBOR [*looking out*]. She's coming now, and let you walk in and keep Fergus, till I speak with her a while.

LAVARCHAM [*going left*]. If I'm after vexing you, itself, it'd be best you weren't taking her hasty or scolding her at all.

CONCHUBOR [*very stiffly*]. I've no call to. I'm well pleased she's light and airy.

LAVARCHAM [*offended at his tone*]. Well pleased is it? [*With a snort of irony.*] It's a queer thing the way the likes of me do be telling the truth and the wise are lying all times!

[*She goes into room left.* CONCHUBOR *arranges himself before a mirror for a moment, then goes a little to the left and waits.* DEIRDRE *comes in poorly dressed with a little bag and a bundle of twigs in her arms. She is astonished for a moment when she sees* CONCHUBOR; *then she makes a curtsey to him, and goes to the hearth without any embarrassment.*]

CONCHUBOR. The gods save you, Deirdre. I have come up bringing you rings and jewels from Emain Macha.

DEIRDRE. The gods save you.

CONCHUBOR. What have you brought from the hills?

DEIRDRE [*quite self-possessed*]. A bag of nuts, and twigs for our fires at the dawn of day.

CONCHUBOR [*showing annoyance in spite of himself*]. And it's that way you're picking up the manners will fit you to be Queen of Ulster?

DEIRDRE [*made a little defiant by his tone*]. I have no wish to be a queen.

CONCHUBOR [*almost sneeringly*]. You'd wish to be dressing in your duns and grey, and you herding your geese or driving your calves to their shed . . . like the common lot scattered in the glens?

DEIRDRE [*very defiant*]. I would not, Conchubor. [*She goes to tapestry and begins to work.*] A girl born, the way I'm born, is more likely to wish for a mate who'd be her likeness . . . a man with his hair like the raven maybe and his skin like the snow and his lips like blood spilt on it.

CONCHUBOR [*sees his mistake and after a moment takes a flattering tone, looking at her work*]. Whatever you wish there's no queen but would be well pleased to have your skill at choosing colours and making pictures on the cloth. [*Looking closely.*] What is it you're figuring?

DEIRDRE [*deliberately*]. Three young men, and they chasing in the green gap of a wood.

CONCHUBOR [*now almost pleading*]. It's soon you'll have dogs with silver chains to be chasing in the woods of Emain, for I have white hounds rearing up for you, and grey horses, that I've chosen from the finest in Ulster and Britain and Gaul.

DEIRDRE [*unmoved, as before*]. I've heard tell in Ulster and Britain and Gaul, Naisi and his brothers have no match and they chasing in the woods.

CONCHUBOR [*very gravely*]. Isn't it a strange thing you'd be talking of Naisi and his brothers or figuring them either, when you know the things that are foretold about themselves and you! Yet you've little knowledge and I'd do wrong taking it bad when it'll be my share from this out to keep you the way you'll have little call to trouble for knowledge or its want either.

DEIRDRE. Yourself should be wise surely.

CONCHUBOR. The like of me have a store of knowledge that's a weight and terror; it's for that we do choose out the like of yourself that are young and glad only. I'm thinking you're gay and lively each day in the year?

DEIRDRE. I don't know if that's true, Conchubor. There are lonesome days and bad nights in this place like another.

CONCHUBOR. You should have as few sad days I'm thinking as I have glad and good ones.

DEIRDRE. What is it has you that way, Conchubor? Ever this place you hear the old women saying a good child's as happy as a king.

CONCHUBOR. How would I be happy seeing age come on me each year when the dry leaves are blowing back and forward at the gate of Emain, and yet this last while I'm saying out when I'd see the furze breaking and the daws sitting two and two on ash-trees by the Duns of Emain, 'Deirdre's a year nearer her full age when she'll be my mate and comrade,' and then I'm glad surely.

DEIRDRE [*almost to herself*]. I will not be your mate in Emain.

CONCHUBOR [*not heeding her*]. It's there you'll be proud and happy and you'll learn that if young men are great hunters yet it's with the like of myself you'll find a knowledge of what is priceless in your own like. What we all need is a place is safe and splendid, and it's that you'll get in Emain in two days or three.

DEIRDRE [*aghast*]. Two days?

CONCHUBOR. I've the rooms ready, and in a little while you'll be brought down there, to be my queen, and queen of the five parts of Ireland.

DEIRDRE [*standing up frightened and pleading*]. I'd liefer stay this place, Conchubor. . . . Leave me this place where I'm well used to the tracks and pathways and the people of the glens. . . . It's for this life I'm born surely.

CONCHUBOR. You'll be happier and greater with myself in Emain. It is I will be your comrade, and I will stand between you and the great troubles are foretold.

DEIRDRE. I will not be your queen in Emain when it's my pleasure to be having my freedom on the edges of the hills.

CONCHUBOR. It's my wish to have you quickly, and I'm sick and weary thinking of the day you'll be brought down to me and seeing you walking into my big empty halls. I've made all sure to have you —and yet all said there's a fear in the back of my mind I'd miss you and have great troubles in the end. It's for that, Deirdre, I'm praying that you'll come quickly. And you may take the word of a man has no lies you'll not find with any other the like of what I'm bringing you in wildness and confusion in my own mind.

DEIRDRE. I cannot go, Conchubor.

CONCHUBOR [*taking a triumphant tone*]. It is my pleasure to have you and I a man is waiting a long while on the throne of Ulster. Wouldn't you liefer be my comrade growing up the like of Emer and Maeve, than to be in this place and you a child always?

DEIRDRE. You don't know me, and you'd have little joy taking me, Conchubor. . . . I'm too long watching the days getting a great speed passing me by, I'm too long taking my will and it's that way I'll be living always.

CONCHUBOR [*drily*]. Call Fergus to come with me. This is your last night upon Slieve Fuadh.

DEIRDRE [*now pleadingly*]. Leave me a short space longer, Conchubor. Isn't it a poor thing I should be hastened away when all these troubles are foretold? Leave me a year Conchubor, it isn't much I'm asking.

CONCHUBOR. It's much to have me two score and two weeks waiting for your voice in Emain, and you in this place growing lonesome and shy. I'm a ripe man and I've great love and yet, Deirdre, I'm the King of Ulster. [*He gets up.*] I'll call Fergus and we'll make Emain ready in the morning. [*He goes towards door on left.*]

DEIRDRE [*clinging to him*]. Do not call him, Conchubor. . . . Promise me a year of quiet. . . . It's one year I'm asking only.

CONCHUBOR. You'd be asking a year next year, and the years that follow. [*Calling.*] Fergus. . . Fergus. . . . [*To* DEIRDRE.] Young girls are slow always; it is their lovers that must say the word. [*Calling.*] Fergus!

[DEIRDRE *springs away from him as* FERGUS *comes in with* LAVARCHAM *and* OLD WOMAN.]

CONCHUBOR [*to* FERGUS]. There is a storm coming and we'd best be going to our people when the night is young.

FERGUS [*cheerfully*]. The gods shield you, Deirdre. [*To* CONCHUBOR.] We're late already, and it's no work the High King to be slipping on stepping stones, and hilly pathways when the floods are rising with the rain. [*He helps* CONCHUBOR *into his cloak.*]

CONCHUBOR [*glad that he has made his decision, to* LAVARCHAM]. Keep your rules a few days longer and you'll be brought down to Emain, you and Deirdre with you.

LAVARCHAM [*obediently*]. Your rules are kept always.

CONCHUBOR. The gods shield you.

[*He goes out with* FERGUS. OLD WOMAN *bolts the door.* DEIRDRE *covers her face.*]

LAVARCHAM [*looking at* DEIRDRE]. Wasn't I saying you'd do it? . . . You've brought your marriage a sight nearer not heeding those are wiser than yourself.

DEIRDRE [*with agitation*]. It wasn't I did it. Will you take me from this place, Lavarcham, and keep me safe in the hills?

LAVARCHAM. He'd have us tracked in the half of a day, and then you'd be his queen in spite of you, and I and mine would be destroyed forever.

DEIRDRE [*terrified with the reality that is before her*]. Are there none can go against Conchubor?

LAVARCHAM. Maeve of Connaught only, and those that are her like.

DEIRDRE. Would Fergus go against him?

LAVARCHAM. He would maybe and his temper roused.

DEIRDRE [*in a lower voice, with sudden excitement*]. Would Naisi and his brothers?

LAVARCHAM [*impatiently*]. Let you not be dwelling on Naisi and his brothers. . . . In the end of all there is none can go against Conchubor, and it's folly that we're talking, for if any went against

Conchubor it's sorrows he'd earn and the shortening of his day of life.

[*She turns away, and* DEIRDRE *stands up stiff with excitement, then goes to the window and looks out.*]

DEIRDRE. Are the stepping stones flooding, Lavarcham? Will the night be stormy in the hills?

LAVARCHAM [*looking at her curiously*]. The stepping stones are flooding surely, and the night will be the worst I'm thinking we've seen these years gone by.

DEIRDRE [*tearing open the press and pulling out clothes and tapestries*]. Lay these mats and hangings by the windows, and at the tables for our feet, and take out the skillets of silver, and the golden cups we have, and our two flasks of wine.

LAVARCHAM. What ails you?

DEIRDRE [*gathering up a dress*]. Lay them out quickly Lavarcham, we've no call dawdling this night. Lay them out quickly; I'm going into the room to put on the rich dresses and jewels have been sent from Emain.

LAVARCHAM. Putting on dresses at this hour and it dark and drenching with the weight of rain! Are you away in your head?

DEIRDRE [*gathering her things together with an outburst of excitement*]. I will dress like Emer in Dundealgan or Maeve in her house in Connaught. If Conchubor'll make me a queen I'll have the right of a queen who is a master, taking her own choice and making a stir to the edges of the seas. . . . Lay out your mats and hangings where I can stand this night and look about me. Lay out the skins of the rams of Connaught and of the goats of the west. I'll put on my robes that are the richest for I will not be brought down to Emain as Cuchulain brings his horse to its yoke, or Conall Cearneach puts his shield upon his arm. And maybe from this day I will turn the men of Ireland like a wind blowing on the heath.

[*She goes into inner room.* LAVARCHAM *and* OLD WOMAN *look at each other; then* OLD WOMAN *goes over, looks in at* DEIRDRE *through chink of the door, and then closes it carefully.*]

OLD WOMAN [*in a frightened whisper*]. She's thrown off the rags she had about her, and there she is in her skin putting her hair in shiny twists. Is she raving Lavarcham, or has she a good right turning to a queen like Maeve?

LAVARCHAM [*putting up hangings, very anxiously*]. It's more than raving's in her mind, or I'm the more astray, and yet she's as good a right as another, maybe, having her pleasure though she'd spoil the world.

OLD WOMAN [*helping her*]. Be quick before she'll come back. . . . Who'd have thought we'd run before her and she so quiet till tonight. Will the High King get the better of her, Lavarcham? If I was Conchubor I wouldn't marry with her like at all.

LAVARCHAM. Hang that by the window. That should please her surely. . . . When all's said it's her like will be the master till the ends of time.

OLD WOMAN [*at the window*]. There's a mountain of blackness in the sky, and the greatest rain falling has been these long years on the earth. The gods help Conchubor, he'll be a sorry man this night reaching his Dun, and he with all his spirits, thinking to himself he'll be putting his arms around her in two days or three.

LAVARCHAM. It's more than Conchubor'll be sick and sorry, I'm thinking, before this story is told to the end.

[*Loud knocking on door at right.*]

LAVARCHAM [*startled*]. Who is that?

NAISI [*outside*]. Naisi and his brothers.

LAVARCHAM. We are lonely women. What is it you're wanting in the blackness of the night?

NAISI. We met a young girl in the woods who told us we might shelter this place if the rivers rose on the pathways and the floods gathered from the butt of the hills.

[OLD WOMAN *clasps her hands in horror.*]

LAVARCHAM [*with great alarm*]. You cannot come in. . . . There is no one let in here, and no young girl with us.

NAISI. Let us in from the great storm. Let us in and we will go further when the cloud will rise.

LAVARCHAM. Go round east to the shed and you'll have shelter. You cannot come in.

NAISI [*knocking loudly*]. Open the door, or we will burst it.

[*The door is shaken.*]

OLD WOMAN [*in a timid whisper*]. Let them in, and keep Deirdre in her room tonight.

AINNLE AND ARDAN [*outside*]. Open. . . . Open. . . .

LAVARCHAM [*to* OLD WOMAN]. Go in and keep her.

OLD WOMAN. I couldn't keep her. I've no hold on her. . . . Go in yourself and I will free the door.

LAVARCHAM. I must stay and turn them out. [*She pulls her hair and cloak over her face.*] Go in and keep her.

OLD WOMAN. The gods help us. [*She runs into inner room.*]

VOICES. Open!

LAVARCHAM [*opening the door*]. Come in then, and ill luck if you'll have it so.

[NAISI *and* AINNLE *and* ARDAN *come in, and look around with astonishment.*]

NAISI. It's a rich man has this place and no herd at all.

LAVARCHAM [*sitting down with her head half-covered*]. It is not, and you'd do best going quickly.

NAISI [*hilariously, shaking rain from his clothes*]. When we've the pick of luck finding princely comfort in the darkness of the night? Some rich man of Ulster should come here and he chasing in the woods. May we drink? [*He takes up flask.*] Whose wine is this that we may drink his health?

LAVARCHAM. It's no one's that you've call to know.

NAISI [*pouring out wine for the three*]. Your own health then and length of life. [*They drink.*]

LAVARCHAM [*very crossly*]. You're great boys taking a welcome
where it isn't given, and asking questions where you've no call to.
. . . If you'd a quiet place settled up to be playing yourself maybe
with a gentle queen, what'd you think of young men prying around
and carrying tales? When I was a bit of a girl, the big men of Ulster
had better manners and they the like of your three selves in the top
folly of youth. That'll be a great story to tell out in Tara that Naisi
is a tippler and stealer, and Ainnle the drawer of a stranger's cork.

NAISI [*quite cheerfully, sitting down beside her*]. At your age you should
know there are nights when a king like Conchubor would spit upon
his arm ring and queens will stick their tongues out at the rising
moon. We're that way this night, and it's not wine we're asking
only. . . . Where is the young girl told us we might shelter here?

LAVARCHAM. Asking me you'd be? . . . We're decent people, and I
wouldn't put you tracking a young girl, not if you gave me the gold
clasp you have, hanging on your coat.

NAISI [*giving it to her*]. Where is she?

LAVARCHAM [*in a confidential whisper, putting her hand on his arm*]. Let
you walk back into the hills, and turn up by the second cnuceen
where there are three together. You'll see a path running on the
rocks and you'll hear the dogs barking in the houses and their noise
will guide you till you come to a bit of cabin at the foot of an ash-
tree. It's there there is a young and flighty girl that I'm thinking is
the one you've seen.

NAISI [*hilariously*]. Here's health then to herself and you!

ARDAN. Here's to the years when you were young as she!

AINNLE [*in a frightened whisper*]. Naisi. . . .

[NAISI *looks up and* AINNLE *beckons to him. He goes over and*
AINNLE *points to something on the golden mug he holds in his hand.*]

NAISI [*looking at it in astonishment*]. This is the High King's. . . . I see
his mark on the rim. Does Conchubor come lodging here?

LAVARCHAM [*jumping up with extreme annoyance*]. Who says it's
Conchubor's? How dare young fools the like of you [*speaking with
vehement insolence*] come prying around, running the world into
troubles for some slip of a girl? What brings you this place straying

from Emain? [*Very bitterly.*] Though you think maybe young men
can do their fill of foolery and there is none to blame them.

NAISI [*very soberly*]. Is the rain easing?

ARDAN. The clouds are breaking. . . . I can see Orion in the gap of the
glen.

NAISI [*still cheerfully*]. Open the door and we'll go forward to the little
cabin between the ash-tree and the rocks. Lift the bolt and pull it.

[DEIRDRE *comes in on left royally dressed and very beautiful. She stands
for a moment, and then as the door opens she calls softly.*]

DEIRDRE. Naisi. . . . Do not leave me, Naisi, I am Deirdre of the
Sorrows.

NAISI [*transfixed with amazement*]. And it is you who go around in the
woods, making the thrushes bear a grudge against the heavens for
the sweetness of your voice?

DEIRDRE. It is with me you've spoken surely. [*To* LAVARCHAM *and*
OLD WOMAN.] Take Ainnle and Ardan, these two princes, into
the little hut where we eat, and serve them with what is best and
sweetest. I have many things for Naisi only.

LAVARCHAM [*overawed by her tone*]. I will do it, and I ask their pardon
I have fooled them here.

DEIRDRE [*to* AINNLE *and* ARDAN]. Do not take it badly, that I am
asking you to walk into our hut for a little. You will have a supper
that is cooked by the cook of Conchubor, and Lavarcham will tell
you stories of Maeve and Nessa and Rogh.

AINNLE. We'll ask Lavarcham to tell us stories of yourself, and with
that we'll be well pleased to be doing your wish.

[*They all go out except* DEIRDRE *and* NAISI.]

DEIRDRE [*sitting in the high chair in the centre for the first time*]. Come to
this stool, Naisi. [*Pointing to the stool.*] If it's low itself the High King
would sooner be on it this night, than on the throne of Emain
Macha.

NAISI [*sitting down*]. You are Fedlimid's daughter that Conchubor has
walled up from all the men of Ulster?

DEIRDRE. Do many know what is foretold, that Deirdre will be the ruin of the Sons of Usna, and have a little grave by herself, and a story will be told forever?

NAISI. It's a long while men have been talking of Deirdre the child who had all gifts, and the beauty that has no equal. Many know it, and there are kings would give a great price to be in my place this night, and you grown to a queen.

DEIRDRE. It isn't many I'd call, Naisi. . . . I was in the woods at the full moon and I heard a voice singing. Then I gathered up my skirts, and I ran on a little path I have to the verge of a rock, and I saw you pass by underneath, in your crimson cloak, singing a song, and you standing out beyond your brothers are called the flower of Ireland.

NAISI [*in a low voice*]. It's for that you called us in the dusk?

DEIRDRE [*in a low voice also*]. Since that, Naisi, I have been one time the like of a ewe looking for a lamb that had been taken away from her, and one time seeing new gold on the stars and a new face on the moon, and all times dreading Emain.

NAISI [*pulling himself together and beginning to draw back a little*]. Yet it should be a lonesome thing to be in this place and you born for great company.

DEIRDRE [*softly*]. This night I have the best company in the whole world.

NAISI [*still a little formally*]. It's yourself is your best company, for when you're queen in Emain you will have none to be your match or fellow.

DEIRDRE. I will not be queen in Emain.

NAISI. Conchubor has made an oath you will surely.

DEIRDRE. It's for that maybe I'm called Deirdre, the girl of many sorrows [*she looks up at him*] . . . for it's a sweet life you and I could have Naisi. . . . It should be a sweet thing to have what is best and richest if it's for a short space only.

NAISI [*very distressed*]. And we've a short space only to be triumphant and brave.

DEIRDRE. You must not go Naisi, and leave me to the High King, a man is ageing in his Dun, with his crowds round him and his silver and gold. [*More quickly.*] I will not live to be shut up in Emain, and wouldn't we do well paying, Naisi, with silence, and a near death? [*She stands up and walks away from him.*] I'm a long while in the woods with my own self, and I'm in little dread of death, and it earned with richness would make the sun red with envy and he going up the heavens, and the moon pale and lonesome and she wasting away. [*She comes to him and puts her hands on his shoulders.*] Isn't it a small thing is foretold about the ruin of ourselves, Naisi, when all men have age coming and great ruin in the end?

NAISI. Yet it's a poor thing it's I should bring you to a tale of blood, and broken bodies and the filth of the grave. . . . Wouldn't we do well to wait, Deirdre, and I each twilight meeting you on the side of the hills?

DEIRDRE. Messengers are coming tomorrow morning or the next morning to bring me down to Conchubor to be his mate in Emain.

NAISI. Messengers are coming?

DEIRDRE. Tomorrow morning or the next surely.

NAISI. Then it isn't I will give your like to Conchubor, not if the grave was dug to be my lodging when a week was by. [*He looks out.*] The stars are out Deirdre, and let you come with me quickly, for it is the stars will be our lamps many nights and we abroad in Alban, and taking our journeys among the little islands in the sea. There has never been the like of the joy we'll have Deirdre, you and I having our fill of love at the evening and the morning till the sun is high.

DEIRDRE [*sinking on his shoulder, a little shaken by what has passed*]. And yet I'm in dread leaving this place where I have lived always. Won't I be lonesome and I thinking on the little hill beyond and the apple trees do be budding in the springtime by the post of the door? . . . Won't I be in great dread to bring you to destruction, Naisi, and you so happy and young?

NAISI. Are you thinking I'd go on living after this night, Deirdre, and you with Conchubor in Emain? Are you thinking I'd go out after hares on the hillside when I've had your lips in my sight?

[LAVARCHAM *comes in as they cling to each other.*]

LAVARCHAM. Are you raving, Deirdre? . . . Are you choosing this night to destroy the world?

DEIRDRE [*very deliberately, letting go of* NAISI *slowly*]. It's Conchubor has chosen this night, calling me to Emain. [*To* NAISI.] Bring in Ainnle and Ardan, and take me from this place where I'm in dread from this out of the footstep of a hare passing.

[NAISI *goes.*]

DEIRDRE [*clinging to* LAVARCHAM]. Do not take it bad I'm going, Lavarcham. It's you have been a good friend and given me great freedom and joy, and I living on Slieve Fuadh, and maybe you'll be well pleased one day, saying you have nursed Deirdre.

LAVARCHAM [*moved*]. It isn't I'll be well pleased and I far away from you. Isn't it a hard thing you're doing, but who can help it? Birds go mating in the spring of the year, and ewes at the leaves falling, but a young girl must have her lover in all the courses of the sun and moon.

DEIRDRE. Will you go to Emain in the morning?

LAVARCHAM. I will not, I'll go to Brandon in the south, and in the course of a piece maybe I'll be sailing back and forward on the seas to be looking on your face, and the little ways you have that none can equal.

[NAISI *comes back with* AINNLE *and* ARDAN *and* OLD WOMAN.]

DEIRDRE [*taking* NAISI'*s hand*]. My two brothers, I am going with Naisi to Alban and the north, to face the troubles are foretold. Will you take word to Conchubor in Emain?

AINNLE. We will go with you.

ARDAN. We will be your servants and your huntsmen, Deirdre.

DEIRDRE. It isn't one brother only of you three, is brave and courteous. . . . Will you wed us Lavarcham, you have the words and customs?

LAVARCHAM. I will not then. . . . What would I want meddling in the ruin you will earn?

NAISI. Let Ainnle wed us. . . . He has been with wise men and he knows their ways.

AINNLE [*joining their hands*]. By the sun and moon and the whole earth, I wed Deirdre to Naisi. [*He steps back and holds up his hands.*] May the air bless you, and water and the wind, the sea, and all the hours of the sun and moon.

CURTAIN

ACT II

Alban, early morning in the beginning of winter. A wood, outside the tent of DEIRDRE *and* NAISI. LAVARCHAM *comes in, muffled in a cloak.*

LAVARCHAM [*calling*]. Deirdre. . . Deirdre. . . .

DEIRDRE [*coming from tent, radiant and mature*]. My welcome, Lavarcham. . . . Whose curagh is rowing from Ulster? I saw the oars through the tops of the trees, and I thought it was you were coming towards us.

LAVARCHAM. I came in the shower was before the dawn.

DEIRDRE. And who is coming?

LAVARCHAM [*mournfully*]. Let you not be startled or taking it bad, Deirdre. It's Fergus bringing messages of peace from Conchubor to take Naisi and his brothers back to Emain. [*Sitting down.*]

DEIRDRE [*lightly*]. Naisi and his brothers are well pleased this place and what would take them back to Conchubor in Ulster?

LAVARCHAM. Their like would go any place where they'd see death standing. [*With more agitation.*] I'm in dread Conchubor wants to have yourself, and to kill Naisi, and that that'll be the ruin of the Sons of Usna. I'm silly maybe to be dreading the like, but those have a great love for yourself have a right to be in dread always.

DEIRDRE [*more anxiously*]. Emain should be no safe place for myself and Naisi, and isn't it a hard thing, they'll leave us no peace Lavarcham, and we so quiet in the woods?

LAVARCHAM [*impressively*]. It's a hard thing surely, but let you take my word and swear Naisi by the earth, and the sun over it, and the four quarters of the moon he'll not go back to Emain for good faith, or bad faith, the time Conchubor's keeping the high throne of Ireland. . . . It's that would save you surely.

DEIRDRE [*without hope*]. There's little power in oaths to stop what's coming, and little power in what I'd do Lavarcham, to change the story of Conchubor and Naisi and the things old men foretold.

LAVARCHAM [*aggressively*]. Was there little power in what you did the night you dressed in your finery and ran Naisi off along with you, in spite of Conchubor, and the big nobles did dread the blackness of your luck? It was power enough you had that night to bring distress and anguish, and now I'm pointing you a way to save Naisi, you'll not stir stick or straw to aid me.

DEIRDRE [*a little haughtily*]. Let you not raise your voice against me Lavarcham, if you have great will itself to guard Naisi.

LAVARCHAM [*breaking out in anger*]. Naisi is it? I didn't care if the crows were stripping his thigh-bones at the dawn of day. It's to stop your own despair and wailing, and you waking up in a cold bed, without the man you have your heart on, I am raging now. [*Starting up with temper.*] Yet there's more men than Naisi in it, and maybe I was a big fool thinking his dangers, and this day, would fill you up with dread.

DEIRDRE [*sharply*]. Let you end such talking is a fool's only, when it's well you know if a thing harmed Naisi it isn't I would live after him. [*With distress.*] It's well you know it's this day I'm dreading seven years, and I, fine nights, watching the heifers walking to the haggard with long shadows on the grass [*with a thickening in her voice*], or the time I've been stretched in the sunshine when I've heard Ainnle and Ardan stepping lightly, and they saying, 'Was there ever the like of Deirdre for a happy and a sleepy queen?'

LAVARCHAM [*not fully pacified*]. And yet you'll go and welcome is it, if Naisi chooses?

DEIRDRE. I've dread going or staying, Lavarcham. It's lonesome this place having happiness like ours till I'm asking each day, will this day match yesterday, and will tomorrow take a good place beside the same day in the year that's gone, and wondering all times is it a game worth playing, living on until you're dried and old, and our joy is gone forever.

LAVARCHAM. If it's that ails you, I tell you there's little hurt getting old, though young girls and poets do be storming at the shapes of age. [*Passionately.*] There's little hurt getting old, saving when you're looking back, the way I'm looking this day, and seeing the young you have a love for breaking up their hearts with folly. [*Going to* DEIRDRE, *making a last attempt.*] Take my word and stop Naisi, and

the day'll come you'll have more joy having the senses of an old
woman and you with your little grandsons shrieking round you,
than I'd have this night putting on the red mouth, and the white
arms you have, to go walking lonesome byeways with a gamey king.

DEIRDRE. It's little joy of a young woman or an old woman I'll have
from this day surely. But what use is in our talking when there's
Naisi on the foreshore, and Fergus with him.

LAVARCHAM [*getting up despairingly*]. I'm late so with my warnings,
for Fergus'd talk the moon over to take a new path in the sky. [*With
reproach.*] You'll not stop him this day, and isn't it a strange story
you were a plague and torment since you were that height to those
did hang their life-times on your voice. . . . [*Overcome with trouble,
gathering her cloak about her.*] Don't think bad of my crying. I'm not
the like of many and I'd see a score of naked corpses and not heed
them at all, but I'm destroyed seeing yourself in your hour of joy,
when the end is coming surely.

[OWEN *comes in quickly, rather ragged, bows to* DEIRDRE.]

OWEN [*to* LAVARCHAM]. Fergus's men are calling you. You were seen
on the path and he and Naisi want you for their talk below.

LAVARCHAM [*looking at him with dislike*]. Yourself's an ill-lucky thing
to meet a morning is the like of this. Yet if you are a spy itself I'll go
and give my word that's wanting surely. [*She goes out slowly.*]

OWEN [*to* DEIRDRE]. So I've found you alone, and I after waiting three
weeks getting ague and asthma in the chill of the bogs, till I saw
Naisi caught with Fergus.

DEIRDRE. I've heard news of Fergus, what brought you from Ulster?

OWEN [*who has been searching, finds a loaf and sits down eating greedily*].
The full moon I'm thinking and it squeezing the crack in my skull.
Was there ever a man crossed nine waves after a fool's wife and he
not away in his head?

DEIRDRE [*absently*]. It should be a long time since you left Emain,
where there's civility in speech with queens.

OWEN. It's a long while surely. It's three weeks I am losing my manners beside the Saxon bull-frogs at the head of the bog. Three weeks

is a long space, and yet you're seven years spancelled with Naisi and the pair!

DEIRDRE [*beginning to fold up her jewels*]. Three weeks of your days might be long surely; yet seven years are a short space for the like of Naisi and myself.

OWEN [*derisively*]. If they're a short space there aren't many the like of you. Wasn't there a queen in Tara had to walk out every morning till she'd meet a stranger and see the flame of courtship leaping up within his eye? Tell me now [*leaning towards her*], . . . are you well pleased that length with the same man snorting next you at the dawn of day?

DEIRDRE [*very quietly*]. Am I well pleased seven years seeing the same sun throwing light across the branches at the dawn of day? [*With abstracted feeling.*] It's a heart-break to the wise that it's for a short space we have the same things only. [*With contempt.*] Yet the earth itself is a silly place maybe, when a man's a fool and talker.

OWEN [*sharply*]. Well go take your choice. Stay here and rot with Naisi, or go to Conchubor in Emain. Conchubor's a swelling belly, and eyes falling down from his shining crown, Naisi should be stale and weary; yet there are many roads, Deirdre [*he goes towards her*], and I tell you I'd liefer be bleaching in a bog-hole than living on without a touch of kindness from your eyes and voice. It's a poor thing to be so lonesome you'd squeeze kisses on a cur dog's nose.

DEIRDRE. Are there no women like yourself could be your friends in Emain?

OWEN [*vehemently*]. There are none like you, Deirdre. It's for that I'm asking are you going back this night with Fergus?

DEIRDRE. I will go where Naisi chooses.

OWEN [*with a burst of rage*]. It's Naisi, Naisi is it? Then I tell you you'll have great sport one day seeing Naisi getting a harshness in his two sheep's eyes and he looking on yourself. Would you credit it, my father used to be in the broom and heather kissing Lavarcham, with a little bird chirping out above their heads, and now she'd scare a raven from a carcass on a hill. [*With a sad cry that brings dignity into his voice.*] Queens get old Deirdre, with their white and long arms

going from them, and their backs hooping. I tell you it's a poor thing
to see a queen's nose reaching down to scrape her chin.

DEIRDRE [*looking out, a little uneasy at his tone*]. Naisi and Fergus are
coming on the path.

OWEN. I'll go so . . . for if I had you seven years I'd be jealous of the
midges and the dust is in the air. [*With a sort of warning in his voice,
muffling himself in his cloak.*] I'll give you a riddle, Deirdre. Why isn't
my father as ugly and as old as Conchubor? You've no answer? . . .
It's because Naisi killed him. [*With a curious expression.*] Think of
that and you awake at night hearing Naisi snoring, or the night
you'll hear strange stories of the things I've done in Alban or in
Ulster either.

   [*He goes out, and in a moment* NAISI *and* FERGUS *come in on the other
   side.*]

NAISI [*gaily*]. Fergus has brought messages of peace from Conchubor!

DEIRDRE [*greeting* FERGUS]. He is welcome. Let you rest Fergus, you
should be hot and thirsty after mounting the rocks.

FERGUS. It's a sunny nook you've found in Alban, yet any man would
be well pleased mounting higher rocks, to fetch yourself and Naisi
back to Emain.

DEIRDRE [*with keenness*]. They've answered? They would go?

FERGUS [*benignly*]. They have not [DEIRDRE *begins to net*], but when
I was a young man we'd have given a lifetime to be in Ireland a
score of weeks, and to this day the old men have nothing so heavy
as knowing it's in a short while they'll lose the high skies are over
Ireland, and the lonesome mornings with birds crying on the bogs.
Let you come this day for there's no place but Ireland where the Gael
can have peace always.

NAISI [*gruffly*]. It's true surely. Yet we're better this place while Conchubor's in Emain Macha.

FERGUS [*giving him parchments*]. These are your sureties with Conchubor's seal. [*To* DEIRDRE, *who stops netting during his speech.*] You'll
not be young always, and it's time you were making yourselves
ready for the years will come, building up a homely Dun beside the
seas of Ireland, and getting in your children from the princes'

wives. It's little joy wandering till age is on you and your youth is gone away, so you'd best come this night, for you'd have great pleasure putting out your foot and saying 'I am in Ireland surely'.

DEIRDRE. It isn't pleasure I'd have while Conchubor is king in Emain.

FERGUS [*almost annoyed*]. Would you doubt the seals of Conall Cearneach and the kings of Meath? [*More gently.*] It's easy being fearful and you alone in the woods yet it would be a poor thing if a timid woman [*taunting her a little*] could turn away the Sons of Usna from the life of kings. Let you be thinking on the years to come, Deirdre, and the way you'd have a right to see Naisi a high and white-haired Justice beside some king of Emain. Wouldn't it be a poor story if a queen the like of you should have no thought but to be scraping up her hours dallying in the sunshine with the sons of kings?

DEIRDRE [*turning away a little haughtily*]. I leave the choice to Naisi. [*Turning back towards* FERGUS.] Yet you'd do well Fergus to go on your own way, for the sake of your own years, so you'll not be saying till your hour of death, maybe it was yourself brought Naisi and his brothers to a grave was scooped by treachery. [*She goes into tent.*]

FERGUS. It's a poor thing to see a queen so lonesome and afraid. [*He watches till he is sure* DEIRDRE *cannot hear him.*] Listen now to what I'm saying. You'd do well to come back to men and women are your match and comrades, and not be lingering until the day that you'll grow weary, and hurt Deirdre showing her the hardness in your eyes. . . . You've been here years and plenty to know it's truth I'm saying.

[DEIRDRE *comes out of tent with a horn of wine. She catches the beginning of* NAISI'*s speech and stops with stony wonder.*]

NAISI [*very thoughtfully*]. I'll not tell you a lie. There have been days a while past when I've been throwing a line for salmon, or watching for the run of hares, that I've had a dread upon me a day'd come I'd weary of her voice [*very slowly*] . . . and Deirdre'd see I'd wearied.

FERGUS [*sympathetic but triumphant*]. I knew it, Naisi. . . . And take my word Deirdre's seen your dread and she'll have no peace from this out in the woods.

NAISI [*with confidence*]. She's not seen it. . . . Deirdre's no thought of getting old or wearied, it's that puts wonder in her ways, and she with spirits would keep bravery and laughter in a town with plague.

[DEIRDRE *drops the horn of wine and crouches down where she is.*]

FERGUS. That humour'll leave her. But we've no call going too far, with one word borrowing another. Will you come this night to Emain Macha?

NAISI. I'll not go, Fergus. I've had dreams of getting old and weary, and losing my delight in Deirdre, but my dreams were dreams only. What are Conchubor's seal and all your talk of Emain and the fools of Meath beside one evening in Glen Masain? We'll stay this place till our lives and time are worn out. It's that word you may take in your curagh to Conchubor in Emain.

FERGUS [*gathering up his parchments*]. And you won't go surely?

NAISI [*gaily*]. I will not. . . . I've had dread, I tell you, dread winter and summer, and the autumn and the spring-time, even when there's a bird in every bush making his own stir till the fall of night. But this talk's brought me ease, and I see we're as happy as the leaves on the young trees and we'll be so ever and always though we'd live the age of the eagle and the salmon and the crow of Britain.

FERGUS [*very much annoyed*]. Where are your brothers? My message is for them also.

NAISI. You'll see them above chasing otters by the stream.

FERGUS [*bitterly*]. It isn't much I was mistaken, thinking you were hunters only.

[*He goes.* NAISI *turns towards tent, and sees* DEIRDRE *crouching down with her cloak round her face.* DEIRDRE *comes out.*]

NAISI. You've heard my words to Fergus? [*She does not answer. A pause. He puts his arm round her.*] Leave troubling, and we'll go this night to Glen da Ruadh where the salmon will be running with the tide.

[DEIRDRE *crosses and sits down.*]

DEIRDRE [*in a very low voice*]. With the tide in a little while we will be journeying again, or it is our own blood maybe will be running away. [*She turns and clings to him.*] The dawn and evening are a little while, the winter and the summer pass quickly, and what way would you and I Naisi, have joy forever?

NAISI. We'll have the joy is highest till our age is come, for it isn't Fergus's talk of great deeds could take us back to Emain.

DEIRDRE. It isn't to great deeds you're going but to near troubles, and the shortening of your days the time that they are bright and sunny and isn't it a poor thing that I, Deirdre, could not hold you away?

NAISI. I've said we'd stay in Alban always?

DEIRDRE. There's no place to stay always. . . . It's a long time we've had, pressing the lips together, going up and down, resting in our arms, Naisi, waking with the smell of June in the tops of the grasses, and listening to the birds in the branches that are highest. . . . It's a long time we've had, but the end has come surely.

NAISI. Would you have us go to Emain, though if any ask the reason we do not know it, and we journeying as the thrushes come from the north, or young birds fly out on a dark sea?

DEIRDRE. There's reason all times for an end that's come. . . . And I'm well pleased, Naisi, we're going forward in the winter the time the sun has a low place, and the moon has her mastery in a dark sky, for it's you and I are well lodged our last day, where there is a light behind the clear trees, and the berries on the thorns are a red wall.

NAISI [*with a new rush of love, eagerly*]. If our time this place is ended, come away without Ainnle and Ardan to the woods of the East, for it's right to be away from all people when two lovers have their love only. Come away and we'll be safe always.

DEIRDRE [*broken-hearted*]. There's no safe place, Naisi, on the ridge of the world. . . . And it's in the quiet woods I've seen them digging our grave, throwing out the clay on leaves are bright and withered.

NAISI [*still more eagerly*]. Come away, Deirdre, and it's little we'll think of safety or the grave beyond it, and we resting in a little corner between the daytime and the long night.

DEIRDRE [*clearly and gravely*]. It's this hour we're between the daytime and a night where there is sleep forever, and isn't it a better thing to be following on to a near death, than to be bending the head down, and dragging with the feet, and seeing one day, a blight showing upon love where it is sweet and tender?

NAISI [*his voice broken with distraction*]. If a near death is coming what will be my trouble losing the earth and the stars over it, and you Deirdre are their flame and bright crown? Come away into the safety of the woods.

DEIRDRE [*shaking her head slowly*]. There are as many ways to wither love as there are stars in a night of Samhain, but there is no way to keep life or love with it a short space only. . . . It's for that there's nothing lonesome like a love is watching out the time most lovers do be sleeping. . . . It's for that we're setting out for Emain Macha when the tide turns on the sand.

NAISI [*giving in*]. You're right maybe. . . . It should be a poor thing to see great lovers and they sleepy and old.

DEIRDRE [*with a more tender intensity*]. We're seven years without roughness or growing weary, seven years so sweet and shining, the gods would be hard set to give us seven days the like of them. . . . It's for that we're going to Emain where there'll be a rest forever, or a place for forgetting, in great crowds and they making a stir.

NAISI [*very softly*]. We'll go surely, in place of keeping a watch on a love had no match and it wasting away.

[*They cling to each other for a moment, then* DEIRDRE *stands up slowly, and goes into the tent with her head bowed down without looking at* NAISI. NAISI *sits with his head bowed.* OWEN *runs in stealthily, comes behind* NAISI *and seizes him round the arms;* NAISI *shakes him off and whips out his sword.*]

OWEN [*screaming with derisive laughter and showing his empty hands*]. Ah Naisi, wasn't it well I didn't kill you that time! There was a fright you got. I've been watching Fergus above—don't be frightened—and I've come down to see him getting the cold shoulder and going off alone. . . . There he is.

[*Voices are heard on the right, and* AINNLE, ARDAN, FERGUS *and* LAVARCHAM *come in. They are all subdued like men at a queen's wake.*]

NAISI [*goes to* FERGUS, *putting up his sword*]. We are going back when the tide turns, I and Deirdre with yourself.

ALL. Going back?

FERGUS. You've a choice wise men will be glad of in the five ends of Ireland.

OWEN. Wise men is it and they going back to Conchubor? I could stop them only Naisi put in his sword among my father's ribs and when a man's done that he'll not credit your oath. Going to Conchubor! I could tell of plots and tricks and spies were well paid for their play. [*He throws up a bag of gold.*] Are you paid, Fergus? [*He scatters gold pieces over* FERGUS.]

FERGUS. He is raving. . . . Seize him. . . .

OWEN [*flying between them*]. You won't. Let the lot of you be off to Emain but I'll be off before you. . . . Dead men, dead men, men who'll die for Deirdre's beauty, I'll be before you in the grave!

[OWEN *runs out with his knife in his hand. They all run after him except* LAVARCHAM, *who looks out and then clasps her hands.* DEIRDRE *comes out to her in a dark cloak.*]

DEIRDRE. What has happened?

LAVARCHAM. It's Owen gone raging mad and he's after splitting his gullet beyond at the butt of the stone. There was ill luck this day in his eye. And he knew a power if he'd said it all.

[NAISI *comes back followed by the others.*]

AINNLE [*coming in very excited*]. That man knew plots of Conchubor's. . . . We'll not go to Emain where Conchubor may love her and has hatred for yourself.

FERGUS. Would you mind a fool and raver?

AINNLE. It's many times there's more sense in madmen than the wise. We will not obey Conchubor.

NAISI. I and Deirdre have chosen, we will go back with Fergus.

ARDAN. We will not go back. . . . We will burn your curaghs by the sea.

FERGUS. My sons and I will guard them.

AINNLE. We will blow the horn of Usna and our friends will come to aid us.

NAISI. It is my friends will come.

AINNLE. Your friends will bind your hands and you out of your wits.

[DEIRDRE *comes forward quickly and comes between* AINNLE *and* NAISI.]

DEIRDRE [*in a low voice*]. For seven years the Sons of Usna have not raised their voices in a quarrel.

AINNLE. We will not take you to Emain.

ARDAN. It is Conchubor has broken our peace.

AINNLE. Stop Naisi going. What way would we live if Conchubor should take you from us?

DEIRDRE [*winningly putting her hands on his shoulders*]. There is no one could take me from you. . . . I have chosen to go back with Fergus. Will you quarrel with me Ainnle, though I have been your queen these seven years in Alban?

AINNLE [*subsiding suddenly*]. Naisi has no call to take you.

ARDAN. Why are you going?

DEIRDRE [*to both of them and the others*]. It is my wish. . . . It may be I will not have Naisi growing an old man in Alban with an old woman at his side, and young girls pointing out and saying 'that is Deirdre and Naisi, had great beauty in their youth'. . . . It may be we do well putting a sharp end to the day is brave and glorious, as our fathers put a sharp end to the days of the kings of Ireland, . . . or that I'm wishing to set my foot on Slieve Fuadh where I was running one time and leaping the streams [*to* LAVARCHAM], and that I'd be well pleased to see our little apple-trees Lavarcham, behind our cabin on the hill, or that I've learned Fergus, it's a lonesome thing to be away from Ireland always.

AINNLE [*giving in*]. There is no place but will be lonesome to us from this out and we thinking on our seven years in Alban.

DEIRDRE. It's in this place we'd be lonesome in the end. . . . [*To* NAISI.] Take down Fergus to the sea. . . . He has been a guest and a hard welcome and he bringing messages of peace.

FERGUS. We will make your curagh ready and it fitted for the voyage of a king. [*He goes with* NAISI.]

DEIRDRE. Take your spears Ainnle and Ardan, and go down before me, and take your horse-boys to be carrying my cloaks are on the threshold.

AINNLE [*obeying*]. It's with a poor heart we'll carry your things this day, we have carried merrily so often and we hungry and cold.

[*They gather up things and go out.*]

DEIRDRE [*to* LAVARCHAM]. Go you too, Lavarcham. You are old and I will follow quickly.

LAVARCHAM. I'm old surely, and the hopes I had my pride in, are broken and torn. [*She goes out, with a look of awe at* DEIRDRE.]

DEIRDRE [*clasping her hands*]. Woods of Cuan, woods of Cuan. . . . It's seven years we've had a life was joy only and this day we're going west, this day we're facing death maybe, and [*goes and looks towards* OWEN] death should be a poor untidy thing, though it's a queen that dies. [*She goes out slowly.*]

CURTAIN

ACT III

Tent below Emain, with shabby skins and benches. There is an opening at each side and at back, the latter closed. OLD WOMAN *comes in with food and fruits and arranges them on table.* CONCHUBOR *comes in on right.*

CONCHUBOR [*sharply*]. Has no one come with news for me?

OLD WOMAN. I've seen no one at all, Conchubor.

CONCHUBOR [*watches her working for a moment, then makes sure opening at back is closed*]. Go up then to Emain, you're not wanting here. [*A noise is heard left.*] Who is that?

OLD WOMAN [*going left*]. It's Lavarcham coming again. . . . She's a great wonder for jogging back and forward through the world and I made certain she'd be off to meet them, but she's coming alone, Conchubor, my dear child Deirdre isn't with her at all.

CONCHUBOR. Go up so and leave us.

OLD WOMAN [*pleadingly*]. I'd be well pleased to set my eyes on Deirdre if she's coming this night, as we're told.

CONCHUBOR [*impatiently*]. It's not long till you'll see her. But I've matters with Lavarcham and let you go on now I'm saying.

[*He shows her out right, as* LAVARCHAM *comes in on the left.*]

LAVARCHAM [*looking round her, with suspicion*]. This is a queer place to find you, and it's a queer place to be lodging Naisi and his brothers, and Deirdre with them, and the lot of us tired out with the long way we have been walking.

CONCHUBOR. You've come along with them the whole journey?

LAVARCHAM. I have then, though I've no call now to be wandering that length to a wedding or a burial or the two together. [*She sits down wearily.*] . . . It's a poor thing the way me and you is getting old, Conchubor, and I'm thinking you yourself have no call to be loitering this place getting your death, maybe, in the cold of night.

CONCHUBOR. I'm waiting only to know is Fergus stopped in the north.

LAVARCHAM [*more sharply*]. He's stopped surely, and that's a trick has me thinking you have it in mind to bring trouble this night on Emain and Ireland and the big world's east beyond them. [*She goes to him.*] . . . And yet you'd do well to be going to your Dun, and not putting shame on her meeting the High King, and she seamed and sweaty, and in great disorder from the dust of many roads. [*Laughing derisively.*] Ah, Conchubor, my lad, beauty goes quickly in the woods, and you'd let a great gasp, I tell you, if you set your eyes this night on Deirdre.

CONCHUBOR [*fiercely*]. It's little I care if she's white and worn, for it's I did rear her from a child should have a good right to meet and see her always.

LAVARCHAM [*put back*]. A good right is it? Haven't the blind a good right to be seeing and the lame to be dancing, and the dummies singing tunes? It's that right you have to be looking for gaiety on Deirdre's lips. [*Coaxingly.*] Come on to your Dun, I'm saying, and leave her quiet for one night itself.

CONCHUBOR [*with sudden anger*]. I'll not go, when it's long enough I am above in my Dun stretching east and west without a comrade, and I more needy maybe than the thieves of Meath. . . . You think I'm old and wise, but I tell you the wise know the old must die, and they'll leave no chance for a thing slipping from them, they've set their blood to win.

LAVARCHAM [*nodding her head*]. If you're old and wise, it's I'm the same, Conchubor, and I'm telling you, you'll *not* have her though you're ready to destroy mankind, and skin the gods to win her. . . . There's things a king can't have, Conchubor, and if you go rampaging this night you'll be apt to win nothing but death for many, and a sloppy face of trouble on your own self before the day will come.

CONCHUBOR. It's too much talk you have. [*Goes right, anxiously.*] Where is Owen, did you see him no place and you coming the road?

LAVARCHAM [*stiffly*]. I seen him surely. . . . He went spying on Naisi, and now the worms is spying on his own inside.

CONCHUBOR [*exultingly*]. Naisi killed him?

LAVARCHAM. He did not then. . . . It was Owen destroyed himself, running mad because of Deirdre. . . . Fools and kings and scholars are all one in a story with her like, and Owen thought he'd be a great man, being the first corpse in the game you'll play this night in Emain.

CONCHUBOR [*turning to her with excitement*]. It's yourself should be the first corpse, but my other messengers are coming, men from the clans that hated Usna.

LAVARCHAM [*drawing back hopelessly*]. Then the gods have pity on us all.

[MEN *come in with weapons.*]

CONCHUBOR. Are Ainnle and Ardan separate from Naisi?

MEN. They are, Conchubor. We've got them off, saying they were needed to make ready Deirdre's house.

CONCHUBOR. And Naisi and Deirdre are coming?

SOLDIER. Naisi's coming surely, and a woman with him is putting out the glory of the moon is rising, and the sun is going down.

CONCHUBOR [*triumphant, to* LAVARCHAM]. That's your story that she's seamed and ugly?

SOLDIER. I have more news. When that woman heard you were bringing Naisi this place, she sent a horse-boy to call Fergus from the north.

CONCHUBOR [*to* LAVARCHAM]. It's for that you've been playing your tricks, but what you've won is a nearer death for Naisi. [*To* SOLDIERS.] Go up and call my fighters, and take that woman up to Emain.

LAVARCHAM. I'd liefer stay this place. I've done my best but if a bad end is coming surely, it would be a good thing maybe I was here to tend her.

CONCHUBOR [*fiercely*]. Take her to Emain; it's too many tricks she's tried this day already.

[*A* SOLDIER *goes to her.*]

LAVARCHAM. Don't touch me. [*She puts her cloak round her and catches* CONCHUBOR's *arm.*] . . . I thought to stay your hand with my stories till Fergus would come to be beside them, the way I'd save yourself, Conchubor, and Naisi and Emain Macha, but I'll walk up now into your halls and I'll say [*with a gesture*]. . . it's here nettles will be growing, and beyond thistles and docks. I'll go into your High Chambers, where you've been figuring yourself stretching out your neck for the kisses of a queen of women, and I'll say it's here there'll be deer stirring, and goats scratching, and sheep, waking and coughing when there is a great wind from the north.

CONCHUBOR [*shaking himself loose*]. Take her away.

LAVARCHAM. I'm going surely, and in a short space I'll be sitting up with many listening to the flames crackling, and the beams breaking, and I looking on the great blaze will be the end of Emain. [*She goes out.*]

CONCHUBOR [*looking out left*]. I see two people in the trees. It should be Naisi and Deirdre. [*To* SOLDIER.] Let you tell them they'll lodge here tonight.

[*He goes off right.* NAISI *and* DEIRDRE *come in on left, very weary.*]

NAISI. Is it this place he's made ready for myself and Deirdre?

SOLDIER. The Red Branch House is being aired and swept and you'll be called there when a space is by. Till then you'll find fruits and drink on this table, and so the gods be with you. [*Goes right.*]

NAISI [*looking round*]. It's a strange place he's put us camping and we come back as his friends.

DEIRDRE. He's likely making up a welcome for us, having curtains shaken out and rich rooms put in order; and it's right he'd have great state to meet us, and you his sister's sons.

NAISI [*gloomy*]. It's little we want with state or rich rooms or curtains, when we're used to the ferns only, and cold streams and they making a stir.

DEIRDRE [*roaming round room*]. We want what is our right in Emain [*looking at hangings*] . . . and though he's riches in store for us it's a shabby ragged place he's put us waiting, with frayed rugs and skins are eaten by the moths.

NAISI [*a little impatiently*]. There are few would worry over skins and moths on this first night that we've come back to Emain.

DEIRDRE [*brightly*]. You should be well-pleased it's for that I'd worry all times, when it's I have kept your tent these seven years, as tidy as a bee-hive or a linnet's nest. If Conchubor'd a queen like me in Emain he'd not have stretched these rags to meet us. [*She pulls hanging, and it opens.*] . . . There's new earth on the ground and a trench dug. . . . It's a grave Naisi, that is wide and deep.

NAISI [*goes over and pulls back curtain showing grave*]. And that'll be our home in Emain. . . . He's dug it wisely at the butt of a hill with fallen trees to hide it. . . . He'll want to have us killed and buried before Fergus comes.

DEIRDRE [*in a faint voice*]. Take me away. . . . Take me to hide in the rocks, for the night is coming quickly.

NAISI [*pulling himself together*]. I will not leave my brothers.

DEIRDRE [*vehemently*]. It's of us two he's jealous. Come away to the places where we're used to have our company. . . . Wouldn't it be a good thing to lie hid in the high ferns together? [*She pulls him left.*] I hear strange words in the trees.

NAISI. It should be the strange fighters of Conchubor, . . . I saw them passing as we came.

DEIRDRE [*pulling him towards the right*]. Come to this side; listen, Naisi!

NAISI. There are more of them. . . . We are shut in and I have not Ainnle and Ardan to stand near me. Isn't it a hard thing that we three who have conquered many may not die together?

DEIRDRE [*sinking down*]. And isn't it a hard thing that you and I are this place by our opened grave, though none have lived had happiness like ours those days in Alban that went by so quick.

NAISI. It's a hard thing surely we've lost those days forever, and yet it's a good thing maybe that all goes quick, for when I'm in that grave it's soon a day'll come you'll be too wearied to be crying out, and that day'll bring you ease.

DEIRDRE. I'll not be here to know if that is true.

NAISI. It's our three selves he'll kill tonight, and then in two months, or three, you'll see him walking down for courtship with yourself.

DEIRDRE. I'll not be here.

NAISI [*hard*]. You'd best keep him off maybe, and then, when the time comes, make your way to some place west in Donegal, and it's there you'll get used to stretching out lonesome at the fall of night, and waking lonesome for the day.

DEIRDRE. Let you not be saying things are worse than death.

NAISI [*a little recklessly*]. I've one word left. . . . If a day comes in the west that the larks are cocking their crests on the edge of the clouds, and the cuckoos making a stir, and there's a man you'd fancy, let you not be thinking that day, I'd be well pleased you'd go on keening always.

DEIRDRE [*half-surprised, turning to look at him*]. And if it was I that died, Naisi, would you take another woman to fill up my place?

NAISI [*very mournfully*]. It's little I know. . . . Saving only that it's a hard and bitter thing leaving the earth, and a worse and harder thing leaving yourself alone and desolate to be making lamentation on its face always.

DEIRDRE. I'll die when you do, Naisi. I'd not have come from Alban but I knew I'd be along with you in Emain, and you living or dead. . . . Yet this night it's strange and distant talk you're making only.

NAISI. There's nothing surely the like of a new grave of open earth for putting a great space between two friends that love.

DEIRDRE. If there isn't maybe it's that grave when it's closed will make us one forever, and we two lovers have had a great space without weariness or growing old or any sadness of the mind.

[CONCHUBOR *comes in on right.*]

CONCHUBOR. I'd bid you welcome, Naisi.

NAISI [*standing up, watching himself*]. You're welcome, Conchubor. . . . I'm well pleased you've come.

CONCHUBOR [*blandly*]. Let you not think bad of this place where I've put you, till other rooms are readied.

H

NAISI [*breaking out*]. We know the room you've readied. We know what stirred you to send your seals, and Fergus into Alban, and to stop him in the north [*opening curtain, and pointing to the grave*] . . . and dig that grave before us. Now I ask what brought you here?

CONCHUBOR. I've come to look on Deirdre.

NAISI. Look on her. You're a knacky fancier and it's well you chose the one you'd lure from Alban. Look on her, I tell you, and when you've looked I've got ten fingers will squeeze your mottled goose neck though you're king itself.

DEIRDRE [*coming between them*]. Hush Naisi, maybe Conchubor'll make peace. . . . Do not mind him Conchubor, he has cause to rage.

CONCHUBOR. It's little I heed his raging, when a call would bring my fighters from the trees. . . . But what do you say, Deirdre?

DEIRDRE. I'll say so near that grave we seem three lonesome people, and by a new made grave there's no man will keep brooding on a woman's lips, or on the man he hates. It's not long till your own grave will be dug in Emain and you'd go down to it more easy if you'd let call Ainnle and Ardan, the way we'd have a supper all together, and fill that grave, and you'll be well pleased from this out having four new friends the like of us in Emain.

CONCHUBOR [*looking at her for a moment*]. That's the first friendly word I've heard you speaking, Deirdre. A game the like of yours should be the proper thing for softening the heart and putting sweetness in the tongue, and yet this night when I hear you, I've small blame left for Naisi that he stole you off from Ulster.

DEIRDRE [*to* NAISI]. Now, Naisi, answer gently and we'll be friends tonight.

NAISI [*doggedly*]. I have no call but to be friendly, I'll answer what you will.

DEIRDRE [*taking* NAISI'*s hand*]. Then you'll call Conchubor your friend and king, the man who reared me up upon Slieve Fuadh.

[*As* CONCHUBOR *is going to clasp* NAISI'*s hand, cries are heard behind.*]

CONCHUBOR. What noise is that?

AINNLE [*behind*]. Naisi . . . Naisi. . . . Come to us, we are betrayed and broken.

NAISI. It's Ainnle crying out in a battle!

CONCHUBOR. I was near won this night, but death's between us now. [*He goes out.*]

DEIRDRE [*clinging to* NAISI]. There is no battle. . . . Do not leave me, Naisi.

NAISI. I must go to them.

DEIRDRE [*beseechingly*]. Do not leave me, Naisi. Let us creep up in the darkness behind the grave. . . . If there's a battle, maybe the strange fighters will be destroyed, when Ainnle and Ardan are against them.

[*Cries are heard.*]

NAISI [*wildly*]. I hear Ardan crying out. Do not hold me from my brothers.

DEIRDRE [*broken after the strain*]. Do not leave me, Naisi. Do not leave me broken and alone.

NAISI. I cannot leave my brothers when it is I who have defied the king.

DEIRDRE. I will go with you.

NAISI. You cannot come. . . . Do not hold me from the fight. [*He throws her aside almost roughly.*]

DEIRDRE [*with restraint.*] Go to your brothers. . . . For seven years you have been kindly, but the hardness of death has come between us.

NAISI [*looking at her aghast*]. And you'll have me meet death with a hard word from your lips in my ear?

DEIRDRE. We've had a dream, but this night has waked us surely. In a little while we've lived too long, Naisi, and isn't it a poor thing we should miss the safety of the grave, and we trampling its edge?

AINNLE [*behind*]. Naisi, Naisi, we are attacked and ruined.

DEIRDRE. Let you go where they are calling! [*She looks at him for an instant coldly.*] Have you no shame loitering and talking and a cruel death facing Ainnle and Ardan in the woods?

NAISI [*frantic*]. They'll not get a death that's cruel and they with men alone. It's women that have loved are cruel only, and if I went on living from this day I'd be putting a curse on the lot of them I'd meet walking in the east or west, putting a curse on the sun that gave them beauty, and on the madder and the stone-crop put red upon their cloaks.

DEIRDRE [*bitterly*]. I'm well pleased there's no one this place to make a story that Naisi was a laughing-stock the night he died.

NAISI. There'd not be many'd make a story, for that mockery is in your eyes this night will spot the face of Emain with a plague of pitted graves. [*He draws out his sword, throws down belt and cloak, and goes out.*]

CONCHUBOR [*outside*]. That is Naisi. Strike him.

[*Tumult.* DEIRDRE *crouches down on* NAISI's *cloak.* CONCHUBOR *comes in hurriedly, and closes tent so that the grave is not seen any more.*]

CONCHUBOR. They've met their death, the three that stole you Deirdre, and from this out you'll be my queen in Emain.

[*A keen of men's voices is heard behind.*]

DEIRDRE [*bewildered and terrified*]. It is not I will be a queen.

CONCHUBOR. Make your lamentation a short while if you will, but it isn't long till a day'll come when you'll begin pitying a man is old and desolate and High King also. . . . Let you not fear me for it's I'm well pleased you have a store of pity for the three that were your friends in Alban.

DEIRDRE. I have pity surely. . . . It's the way pity has me this night, when I think of Naisi, that I could set my teeth into the heart of a king.

CONCHUBOR. I know well pity's cruel, when it was my pity for my own self destroyed Naisi.

DEIRDRE [*more wildly*]. It was my words without pity gave Naisi a death will have no match until the ends of life and time. [*Breaking out into a keen.*] But who'll pity Deirdre has lost the lips of Naisi from her neck, and from her cheek forever: who'll pity Deirdre has lost the twilight in the woods with Naisi, when beech-trees were silver and copper, and ash-trees were fine gold?

CONCHUBOR [*bewildered*]. It's I'll know the way to pity and care you, and I with a share of troubles has me thinking this night, it would be a good bargain if it was I was in the grave, and Deirdre crying over me, and it was Naisi who was old and desolate.

[*A keen rises loudly over the grave.*]

DEIRDRE [*wild with sorrow*]. It is I who am desolate, I, Deirdre, that will not live till I am old.

CONCHUBOR. It's not long you'll be desolate, and I seven years saying, 'It's a bright day for Deirdre in the woods of Alban,' or saying again, 'what way will Deirdre be sleeping this night, and wet leaves and branches driving from the north?' Let you not break the thing I've set my life on, and you giving yourself up to your sorrow when it's joy and sorrow do burn out like straw blazing in an east wind.

DEIRDRE [*turning on him*]. Was it that way with *your* sorrow, when I and Naisi went northward from Slieve Fuadh and let raise our sails for Alban?

CONCHUBOR [*after a moment*] . There's one sorrow has no end surely, that's being old and lonesome. [*With extraordinary pleading.*] But you and I will have a little peace in Emain, with harps playing, and old men telling stories at the fall of night. . . . I've let build rooms for our two selves Deirdre, with red gold upon the walls, and ceilings that are set with bronze. There was never a queen in the east had a house the like of your house, that's waiting for yourself in Emain.

SOLDIER [*running in*]. Emain is in flames. Fergus has come back and is setting fire to the world. Come up Conchubor, or your state will be destroyed.

CONCHUBOR [*angry and regal again*]. Are the Sons of Usna buried?

SOLDIER. They are in their grave, but no earth is thrown.

CONCHUBOR. Let me see them. Open the tent. [SOLDIER *opens back of tent and shows grave.*] . . . Where are my fighters?

SOLDIER. They are gone to Emain.

CONCHUBOR [*to* DEIRDRE]. There are none to harm you. Stay here until I come again. [*Goes out with* SOLDIER.]

[DEIRDRE *looks round for a moment, then goes up slowly and looks into grave. She crouches down and begins swaying herself backwards and forwards keening softly. At first her words are not heard, then they become clear.*]

DEIRDRE. It's you three will not see age or death coming, you that were my company when the fires on the hill-tops were put out and the stars were our friends only. I'll turn my thoughts back from this night—that's pitiful for want of pity—to the time it was your rods and cloaks made a little tent for me where there'd be a birch tree making shelter, and a dry stone: though from this day my own fingers will be making a tent for me, spreading out my hairs and they knotted with the rain.

[LAVARCHAM *and* OLD WOMAN *come in stealthily on right.*]

DEIRDRE [*not seeing them*]. It is I Deirdre will be crouching in a dark place, I Deirdre that was young with Naisi, and brought sorrow to his grave in Emain.

OLD WOMAN. Is that Deirdre broken down that was so light and airy?

LAVARCHAM. It is, surely, crying out over their grave. [*She goes to* DEIRDRE.]

DEIRDRE. It will be my share from this out to be making lamentation on his stone always, and I crying for a love will be the like of a star shining on a little harbour by the sea.

LAVARCHAM [*coming forward*]. Let you rise up Deirdre, and come off while there are none to heed us the way I'll find you shelter, and some friend to guard you.

DEIRDRE. To what place would I go away from Naisi? What are the woods without Naisi, or the seashore?

LAVARCHAM [*very coaxingly*]. If it's keening you'd be come till I find you a sunny place where you'll be a great wonder they'll call the queen of sorrows, and you'll begin taking a pride to be sitting up pausing and dreaming when the summer comes.

DEIRDRE. It was the voice of Naisi that was strong in summer, the voice of Naisi that was sweeter than pipes playing, but from this day will be dumb always.

LAVARCHAM [*to* OLD WOMAN, *also sobbing*]. She doesn't heed us at all. We'll be hard set to rouse her.

OLD WOMAN. If we don't the High King will rouse her coming down beside her with the rage of battle in his blood, for how could Fergus stand against him.

LAVARCHAM [*touching* DEIRDRE *with her hand*]. There's a score of woman's years in store for you, and you'd best choose will you start living them beside the man you hate, or being your own mistress in the west or south.

DEIRDRE. It is not I will go on living after Ainnle and after Ardan. After Naisi I will not have a lifetime in the world.

OLD WOMAN [*with excitement*]. Look, Lavarcham! There's a light leaving the Red Branch. Conchubor and his lot will be coming quickly with a torch of bog-deal for her marriage throwing a light on her three comrades.

DEIRDRE [*startled*]. Let us throw down clay on my three comrades. Let us cover up Naisi along with Ainnle and Ardan, they that were the pride of Emain. [*Throwing in clay.*] There is Naisi was the best of three, the choicest of the choice of many. It was a clean death was your share Naisi, and it is not I will quit your head when it's many a dark night among the snipe and plover that you and I were whispering together. It is not I will quit your head Naisi, when it's many a night we saw the stars among the clear trees of Glen da Ruadh, or the moon pausing on the edges of the hills.

OLD WOMAN. Conchubor is coming surely. I see the glare of flames throwing a light upon his cloak.

LAVARCHAM [*eagerly*]. Rise up Deirdre and come to Fergus, or be the High King's slave forever.

DEIRDRE [*imperiously*]. I will not leave Naisi who has left the whole world scorched and desolate, I will not go away when there is no light in the heavens, and no flower in the earth under them, but is saying to me, that it is Naisi who is gone forever.

CONCHUBOR [*behind*]. She is here. . . . Stay a little back.

[LAVARCHAM *and* OLD WOMAN *go into the shadow on left as* CONCHUBOR *comes in.*]

CONCHUBOR [*with excitement, to* DEIRDRE]. Come forward and leave Naisi the way I've left charred timber and a smell of burning in Emain Macha, and a heap of rubbish in the storehouse of many crowns.

DEIRDRE [*more awake to what is round her*]. What are crowns and Emain Macha when the head that gave them glory is this place Conchubor, and it stretched upon the gravel will be my bed tonight?

CONCHUBOR. Make an end with talk of Naisi, for I've come to bring you to Dundealgan since Emain is destroyed. [*Makes a movement towards her.*]

DEIRDRE [*with a tone that stops him*]. Draw a little back from Naisi who is young forever. Draw a little back from the white bodies I am putting under a mound of clay and grasses that are withered—a mound will have a nook for my own self when the end is come.

CONCHUBOR [*roughly*]. Let you rise up and come along with me in place of growing crazy with your wailings here.

DEIRDRE. It's yourself has made a crazy story, and let you go back to your arms, Conchubor, and to councils where your name is great, for in this place you are an old man and a fool only.

CONCHUBOR. If I've folly I've sense left not to lose the thing I've bought with sorrow and the deaths of many. [*He moves towards her.*]

DEIRDRE. Do not raise a hand to touch me.

CONCHUBOR. There are other hands to touch you. My fighters are set round in among the trees.

DEIRDRE [*almost mockingly*]. Who'll fight the grave, Conchubor, and it opened on a dark night?

LAVARCHAM [*eagerly*]. There are steps in the wood. . . . I hear the call of Fergus and his men.

CONCHUBOR [*furiously*]. Fergus cannot stop me. . . . I am more powerful than he is though I am defeated and old.

[*A red glow is seen behind the grave.*]

FERGUS [*comes in to* DEIRDRE]. I have destroyed Emain, and now I'll guard you all times, Deirdre, though it was I, without knowledge, brought Naisi to his grave.

CONCHUBOR. It's not you will guard her, for my whole armies are gathering. Rise up, Deirdre, for you are mine surely.

FERGUS [*coming between them*]. I am come between you.

CONCHUBOR [*wildly*]. When I've killed Naisi and his brothers is there any man that I will spare? . . . And is it you will stand against me, Fergus, when it's seven years you've seen me getting my death with rage in Emain?

FERGUS. It's I surely will stand against a thief and traitor.

DEIRDRE [*stands up and sees the light from Emain*]. Draw a little back with the squabbling of fools when I am broken up with misery. [*She turns round.*] . . . I see the flames of Emain starting upward in the dark night, and because of me there will be weasels and wild cats crying on a lonely wall where there were queens and armies, and red gold, the way there will be a story told of a ruined city and a raving king and a woman will be young forever. [*A pause. She looks round.*] . . . I see the trees naked and bare, and the moon shining. Little moon, little moon of Alban, it's lonesome you'll be this night, and to-morrow night, and long nights after, and you pacing the woods beyond Glen Laid, looking every place for Deirdre and Naisi, the two lovers who slept so sweetly with each other.

FERGUS [*going to* CONCHUBOR's *right and whispering*]. Keep back or you will have the shame of pushing a bolt on a queen who is out of her wits.

CONCHUBOR. It is I am out of my wits, with Emain in flames, and Deirdre raving, and my own heart gone within me.

DEIRDRE [*in a high and quiet tone*]. I have put away sorrow like a shoe that is worn out and muddy, for it is I have had a life that will be envied by great companies. It was not by a low birth I made kings uneasy, and they sitting in the halls of Emain. It was not a low thing to be chosen by Conchubor, who was wise, and Naisi had no match for bravery. . . . It is not a small thing to be rid of grey hairs and the loosening of the teeth. [*With a sort of triumph.*] . . . It was the choice of lives we had in the clear woods, and in the grave we're safe surely. . . .

CONCHUBOR. She will do herself harm.

DEIRDRE [*showing* NAISI's *knife*]. I have a little key to unlock the prison of Naisi, you'd shut upon his youth forever. Keep back Conchubor, for the High King who is your master has put his hands between us. [*She half turns to the grave.*] . . . It was sorrows were fore-told, but great joys were my share always, yet it is a cold place I must go to be with you, Naisi, and it's cold your arms will be this night that were warm about my neck so often. . . . It's a pitiful thing to be talking out when your ears are shut to me. It's a pitiful thing, Conchubor, you have done this night in Emain, yet a thing will be a joy and triumph to the ends of life and time.

[*She presses knife to her heart and sinks into the grave.* CONCHUBOR *and* FERGUS *go forward; the red glow fades leaving the stage very dark.*]

FERGUS. Four white bodies are laid down together, four clear lights are quenched in Ireland. [*He throws his sword into the grave.*] . . . There is my sword that could not shield you, my four friends that were the dearest always. The flames of Emain have gone out: Deirdre is dead and there is none to keen her. That is the fate of Deirdre and Naisi next the Children of Usna and for this night Conchubor, our war is ended. [*He goes out.*]

LAVARCHAM. I have a little hut where you can rest Conchubor, there is a great dew falling.

CONCHUBOR [*with the voice of an old man*]. Take me with you, I'm hard set to see the way before me.

OLD WOMAN. This way, Conchubor.

LAVARCHAM. Deirdre is dead, and Naisi is dead, and if the oaks and stars could die for sorrow it's a dark sky and a hard and naked earth we'd have this night in Emain.

CURTAIN

APPENDIX

WHEN THE MOON HAS SET[1]

A PLAY IN ONE ACT

(1900–1903; unpublished)

[1] 'I wrote one play—which I have never published—in Paris, dealing with Ireland of course, but not a peasant play, before I wrote *Riders to the Sea*,' Synge wrote to Leon Brodzky on 12 December 1907.

'I wish to be emphatic about this play. It is just the kind of work which some theatrical experimenter with no literary judgment or indifferent to literature would be glad to get. It is quite complete. It might have a slight stage success with a certain kind of very modern audience. It was Synge's first play, he read it to Lady Gregory and myself in either two or three acts. He has since then, at what date I cannot now remember, though certainly not very recently, reduced it to one act. It is morbid and conventional though with an air of originality. The only thing interesting about it is that it shows his preoccupation with the thought of death. He knew my opinion about it at the time. It was after its rejection by us he took to peasant work.' W. B. Yeats, from a Memorandum to Synge's executors, 1909.

No title-page or list of characters exists for this play, but it is evident from his diaries that Synge had chosen this title for the one-act version of the play he completed in May 1903.

Old family library in country house; many books are in shelves round the walls. A turf fire has burnt low in the fireplace, which is on one side, with a large portrait above it. The principal door is on the right, but there is another in the back wall partly covered with a curtain and opening with two battants into the open air. Small window near the fireplace; another to the right of the end-door; both have the blinds down. A large lamp heavily shaded is burning near the table. A large bow of black crepe is resting on one of the chairs near the fire. BRIDE, *a young maid, is kneeling down settling the turf fire.* COLM *comes in on the left, wearing a big coat buttoned up to his chin.*

COLM [*looking round the room*]. Sister Eileen has gone to bed?

BRIDE. She has not, your honour. She's been in a great state fearing you were lost in the hills, and now she's after going down the hollow field to see would there be any sound of the wheels coming.

COLM. I came in the other way so she could not have heard me. [*Goes to large window*] Is she long gone?

BRIDE. A while only.

COLM. I wonder if I could find her. . . .

BRIDE. You could not, your honour, and you'd have a right to be sitting here and warming your feet, the way it's proud and happy she'll be to see you when she turns in from the shower is coming in the trees.

COLM [*pulling up the blind*]. I hope she will not miss her way. Perhaps if she sees the door open she will turn back. [*He stands looking out.*]

BRIDE [*a little impatiently*]. She'll be coming in a minute I'm telling you, and let you be taking your own rest. You're wanting it surely, for we were thinking it's destroyed you'd be driving alone in the night and the great rain, and you not used to anything but the big towns of the world. [*She pulls a chair to the fire.*]

[COLM *comes over to the fire, wearily. He begins taking off his coat and heavy boots.* BRIDE *lifts up the bow of crepe from his chair.*]

BRIDE [*showing it to him*]. Isn't it a fine bow she's made with bits of rags that we found? I was watching her do it, and I'm telling you she's a wonder surely.

COLM [*with reserve*]. She is clever with her fingers.

BRIDE. Wait till your honour sees the way she has the room beyond, with fine flowers in it, and white candles, and grand clothes on the bed, and your poor uncle lying so easy with his eyes shut you'd be thinking it was an old man in his sleep. [*Turning to the fire with a sigh.*] Ah, it's a long way any person would go seeking the like of Sister Eileen, and it's very lonesome your honour'll be tomorrow or the next day when she is gone away to the town.

COLM. She will stay for the funeral.

BRIDE. And what day, if myself may ask, will the funeral be?

COLM. I have settled it for Friday, but it was not easy, there were so many things to arrange.

BRIDE. It's great trouble the rich do have when there is even an old man to be buried, and it was that, I'm thinking, kept you the whole evening in the town.

COLM. It kept me a good while, but I went wrong coming home, and took the road through the bogs to the graveyard of Glan-na-nee.

BRIDE. The Lord have mercy on us! There does be no one at all passing that way but a few men do be carting turf, and isn't it a great wonder your honour got home safe, and wasn't lost in the hills?

COLM. I hardly knew where I was, but I found a woman there who told me my way.

BRIDE. It was a lonesome place for a woman, God help her, and the night coming.

COLM. She was nearly crazy I think, but she must have known the trap for she called out to me by my name and asked about my uncle.

BRIDE [*greatly interested*]. And was it much she said to your honour?

COLM. At first she spoke sensibly and told me how I was to go, but when she tried to say something else she had on her mind she got so confused I could not follow her. Then the mare got frightened at a sort of cry she gave, and I had to come away.

BRIDE. She was a big tall woman I'm thinking, with a black shawl on her, and black hair round her face? [*She begins blowing the fire with her mouth.*]

COLM. Then you know who she is?

BRIDE. She's Mary Costello, your honour. [*She goes on blowing.*]

COLM. A beggar woman?

BRIDE [*indignantly*]. Not she a beggar woman. . . . She's a Costello from the old Castilian family, and it's fine people they were at one time, big wealthy nobles of the cities of Spain, and herself was the finest girl you'd find in the whole world, with nice manners, and white hands on her, for she was reared with the nuns, as it's likely you've heard tell from his honour, God rest his soul.

COLM. If he ever spoke of her I do not remember it. Why should he have told me about her?

BRIDE. It's a long story, and a sad pitiful story. I'd have a right to tell you one day maybe if the Lord Almighty keep us alive, but Sister Eileen will be coming now, and the two of you won't be needing the like of that to trouble you at all. [*She stands up and sweeps up the hearth.*]

COLM. Has she been long out of her mind?

BRIDE. A long while in and out of it. It's ten years she was below in the Asylum, and it was a great wonder the way you'd see her in there, not lonesome at all with the great lot were coming in from all the houses in the country, and herself as well off as any lady in England, France, or Germany, walking round in the gardens with fine shoes on her feet. Ah, it was well for her in there, God help her, for she was always a nice quiet woman, and a fine woman to look at, and I've heard tell it was 'Your Ladyship' they would call her, the time they'd be making fun among themselves.

COLM. I wonder if I ever saw her before. Her face reminded me of something, or someone, but I cannot remember where I have met it.

BRIDE [*going up to the portrait over the fireplace*]. Let you come and look here, your honour, and I'm thinking you'll see.

COLM [*going over*]. Yes, that is the woman. But it was done years ago.

BRIDE. Long years surely, your honour, and it's time the whole thing was forgot, for what call has any man to be weighing his mind with the like of it and he storing sorrows till the judgment day?

[*She goes over to window.* COLM *takes down picture and looks at it closely in the lamp-light.*]

BRIDE [*looking out*]. Sister Eileen's coming now, and I'll be going off to my bed, for I'm thinking the two of you won't be needing me, and it's a right yourselves would have to be going to rest, and not sitting here talking and talking in the dark night, when people are better sleeping, and not destroying their souls, pausing and watching and they thinking over the great troubles of the world.

[*She goes out, and in a moment* SISTER EILEEN *comes in quickly from the door which leads into the open air. She is pleased and relieved when she sees* COLM.]

SISTER EILEEN. You have come back? I was afraid something had happened.

COLM. I have been in some time.

SISTER EILEEN. I thought I would hear the wheels, and I went right down to the lake the night is so beautiful. . . . You have arranged everything?

COLM. I sent a number of telegrams, and waited for answers. He is to be buried on Friday at Glan-na-nee, and the coffin will come down tomorrow.

SISTER EILEEN. When the storm broke I was sorry you had gone; you must have got very wet on the road across the mountains.

COLM. It rained heavily on Slieve na-Ruadh, but I am nearly dry again.

SISTER EILEEN. I was out for a little while getting flowers for your uncle's room, but I did not find many they were so broken with the rain.

COLM. Then you saw what a change the rain has made among the trees.

SISTER EILEEN. It has ended the spring. I was just thinking what a difference there is since I arrived here three months ago, with the moonlight shining everywhere on the snow.

COLM. It seems like three years since you telegraphed for me, we have made such a world for ourselves.

SISTER EILEEN [*changing the subject*]. What have you got there?

COLM. It is the picture from that corner. [*He turns it round to her.*] I saw her tonight at the graveyard of Glan-na-nee.

SISTER EILEEN. What took you out there, surely that was not your way?

COLM. I went wrong coming home, and this woman put me right. Do you know anything of the woman?

SISTER EILEEN. I have heard a good deal about her, perhaps more than you have.

COLM. Bride has been telling me that she was a long time in the Asylum, and that she was connected in some way with my uncle.

SISTER EILEEN. He wanted to marry her although she was beneath him, but when it was all arranged she broke it off because he did not believe in God.

COLM. And after that she went mad?

SISTER EILEEN. After that. And your uncle shut himself up. He told me it was nearly twenty years since it happened, and yet he had never spoken of it to anyone. I do not think he would have told me if it had not been for his dislike of religious orders and the clothes I wear.

COLM. You mean he told you as a warning. . . . And yet I suppose you take her as an example to be followed.

SISTER EILEEN. She did what was right. No woman who was really a Christian could have done anything else. . . .

COLM. I wish you had seen her tonight screaming and crying out over the bogs.

SISTER EILEEN. I do not want to see her. . . . I have seen your uncle for three months and his death today. That is enough.

COLM. It is far from enough if it has not made you realize that in evading her impulses this woman did what was wrong and brought this misery on my uncle and herself.

SISTER EILEEN [*giving him back the picture*]. We cannot argue about it. We do not see things the same way. . . . Has she changed a great deal since that was done?

COLM. Less than he has. [*He hangs picture up again.*] He was right in thinking that their story is a warning. . . . At that time they were about the ages we are tonight, and now one is a mad woman, and the other has been tortured to death—[*Some one knocks.*] Come in!

[BRIDE, *half rolled in a shawl, as if she was not fully dressed, comes in with a telegram.*]

BRIDE [*giving it to* SISTER EILEEN]. That has just come for you now, Sister Eileen. It came into town after Mr. Colm had gone away, and they gave it to an old man was driving out west with an ass and cart.

[SISTER EILEEN *takes it and reads it left.* BRIDE *takes* COLM *right.*]

BRIDE [*whispering*]. I heard from the old man he seen Mary Costello coming in great haste over the hills, so let your honour not be afeard if you hear her singing or laughing, or letting a shout maybe in the darkness of the night.

COLM. Is there nothing one can do for her?

BRIDE. Nothing at all your honour. It's best to leave her alone. [*She goes towards the door.*]

SISTER EILEEN [*turning to her, in a low voice*]. Can some one drive me into the town tomorrow? I must go to Dublin by the first train in the morning.

BRIDE. We can surely, Sister Eileen. And what time will we send to meet you coming back?

SISTER EILEEN. I am not coming back.

BRIDE. Well the Lord speed you Sister Eileen, and that the Almighty God may stretch out a holy hand to preserve and prosper you, and see you safe home. [*Turning to the door.*] It's lonesome you'll be leaving the lot of us behind you, and you after bringing a kind of a new life into this house was a dark quiet place for a score of years, and will be dark again maybe from this mortal night. [*She goes out left.*]

COLM [*with a change in his voice*]. What is this talk of your leaving me tomorrow?

SISTER EILEEN. Someone has told the Mother Superior your uncle is dead, and she telegraphs—as she puts it—that she is short of nurses and will need me for a new case tomorrow.

COLM. Cannot you stay a little longer?

SISTER EILEEN. I am afraid not possibly. . . . [*Looking up at the clock.*] I must soon go and pack up.

COLM. Telegraph to the Mother Superior that you cannot leave me till the funeral is over. . . . Then I will have you three days more.

SISTER EILEEN. I cannot. . . . There is no use talking about it.

COLM. We must talk about it till I make you decide with your whole mind whether you will obey the earth, or repeat the story of the mad woman and my uncle.

SISTER EILEEN [*severely*]. If you say what I think you are wishing to say, I will have to leave you and not speak to you any more. That is all you will gain.

COLM [*sternly, locking door*]. You shall not go till I have said what I have to say. Then if you are weak enough to give up your share of what is best in life, you may go where you will.

SISTER EILEEN [*piteously*]. I wish you would not spoil the last night we are together.

COLM. It may not be the last. . . .

SISTER EILEEN [*goes over and lights candle, picks up bow of crepe*]. Please open the door, and let me go to bed. I have been very wrong to allow you to talk to me as I have done, but I will go back to my true life tomorrow, and I will ask to be forgiven.

COLM. And you think that you will forget this place and what has been said here?

SISTER EILEEN. It is only those who do the will of God who are happy; that is all I know.

[*A burst of hysterical laughter is heard outside, and then a sob and a scrap of singing. A moment afterwards the door is pushed open and* MARY

COSTELLO *comes in, dazzled with the light, and goes over left without seeing* COLM *or* SISTER EILEEN. *She goes over to the bureau in the corner and sees that one of the drawers is open and pounces on it. She finds a ring case, and takes out two rings and puts them on her fingers, making the stones sparkle in the lamp light; she finds a bundle of white linen, takes out a silk dress and makes a movement as if she is going to throw it over her head. Before she does so she looks round stealthily, and sees* COLM *and* SISTER EILEEN. *She drops the dress on the floor with a cry, picks up her shawl and runs to the door, then stops, and turns towards them.*]

MARY. A nun is it? What right have the like of you to be walking out through the world and looking on us when it isn't any harm we're doing? What right have the nuns I'm saying to be meddling with the world? [*She recognizes* COLM.] I seen that man tonight, God bless him, and he driving round on the roads. [*She goes up to him.* SISTER EILEEN *has involuntarily drawn close to* COLM. MARY *looks from one to the other with a peculiar smile.*] You're a fine handsome woman, God bless you, a fine beautiful woman I'm saying, and let you not mind them at all. [*She puts her hand pleadingly on* SISTER EILEEN'S *arm.*] Sure you won't mind them, Sister, tell me out you won't mind them at all?

SISTER EILEEN. Who shall I not mind?

MARY [*throwing up her hands, and then clasping them together and turning half round with a shriek of laughter*]. 'Who shall I not mind?' says she. 'Who shall I not mind?' It's a long while since I was in school Sister, yet it's well I know the like of that. It's well I know you've no call to mind what the priests say, or the bishops say, or what the angels of God do be saying, for it's little the like of them knows of women or the seven sorrows of earth. [*With anguish in her voice. She sinks her head and sees the bow of crepe in* SISTER EILEEN'S *hand.*] ... Who is it is dead, Mister, if that's the token of death?

COLM. My uncle, Colm Sweeny.

MARY [*indifferently*]. And a long rest behind him, why would that trouble me now? I was afeard it was my little children [*she looks up to* COLM, *and speaks piteously*]—for if I was never married your honour, and have no children I do be thinking it's alive they must

be if I never had them itself. . . . [*Raising her voice to a plaintive cry.*]
I do see them sometimes when my head's bad and I do be falling
into my sleep. . . . There are five children, five children that wanted
to live, God help them, if the nuns and the priests with them had let
me be [*swaying herself with anguish*]. . . . They're always nice your
honour, with clean faces, and nice frocks on them and little sticks in
their hands. But I wouldn't like them to begin to die on me, for I'm
not like all the rest of you [*covering her face with her hands*] . . . and
it's queer things I do be seeing the time the moon is full. [*She bends
her head sobbing piteously.*]

SISTER EILEEN. Don't mind them now, Mary, there isn't anything to
frighten you here.

MARY [*still sobbing*]. Oh, my head's perished with the night wind, and
I do be very lonesome the time I do be going the bog road, with the
rabbits running round on it and they drowned with the dew. [*She
looks up piteously at* SISTER EILEEN, *sees the little cross she has hanging
round her neck; she takes the cross in her hand.*] Will you give me the
little cross you have Sister, for I've lost the one I had and I do be
wanting the like of it to sit and hold in my hand. [SISTER EILEEN
gives it to her.] . . . May the Almighty God reward you Sister, and
give you five nice children before you die. [*She gives her the rings.*]
. . . May his blessing be on them rings, and they going on your hand,
and his blessing be on your hand and it working with the linen when
the time is come. [*She looks at the crucifix in her hand.*] . . . This will
be a quiet thing to be looking on, and it'll keep me still the long
evenings when the moon is low, and there do be white mists passing
on the bog, the time the little children I have do be lepping, and
crying out to each other, and making games in the dark night, and no
Christian waking but myself only, and the white geese you'd hear a
mile or maybe two mile and they making a great stir over the bog.
[*She moves towards the door.*] . . . I'll be going now I'm thinking, for
I've a long way and this will be keeping me company in the dark
lane through the wood. God save you kindly the two of you. There's
great marrying in the world but it's late we were surely, and let
yourselves not be the same. Let you mind the words I was saying,
and give no heed to the priests or the bishops or the angels of God,
for it's little the like of them, I was saying, knows about women or
the seven sorrows of the earth. [*She goes out.*]

[SISTER EILEEN *goes over and puts the linen and other things back into the drawer.*]

COLM. Another voice has cried out to you. In a few years you will be as old as she is. There will be divine nights like this night and birds crying in the heather, but nothing will reach you, as nothing reaches my uncle at the other side of the hall. [*He goes over to her.*] I am not a woman and I cannot judge of all your feelings, yet I know you have a profound impulse for what is peculiar to women. You realize that the forces which lift women up to a share in the pain and passion of the world are more holy than the vows you have made. [*She stands before him motionless; he speaks more tenderly.*] Before this splendour of the morning you cannot lie. You know that the spirit of life which has transfigured the world is filling you with radiance. Why will you worship the mania of the saints when your own existence is holier than they are. People renounce when they have not power to retain; you have power and courage. . . . I implore you to use them.

SISTER EILEEN. I don't know what to do. . . . You are giving me such pain and yet. . . .

COLM. There is the first note of the birds. . . . When the sun comes over that ridge I will ask you to be my wife. . . . You cannot refuse. The trees might as well refuse to grow fragrant and green when it is May, or the birds to sing before the dawn. . . . There are the larks, and the wrens. . . . You have half an hour. . . . I will not touch you. . . . I will not try to persuade you. It is quite unnecessary. The world will persuade you. The breath that drew out this forest of leaves and sent quivering voices to chant in them, is making of you also a beautiful note in the world. . . . There is the willow warbler, you have a quarter of an hour. Will you go and put this dress about you. I am not in a humour for blasphemy.

[SISTER EILEEN *takes the green dress and goes out without looking at him. He looks out for an instant, then packs the rest of the papers into the bureau drawer. He goes back to the window. In a moment* SISTER EILEEN *comes in behind him in a green silk dress which is cut low at the neck. She reaches the window just as the red morning light sweeps into the room.*]

SISTER EILEEN [*in a low voice*]. Colm, I have come back to you.

COLM [*turning towards her*]. You are infinitely beautiful, and you have done a great action. It is the beauty of your spirit that has set you free, and your emancipation is more exquisite than any that is possible for men who are redeemed by logic. You cannot tell me why you have changed. That is your glory. As a moth comes out to a new sphere of odour and colour and flight, so you have come out to live in a new sphere of beautiful love. . . . Listen to the tumult the birds are making in the trees. That is our marriage hymn. Without love this world would be a loathsome sandhill, and a soul without love is not a great deal better. . . . Speak to me. I want to hear you, your voice will have new cadence from today.

SISTER EILEEN. I have left my veil in the room where your uncle is lying. . . . I seem to be in a dream that is wider than I am. I hope God will forgive me. I cannot help it.

COLM. How many people ask to be forgiven for the most divine instant of their lives. Let us be wiser than they are. [*He takes up one of the rings.*] Here is the ring that was the sorrowful heirloom of my uncle. Give me your hand. I, the male power, have overcome with worship you, the soul of credulous feeling, the reader of the saints. From our harmonized discord new notes will rise. In the end we will assimilate with each other and grow senseless and old. We have incarnated God, and been a part of the world. That is enough. [*He takes her hand.*] In the name of the Summer, and the Sun, and the Whole World, I wed you as my wife. [*He puts the ring on her finger.*]

CURTAIN

GLOSSARY AND
GUIDE TO PRONUNCIATION

agents—landlord representatives empowered to evict tenants failing to pay their rent

agradh—*pr.* u'grah; oh love

Alban—Scotland, from the genitive form of Alba

Annagolan—*pr.* Annagoulan, as in out

banbhs—*pr.* bannuvs, or bonnivs; young pigs

black hags—cormorants

blackthorn—walking-stick made from stem of the blackthorn shrub

blather—foolish talk, nonsense

bona fides—*pr.* as in sides; genuine travellers exempt from licensing hours

boreen—narrow lane or passage between stone walls or high earth banks

Bride—*pr.* Bridee; version of the name Bridget

butt—bottom or end (of his tailpocket, of the ditch, of a rope, etc.)

Cearneach—*pr.* Carnah

cholera morbus—bilious diarrhoea and stomach cramps

cleeve—basket or hamper

cnuceen—*pr.* knockeen; a little hill

cockshot-man— man at fair whose blackened face is the target for wooden balls thrown by competitors

conceit—liking or preference

Conchubor—*pr.* Connahar or, more often by Synge, Conor

creel cart—turf-cart with open or grated sides

curagh—small canoe made of wickerwork covered with hides (by Synge's time with tarred canvas), the shape varying from district to district

Deirdre—*pr.* Dare'dra

destroyed—bothered or exhausted, not necessarily as in *The Playboy*, killed

Doul—*pr.* as in out

dreepiness—described by Synge as that red-nosed look people get when they have a bad cold in the head

dun—hill-fort, often in ancient times a royal residence

-een—*pr.* yeen; diminutive suffix, e.g. houseen, Shaneen, supeen

Emain Macha—*pr.* Evin Vaha; fort near Armagh

Emer—*pr.* Eemer

felts—thrushes

frish-frash—Indian meal and raw cabbage boiled down as thin as gruel

from the licence—to avoid paying for a dog licence

gallous—mischievous, spirited, plucky

gob—mouth

gripe of the ditch—grasp or hollow of the ditch

griseldy—grisly

haggard—farmyard, or walled field next to farmyard

hooshing—lifting up or removing

jobber—livestock dealer

jobbing jockies—men who travel about breaking in horses

keen—a lament for the dead

Kilmainham—a large prison in Dublin

knacky fancier—ingenious or artful chooser

Lavarcham—*pr.* Lower'kem (as in allow)

letting on—pretending

loy—a long narrow spade

lug—ear

madder and stone-crop—vegetable dyes of red and orange

mitch off—play truant

Naisi—*pr.* Nee'shi

the old hen—influenza

parish public—licensed public-house

parlatic—paralytic from drink

paters—the Lord's Prayer

peelers—policemen, nicknamed after Sir Robert Peel

polis—the police

pot-boy—serving-man

poteen—*pr.* potyeen; illegally distilled whisky

a power of—many, a great deal of

Samhain—*pr.* sow'in (as in allow); All Souls' Day, 1 November, the beginning
of winter

scribes of bog—long stretches of wasteland, where turf-cutting took place

shebeen—usually an unlicensed house selling poteen; in *The Playboy* used more
generally as a low wayside public-house

shift—chemise, a woman's undergarment like a slip, worn next to the skin and
reaching to the knees

skelping—beating

Slieve Fuadh—*pr.* Sleeve Foo'a

sluig—ditch or piece of muddy ground

small farmers—poor farmers possessing very small farms, as opposed to
strong farmers

sop of grass tobacco—tuft of uncured tobacco leaf

spancelled—tied together

spavindy—lame or halting from the spavin, a disease of the hock-joint

streeleen—trail or stream of talk

streeler—loiterer, slovenly person

swiggling—swaying and wriggling

thraneen—withered stalk of grass, i.e. a worthless thing

tight—well-made and healthy

trick-o'-the-loop—game at the fair in which spectator must guess centre loop
in a leather belt

turbary—the right of cutting peat

union—the workhouse

Usna—*pr.* Uish'na

wake—the 'watching of the dead' before burial, frequently an occasion for all-
night social gatherings

warrant—a certainty

wattle—a small switch

winkered mule—mule with blinkers